ISLAMIC LAW

ISLAMIC LAW

From Historical Foundations to Contemporary Practice

Mawil Izzi Dien

Edinburgh University Press

ATLANTIC®
PUBLISHERS & DISTRIBUTORS

ATLANTIC®

PUBLISHERS & DISTRIBUTORS
7/22, Ansari Road, Darya Ganj
New Delhi – 110 002
Tel: 2327 3880, 2327 5880, 2328 0451
Fax: 91-11-2328 5873
E-mail: info@atlanticbooks.com
Website: www.atlanticbooks.com

Published in India by
Atlantic Publishers and Distributors, New Delhi
in association with
Edinburgh University Press Ltd
22 George Square, Edinburgh, U.K.

First published 2004 by Edinburgh University Press Ltd
First Indian Reprint 2005

ISBN 81-269-0552-2

Typeset in Goudy by
Koinonia, Manchester, and
printed in India by
Pushp Print Services, Delhi

Contents

PART THREE
The source-tuners

PART FOUR
The legal mechanisms for understanding the law

PART FIVE
Legal authority and the future of Islamic law

Acknowledgements

My deepest thanks go first to the divine will, which decreed that my work would be fortunate enough to be seen by others, and to all those who assisted me during the preparation of this book. All my family members deserve acknowledgement for their help and patience, particularly my father, who has been a major source of inspiration when I see him working relentlessly on his many books, and my two brothers Asal and Saad for their support and encouragement. My thanks also go to the Oxford Centre for Islamic Studies for granting me a fellowship which helped me a great deal. I would like to give special thanks to Dr Farhan Nizami, Dr Basil Mustafa, Professor Muhammad Talib, Professor James Piscatori and all the kind staff of the Centre. I am greatly in debt also to all those who assisted me while I was in Oxford, particularly Dr Christopher Melchert for his various discussions, and Professor Clive Holes for his friendship and kindness.

My thanks also go to Professor Saleem al-Hassani and Professor Qasim al-Samarrai, the grand Mufti of Brunei Sheikh Abd al-ʿAziz b. Junayd, and Dr Ayman Shihadha. My gratitude also needs to be recorded to all my students who helped me in one way or another, particularly Dr Shukriji Ramich Abd Allah al-Judayʿ Amr Khalid, Bilal Philips and Nasir al-Lughani. Special thanks go to Pat Sinclair, Dr Dawood El Alami, Professor D. P. Davies, Professor C. E. Bosworth, Professor J. D. Latham and all my departmental colleagues. Finally, my thanks are due to the EUP team, particularly to Professor Carole Hillenbrand for her advice and constructive remarks, Nicola Carr for her great help, and Ivor Normand and Eddie Clark for saving me from errors.

Points of methodology

Transliteration system

All transliterated words (except the names of people) and book titles have been italicised.

Consonants

ء	'	ز	*z*	ق	*q*
ب	*b*	س	*s*	ك	*k*
ت	*t*	ش	*sh*	ل	*l*
ث	*th*	ص	*ṣ*	م	*m*
ج	*j*	ض	*ḍ*	ن	*n*
ح	*ḥ*	ط	*ṭ*	ه	*h*
خ	*kh*	ظ	*ẓ*	و	*w*
د	*d*	ع	'	ي	*y*
ذ	*dh*	غ	*gh*	ة	*a* (in construct state *-at*)
ر	*r*	ف	*f*		

The definite article ال is written as *al* with hyphen, even when used before sun letters and after vowels, e.g. Abu al-Salt (*not* Abū S-Salt). However, *wa-al-* is written as *wa al-*. It is always written in lower case unless it is at the beginning of a sentence or as normally required, such as being the first part of a proper name.

Vowels

Short:		Long or		Doubled	*iyya*
َ	*a*	ا	*ā*	final form ي	*i*
ُ	*u*	و	*ū*	Diphthongs و	*aw*
ِ	*i*	ي	*ī*	ي	*ay*

Exceptions

- The names of well-known places, e.g. Mecca, Medina, Iraq.
- The most often-used words have been written as indicated (without italics), e.g. hadith, salah, hajj, zakah. However, the initials of Qur'an and Sunna are capitalised.
- Well-known Arabic names such as those denoting densities or groups are written in their original Arabic pronunciation; thus: *Umawi*, not Umayyad, and *Khawārij*, not Kharijites.
- 'Abd is written without (')
- Muḥammad and Aḥmad have no (.) under *h*.
- No macron over the last *i* in names and *fi*.

Introduction

Islamic law, in whichever sense we take the term, is sometimes unclear, both in its content and in its historical order. Perhaps the main reason that contributes to this lack of clarity is that it is 'religious' and therefore carries with it all the ambiguity that any world religion entails. Being Islamic makes it so diversified in its texture, viscosity and characteristics that it often carries a claim to originality and sole right of production. Like oil, it is sometimes almost impossible to trace its origin and the cradle of its inception. However, like oil, it generates human life, even if it is highly inflammable when not treated with care and respect. Trying to study Islamic law with preconceived ideas of Islamic love or non-Islamic hate can lead to false conclusions. This represents the second point of difficulty in understanding Islamic law. Muslims see it as the word of God and therefore divine and beyond question. This attitude often fogs the vision and leads to a grave misunderstanding of the real objectives and visions of the law. Western scholarship views it as 'fabricated' or at best a human 'phenomenon' that needs to be studied. There is no doubt that each approach has its own strengths and prejudices, whether historical or methodological; and there is perhaps a need to combine the two approaches to gain a full sense of Islamic law.

This volume therefore aims to examine Islamic law from both a Western and an Islamic perspective and to offer fresh ideas about Islamic law at a structural and presentational level. It is primarily aimed at providing an overview of the law as it stands and exploring its main principles in theory and practice. Because the work is intended as an academic source, the use of Arabic terms and jargon has been minimised. Those that are included are explained in the Glossary, parts of which are taken from this book or other sources, such as *The Encyclopaedia of Islam*. I have referred to *The Encyclopaedia of Islam* (EI^1, EI^2) as the main source of Western scholarship, while I have utilised selected Islamic books that appear to me to offer a good representation of the traditional Islamic books.

I have examined the sources, the content and the actual relationship between the text and the scholastic legislation of Islamic law. This volume explores the dialectical relationship between the text and academic theory and interpretation that can be observed throughout the history of Islamic law, including its formative periods. Regarding the sources of the law, this book suggests a contrasting viewpoint from that of some classical Muslim academics, whose perception of the term 'sources of legislation' is confined to the Qur'an, Sunna, consensus and in some cases public interest. All other sources are seen as simply mechanisms devised by scholars to interpret the law.

On a practical level, the book approaches the subject from the conviction that today Sunni Islamic law is in need of serious reconsideration to render it appropriate for contemporary society, particularly as it lacks a consistent and unanimous source of authority that can be accepted by Muslims generally. It might be helpful to add here that, although the historical development of the law has not been ignored, there is a heavier focus on the law itself and its *modus operandi*. The theoretical debates on issues such as public interest and legal necessity have been considered and some practical cases examined individually in an attempt to provide examples for the future development of Islamic law.

Due to the nature and size of this volume, we have been unable to discuss practical details of the law, such as those related to the family, criminal activity, contracts, political or international conduct. It is hoped that these will be the subjects of a future volume.

The layout of the book

This book is divided into five parts and eleven chapters. The first part examines the historical background, focusing on the early period of Islam during the life of Muhammad, when the notion of regulatory principles and ideas was being initiated. Although many classical historians separate the life of the Prophet Muhammad from that of the orthodox caliphs, the fact remains that this whole era represents the formative period of 'basic Islam'. The divine nature of Islamic law has created the illusion that its development was 'frozen', which led scholars such as Coulson to maintain that Muslim jurisprudence in its traditional form provides an extreme example of a legal science that is divorced from historical consideration. Islamic law may have appeared static, but it is analogous to a slow-moving glacier that adapts its shape to local terrain and alters to accommodate whatever undulations are met en route. The main strength of Islamic law, that has given it the power to erode all non-Islamic customs and practices, lies in the fact that all Islamic legal forms have been constructed on the notion of public interest, *maṣlaḥa*. This aimed to minimise the hardship of human life, be it the old desert life of Arabia, urban medieval life in Iraq and Syria, or the modern affluent society of Europe.

The second part examines the *sharī'a*, which sets out the rules and regulations governing the life and death of Muslims. The concept of the divine nature of the sources in Islamic law is important from the point of view of 'authority'. For this reason, it was decided for classification purposes to separate the sources into 'divine' and 'human', followed by a third part which discusses the sources that appear to 'fine-tune' or act as 'fillers' for those gaps that the sources could not fill. These include the notions of public interest and necessity, without which the sources could not function adequately and would remain as ill-tuned instruments.

The fourth part focuses on the legal mechanisms devised by scholars to understand the law. Here, I have tried for the most part to explain the classical Islamic concepts, in the hope that future studies of Islamic law could focus on these concepts as the bedrock of Islamic law rather than interpreting and evaluating it in terms of non-Islamic notions of what represents the law.

The fifth and final part addresses 'authority' in the Sunni Islamic world. This is one of the law's weakest points. Islamic 'authority' is examined by providing samples of its diverse forms, be they official, individual or composed of groups. The future of Islamic law is also discussed here, in the light of its present authority and 'heated' incidents in the contemporary Muslim world.

PART ONE

Historical background

1

The law of the Prophet and his companions

Islam was born in Arabia some 1,400 years ago, at a time when society comprised simple, spontaneous, nomadic peoples who provided the human element for the monotheistic creed. Consequently, as the legislative and ethical stipulations of Islam, the *shari'a* was trained like a vine to fit the needs and divergences of such social structures; the modest nature of this continued during all the periods from the Prophet's life up to the tragic end of the last orthodox caliph, Ali (d. 40/660).[1] The Islamic legal forms were structured on the notion of public interest, *maṣlaḥa*, which aimed to minimise the hardship, *raf' al-ḥaraj*, of desert life. The era of the Prophet was one of revelation, wherein was initiated a legal tidal wave that maintained its momentum for many centuries.

The legal essence of Islam was embedded in the revelation, as represented by the Qur'an and the guidelines of the Prophet. The distinctive features of early Islamic law were inherent in the fresh legal instructions, *forensis doctrina*, which had been given directly by God. Even the prophetic individual opinion was based on the revelation of God's words, *waḥi*. The flavour of this divine revelation did in fact differ from one location to another, thus creating a variation in approach between the towns of Mecca and Medina. This was due not only to diverse geographical factors but also to the changing circumstances of the new faith. During the thirteen years that Muhammad spent in Mecca, the essence of the Qur'an and its instructions were focused on doctrine and ethics, with little reference to the practical element of human need. The duration of the Prophet's life was undoubtedly the most central period in the history of Islamic jurisprudence, being the only time of divine revelation.

Islamic law entered a new phase subsequent to the Prophet's flight to *Yathrib*,[2] when an Islamic state was established. This heralded an era wherein the practicalities of legislation had to be addressed. The new Islamic state required legal answers for all its perplexities, with regard not only to practical cases such as family, crimes, holy war and inheritance but also to matters relevant to ritual and worship. It is interesting to observe the embryonic stage of legislation during this period, which was conceived to accommodate evolving human needs and to institute unprecedented legislative principles for the future of an Islamic religious society. The implementation of practical legislation often occurred as a response to direct questions that Muslims would ask the Prophet.[3]

The circumstances that accompanied the revelation of certain verses were termed *asbāb al-nuzūl*, which literally designates the reasons for that revelation. This became a fundamental element in the Islamic exegesis of Qur'anic verses. However, there were a large number of verses unlinked to any historical context, these being revealed as general principles that were enacted without known or specified circumstances. The legislation of zakah is an example of a general principle that did not come about as a result of any question or practical problem raised by the Islamic community. Occasionally, there is evidence of the combination of both factors within one verse, and it is difficult to ascertain if a statement is intended as an explanation of the text or as the reason for its revelation.

Zarqāni provides a detailed account of the meanings and forms of *asbāb al-nuzūl*, while offering a guideline for the identification of both verse forms. He states: 'if two phrases [of narration] are relevant to the same subject and one of them states clearly that it is the reason for revaluation whereas the other does not, the first should be taken as the reason for the revelation and the second as merely an explanation of the meaning'.[4] The example that Zarqāni provides here refers to a hadith narrated by Muslim (d. 261/875)[5] thus: Jābir[6] said: 'the Jews used to say that if a man has sexual intercourse with his wife from behind, then their child will be born squint-eyed'.

In explanation of this point, Zarqāni indicates the following Qur'anic verse: 'your women are like a tilth for you which you may approach from whichever [position] you may wish'.[7] He adds that Ibn 'Umar[8] explained this verse as the prohibition of anal sex with women. However, what is considered as a reason for revelation here is the first statement made by Jābir, because it clearly indicates that it was an explanation of the reason for revelation. This is unlike the statement of Ibn 'Umar, which merely explains the meaning of the verse.[9]

Although during his lifetime, on most occasions, the Prophet used his own judgement in a legislative manner, he also permitted his followers to do so, and indeed he often approved of their exercising of individual opinion, *ijtihād*. This is evident in the case where he accepted the ransom for the captives of the battle of Badr. When he consulted his close advisors, he was offered conflicting advice; however, he chose the view of Abu Bakr (570–634) and accepted the ransom. The Prophet is reported to have encouraged the practice of individual opinion among his companions; a tendency that proved to be useful for them after his death. When the Prophet sent Mu'ādh as a judge for Yemen,[10] he asked him how he would judge between people. Mu'ādh responded by stating that he would refer to the Book of God and the tradition of the Prophet or Sunna. When the Prophet asked for his reaction if he might fail to find his answers there, Mu'ādh stated: 'I will use my best judgment'.[11] The Prophet was very pleased with his considered reply and begged God to bless Mu'ādh.[12]

Following the death of the Prophet, his companions could only fall back on their own resources. They had to evaluate and deal with social, political and economic dilemmas, the nature of which was quite removed from the more simplistic problems that manifested themselves in the days when Islam existed within the confines of Mecca and Medina. It could be true that they never regarded him as divine or non-human; but he was the Prophet of God, and as such he represented the only direct contact with God. His death created a vacuum of some magnitude for Muslims, who were used to being inspired by him as a role model and the source of God's legislation. The words of Abu Bakr were a motivating factor for the Muslim population; on hearing the news of the Prophet's death, he declared: 'for those who worship Muhammad, Muhammad is dead; for those who worship Allah, He is ever living'. The method employed by the companions of the Prophet to achieve this adherence to the word of God were reliant on the Qur'an and the legacy of His Prophet.

The Sunna, or the tradition of Muhammad, became the second reference for Muslims who sought answers for their enquiries. Yet the Sunna was still insufficient in providing clarification of the increasingly perplexing circumstances which arose as society expanded and new lands were conquered. The need for a fresh legal mechanism was urgent, and *ijtihād* or individual opinion fitted the requirements. This methodology developed as a practical source based on the Qur'an, Sunna and a general awareness of Islam. As an independent source of legislation, it represented a new vehicle through which to reach legal solutions for a variety of cases. Such an instrument existed only in an embryonic form at the time of the Prophet, and he himself acknowledged its value in circumstances where the text offered no solution. It was inevitable that, as the heart of *ijtihād* lay within personal opinion, occasional disagreement, *khilāf*, would occur, a concept unknown during the Prophet's lifetime. However, views that sometimes lead to conflict, more frequently lead to agreement. Consensus, *ijmā'*, was another innovative and major legal development that took place at this juncture.

The vast majority of legal injunctions were formed as consultative legislation; this was particularly so with regard to cases that were relevant to public matters during the era of Abu Bakr (r. 632–4) and 'Umar (r. 634–44).[13] For example, when Iraq was conquered, 'Umar looked for the advice of the Prophet's companions regarding the distribution and use of its land. He was unsure whether to leave it in the hands of the original owners or distribute it among the conquerors. After consultation, the decision reached was that the land should remain with the owners since they possessed the necessary skills for its future cultivation, whereas the nomadic conquerors lacked such aptitude and experience.[14] The methodology followed by the companions in order to resolve their problems entailed the discerning of the actual reason for an injunction in the light of public interest. Often, some textually prescribed injunctions were suspended on the grounds that they lacked the circumstances and spirit of legislation that the Qur'an and Prophetic instruction required for their application. Legal texts generally cite the following four examples of such suspension during this period:

1. The suspension of the share of the people whose hearts need to be reconciled, on the pretext that shares used to be granted to them on the basis that they would represent a threat to Muslims.[15] When Islam increased in strength, the reason for the injunction became no longer valid, then the text was not applicable (although not cancelled).
2. The suspension of the punishment for theft, which was again prescribed by the Qur'anic text.[16] Accordingly, 'Umar did not amputate the hands of some poor people who had stolen a female camel while working for Ḥāṭib b. Abu Balta'a. 'Umar's justification for not applying the instruction of the text was based on the grounds that the time when the act was committed was one of famine; thus necessity can justify what is prohibited.
3. Ali, the fourth caliph, designated a special sanctuary wherein lost camels could be kept at the expense of the Muslim treasury. This contradicts the Prophet's instruction to leave lost camels wandering free since they are able to fend for themselves. While such an action was straightforward in the days of the Prophet, the situation during Ali's era was different in that the number of straying camels had increased markedly and there were also more untrustworthy people to contend with.[17]
4. At the time of the Prophet, the process of divorce would be spread over three pronouncements and take many months, even if the man declared his intention three times at one session. During 'Umar's era, he decided that those who declared divorce on their wives in one session should bear the consequence of that declaration. His reasoning regarding this issue was based on his wish to control the misuse of divorce pronouncements.[18]

All the above cases provided important precedents upon which Muslim lawyers justified future individual opinions and the concepts of necessity and public interest as part of the process of text-interpretation.

When Mu'āwiya b. Abu Sufyān became caliph (AD 662), Islamic law witnessed a fundamental change in its establishment when the government system was forcibly altered from selection on merit to hereditary succession. In conjunction with this change of policy, the legal system had to adapt to the inevitable social transformation from a basic nomadic lifestyle to a settled and urban one, a movement that was accelerated by the accumulation of wealth and power. This increase of acquisitive values was accompanied by a subsequent plunge into the mundane and materialistic, far removed from the previous mystical, romantic, desert way of life. Despite this, the prophetic tidal wave continued to carry with it the main substance of Arabic society, imbued with the theology of belief in one God, Allah. The discovery of new cultures and systems of life required the alteration of many common Arabic practices, but the old nomadic way basically remained a paradigm from which the Islamic vision of life was produced. The two cities of Mecca and Medina represented the cradle of an Islamic vision for the new way of life.

How did the way of life in Muslim society continue to develop over the next few generations? Was the newly developed legal system divorced from historical considerations, as Coulson maintains?[19] Or was it evolving as a historical phenomenon, closely linked to social progress? In essence, these questions are difficult to answer since the study of the caliphate, its institution and subsequent development has never been attempted in its entirety until now.[20] However, it can be observed that in principle there seem to be two main views in analysing the relationship between the prophetic period and the later development of Islamic law.

Traditional Muslim opinion perceives a continuous relationship between the periods of the Prophet, the caliphs and the development of the law.[21] Conversely, Western scholars, such as Goldziher and Schacht, maintain that the structure which emerged during later periods of Islamic law reflected local practice and the ongoing ideology of local scholars.[22] Schacht maintains Islamic law to be 'a unique phenomenon different from all other forms of law'.[23] He also states: 'the classical theory of Islam was influenced by foreign elements which were so thoroughly assimilated and Islamicised that they hardly seem to reveal a trace of their origin'.[24] Wansbrough argues that the Qur'an, like the hadith, must be recognised as the end product of two centuries of community experience.[25] Coulson views Islamic law through the lens of 'an ongoing evolution that had begun in the time of Muhammad'.[26] Hallaq, on the other hand, asserts that Islamic legal theory recognised a variety of sources and methods from which the law can be derived; and, with the exception of the Qur'anic legal reform, the Prophet generally followed the existing pre-Islamic Arab practices.[27]

The diverse theories in interpreting the formation of Islamic law represent variant angles from which that formation was perceived. However, this legislative development was initiated by a divine 'big bang', which fashioned a cultural wave that has maintained its impetus over the last fourteen centuries, creating a wide variety of legal cultures in its wake. Although our main imperative in this study is not so much to examine the history of Islamic law as to ascertain its essence, we have to accept that 'the law' was the outcome of a religious textual event that clearly contributed to the shaping of human legal life. The fact that

Muslim scholars started the documentation of the tradition of the Prophet very early is by itself an indication of such influence. Sunna's documentation is important because it has a major influence on the legal structure of the society and state.

Any form of new legal growth, whether organic or inorganic, is bound to be noticed since the tradition of the Prophet was not merely hidden in the hearts or memory of the scholars. It was alive in the practice of daily social life. The fact that there is a canonical documentation of Sunna going back to the date of 'Umar b. Abd al-Azīz is evidence by itself that there was great value given to Sunna and to all that is based upon it, and that the law cannot grow independently. Abu al-Zinād, a colleague of Muhammad b. Shihāb al-Zuhri (d. 124/742), recorded the latter's thorough documentation in the following terms: 'We used to write down only legal matters, *al-ḥalāl wa al-ḥarām*, while al-Zuhri wrote down everything he heard'. Al-Zuhri is supposed to have widened the concept of Sunna common to his time by recording everything traced back to the Prophet, even if it was a personal statement made by the Prophet's companions, while his colleagues argued that such a hadith did not form Sunna.[28] Such a criticism of Zuhri's methodology by his contemporaries indicates that the Sunna of the Prophet was valued as a distinguished source of *sharī'a*, more so than the Sunna of his companions. Malignant growth within the prophetic Sunna would soon be noticed and removed.

Notes

1 In 36/656 and 37/657, Ali was already sixty years old. In 11/633, he was a little over thirty: *EI*[2], '*Ali*', by L. Veccia Vaglieri, i, p. 381b.

2 The old name for Medina.

3 Zarqāni, *Manāhil al-'Irfān*, Cairo, n.d., 1, p. 114; Qaṭṭān, *Mabāḥith fi 'ulūm al-Qur'an*, 3rd edn, Beirut, n.d., p. 75; Zaydān, *al-Madkhal li dirāsat al-sharī'a al-Islāmiyya*, Beirut, 1990, p. 92.

4 Zarqāni, p. 115.

5 Muslim b. al-Ḥajjāj, one of the early authentic collectors of the tradition of the Prophet of Islam. *EI*[2], '*Muslim b. al-Ḥajjāj*', by G. H. A. Juynboll, i, p. 53.

6 Jābir b. Abd Allah al-Anṣāri (AD 607–697/16 BH–78 AH), a companion of the Prophet and an eminent narrator of hadith. Zirikli, *Al-A'lām: qāmūs tarājim li ashlar al-rijāl*, 10 vols, Beirut, 1954–9, 2, p. 104.

7 Qur'an: ii: 223.

8 The son of the second orthodox Caliph 'Umar b. al-Khaṭṭāb (d. 73/693) and one of the most prominent personalities of the first generation of Muslims, and one of the authorities most frequently quoted for Traditions. *EI*[2], '*Abd Allah b. 'Umar*', by L. Veccia Vaglieri, vii, p. 691.

9 Zarqāni, p. 115.

10 *EI*[2] states: 'If we were to believe without careful thought the Muslim writers who touch on the Islamisation of *Yemen*, we would accept that in 8/628 the governor in

San'ā', a Persian by the name of Badhān, embraced Islam and the whole of the country immediately followed suit. *EI*[2], 'Yaman', by A. Grohmann et al., xi, p. 269a.
11 Mu'ādh b. Jabal (AD 603–639/20 BH–18 AH), Zirikli, 8, p. 166.
12 This hadith is recorded by a few books of hadith, including Abu Dāwūd in his *Sunan*, 3, p. 412, and Ibn Qayyim al-Jawziyya in *A'lām al-muwaqqi'īn*, Beirut, 1991, 1, p. 154. The hadith is often used to support the concept of *qiyās*. see Fāḍil Abd al-Wāḥid, *Uṣūl al-Fiqh*, Amman, 1998.
13 Abu Bakr was selected to rule after the death of the Prophet. He was then succeeded by 'Umar.
14 Al-Qāḍi Abu Yūsuf Ya'qūb b. Ibrāhīm, *al-Kharāj*, ed. Muhammad Ibrāhīm al-Banna, Cairo, 1981, p. 73, ed. Iḥsān 'Abbās, Beirut, 1985, p. 117.
15 Qur'an: ix: 60.
16 Qur'an: v: 38.
17 Ibn Qayyim Al-Jawziyya, *A'lām al-Muwaqqi'īn*, 2, p. 17; Zaydān, *al-Madkhal*, pp. 102–5.
18 Ibid.
19 Coulson, *History of Islamic Law*, Edinburgh, 1964, p. 1.
20 *EI*[2], '*Khilāfa*', by P. M. Holt, v, p. 7.
21 Yūsuf al-Sibā'i provides an overview of this with a critique for the Western view in his book *Al-sunna wa makanatuha fi al-tashrī' al-islāmi*, Beirut, 1998.
22 *EI*[2], '*Sharī'a*', by N. Calder and M. B. Hooker, vii, p. 323.
23 Joseph Schacht and C. E. Bosworth, *The Legacy of Islam*, Oxford, 1974, p. 392.
24 Joseph Schacht, *The Origins of Mohammadan Jurisprudence*, Oxford, 1950.
25 *EI*[2], '*Sharī'a*', by N. Calder and M. B. Hooker, vii, p. 324.
26 Coulson, pp. 2–4; pp. 21–3.
27 W. B. Hallaq, *A History of Islamic Legal Theories*, Cambridge, 1997, p. 1.
28 *EI*[2], '*Zuhri*', by M. Lecker, xi, p. 565.

2

After the orthodox caliphs

By the end of the year AH 41, Islam was deeply rooted in the hearts and minds of believers. The format of Islamic law, *fiqh*, was based on the concepts and views that had been inherited from both the Prophet and his companions, namely Abu Bakr, 'Umar, 'Uthmān and 'Ali. The death of 'Ali was attributable to the political conflict that emerged in Muslim Arabic society following the killing in 35/655 of 'Uthmān, the third Rightly-Guided Caliph.

However, despite the unstable political environment, the continuity of the law of Islam appears to have remained unaffected. Muslim jurists followed in the methodological footsteps of the Prophet and his orthodox companions, referring both to the Book and the tradition of the Prophet. They also exercised their own individual opinion, *ijtihād*, by considering the reasons behind previously made injunctions and by taking public interest into account. This period can be viewed as crucial to the laying of the foundation of Islamic law. The small candle, which was lit at the time of the Prophet, became a torch during the era of the orthodox companions. With the political and military expansion of Islam, this pensive fire gained momentum and spread throughout the Muslim lands. Inevitably, offshoots from the initial flame developed some individual characteristics, and there emerged disagreement among scholars concerning a variety of legal cases. This, coupled with the widespread narration of the tradition, led to the creation of two basic viewpoints with regard to how the law should be understood. The first school of thought resorted to the texts only, while the second recognised the need for individual reasoning in order to reach an injunction beside the text.

By this time, Islam existed not only in Mecca and Medina, but had reached as far as Egypt and Syria.[1] Islamic legal theology was no longer purely that of the Prophet, and the law was influenced by the developed theology which reflected the political differences initiated by the assassinations of 'Uthman and 'Ali. The importance of *Khawārij* lies particularly, from the point of view of the development of dogma, in the formulation of questions relevant to the theory of the caliphate and to justification (for salvation) by faith or by work.[2]

A further factor, leading to the diversity of Islamic law, lay in the spread of

Muslim schools of thought to various parts of the globe. Such diversity represented not only a 'clustering' effect of the law but also a geographical evolution that had been generated by contrasting individual situations as they emerged in various parts of the Muslim world. The early variation in the understanding of the text created differing local cultural laws which were generated by the dialectical interplay between the knowledge of the scholars and the locations where they lived or to which they travelled.

The Prophet's town of Medina was home to Abd Allah b. 'Umar (d. 73/693), who was well known for his verbal adherence to the text. Abd Allah b. 'Abbās (d. 68/686–8) also resided there, and these two scholars represent a direct link to the mainstream of Islam via their close relationship to the Prophet, the former being the brother-in-law of Muhammad and the latter his uncle. Such traditional direction of thought continued the tendency of strictly adhering to the text in the deduction of injunctions, and this cemented the establishment of cultural law in the locality. In the south of Iraq, Basra subscribed to the views of Abu Mūsa al-Ash'ari, Anas b. Mālik and Muhammad b. Sīrīn. Inevitably, the formulation of the law in that locality was affected by the ethos of Basra, which was an environment influenced by both urbanism and nomadism.[3] In Syria, a country of agricultural villages closely bordering each other,[4] people depended upon the juristic opinions of Mu'ādh b. Jabal and 'Ubāda b. al-Ṣāmit and their students, such as Abu Idrīs al-Khawlāni and 'Umar b. Abd al-'Azīz.[5] The Islamic law of Egypt, a culturally rich country, was formed following the legal decisions of Abd Allah b. 'Amr b. al-'Āṣ.[6]

One can clearly observe a relationship not only between the geographic location and the format of law but also between the personalities of the scholars and their individual attitudes towards the law. Abd Allah b. 'Umar and his followers created a legal attitude that did not divert from the text; and this is perhaps understandable, given the nature of their non-complex society. This strict adherence to the Qu'ran and Sunna of the Prophet was upheld further by future generations. Sālim, the son of Abd Allah b. 'Umar, was also a venerated scholar who continued his father's methodology. Once, when asked by a man to give his opinion in a legal case, he replied: 'I did not hear anything', meaning that he had had no information either from his father or from other scholars. The man pressed further: 'Give me your opinion, and Allah will reward you'. Sālim again refused to pass comment. The man was adamant: 'Please tell me your opinion, and I will accept it'. Sālim went on to justify his decision to remain non-committal: 'If I tell you my opinion, you will leave, and if I change my mind, I will not know where to find you'.[7] Sālim was afraid to exercise his individual opinion because he did not have confidence in its accuracy or its permanence.

Scholars who were not hesitant to proffer personal advice and opinion maintained that, if there was no available text relevant to the issue in hand, then legal opinion was valid, as *sharī'a* was inherent in the eventual decision. Such action did indeed cater for the interests of people, and this was evident in the methodologies employed by the companions such as 'Umar and 'Ali. It can be said that the school of the text had its origins in Medina, while that of individual opinion flourished in Kūfa and Iraq. Needless to say, physical distance played a major role in the formulation of the latter school, since Medina represented the heart of Islam, and at that time Kūfa as a newly built town[8] would have been perceived as a totally different part of the world, in terms of both culture and accessibility. However, this observation should not detract from the fact that the scholars themselves exercised personal and sometimes 'charismatic' influence upon such attitudes. Doubtless the personality and social background of each scholar would have had a considerable impact on the methodology and practice of local law; yet Medina remained the shell for the textual traditionalist, while Kūfa become the harbour for diversity of opinion. The home of the Prophet was a simple desert-edge town, in contrast to Kūfa, which developed a more multi-cultural civilisation due to its status as a major new Iraqi town. Ibrahīm al-Nakh'i (b. c. 50/670, d. c. 96/717)[9] was based there and was influential in the initial establishment of one of the best-known schools of thought in our time, the principles of which continue to endure in India, Pakistan, Iraq and a large portion of the Islamic world – the Ḥanafi school.

During the Umawi period (AD 661–717), Islam spread beyond the Arabic lands, causing Islamic law to expand rapidly. This led to the widening of opinion between various scholars, creating the opposite concept of consensus, the *khilāf* or legal disagreement. The narration of hadith became popular and led to fabrication of problems that affected the process of *fatwa* among Muslim scholars. The most distinctive development during this period was the emergence of two legal methodologies: one which focused on the text, the other on individual opinion. There were also local 'living traditions' which contributed to the development of the schools of law. These living traditions were not directly dependent on the prophetic hadith and Qur'an,[10] but it is certain that they were heavily influenced by them. At least they benefited from the prophetic paradigm of interpreting the text in daily life. Both the Qur'an and hadith accepted human endeavour to deduce the 'truth' when no divine revelation could be found. The process of agreement and disagreement continued during the period of the *'Abbāsi* administration (AD 717–833), causing the law to be further developed through a complex dialectical process between individual human rationale and the text which claimed to have divine authority.

The creation of the four schools in the Sunni branch of law and the centralisation of the law around the concept of *imāma* for the Shī'a were among the natural results of the dialectical interplay between the text and individual opinion. Abu Ḥanīfa al-Nu'mān b. Thābit (80/699–150/767) was the eponym of the Ḥanafi school and he became a foremost authority on Islamic religious law in Kūfa, following the death of his master Ḥammād (d. AH 120).[11] He began his young adult life as a businessman, like his ancestors, dealing in textiles and earning himself a reputation for fair and honest trading. In order to commit himself to the study of Islamic law, he relinquished his profession and concentrated on academic achievement. Abu Ḥanīfa was greatly influenced by Ḥammād, and he went on to meet four companions, including Anas b. Mālik (d. 91/709). He was a highly principled man, and he is renowned for the stand he made in rejecting the post of chief judge offered to him by the Umawi caliph Marwān b. Muhammad. The penalty for this 'slight' to the dynasty entailed 110 public lashes, which were incurred by Abu Ḥanīfa as a result of his reluctance to take up the post in which he would have had to pass judgement on people. No doubt his refusal also reflected his political standpoint towards the Umawis as well as his legal attitude as a public lawyer.

In AH 132, the 'Abbāsis overthrew the opposing Umawi dynasty, and Abu Ḥanīfa was again offered the post by caliph Abu Ja'far al-Manṣūr (d. AH 158), who wanted him to take charge of justice in Baghdad. Once more, the position was refused, and consequently Abu Ḥanīfa was imprisoned until his death. Schacht suggests that he had compromised himself by passing unguarded remarks of a negative nature against the dynasty. He views Abu Ḥanīfa as superior to his contemporary scholars and maintains that this was due to his role as a theoretical systematiser, which enabled him to make considerable progress in his technical legal thought. One of Abu Ḥanīfa's main strengths lay in his ability to blend his own legal views with the customary traditional stream of thought. Because his legal and political opinion tended to be unfettered by restrictive dogma, he faced some criticism and was often accused of being opposed to the tradition of the Prophet.

The fact that he was not involved with the administration of justice provided him with freedom from political responsibility as well as from the burden of conscience when exercising law in court. The systematic consistency of his doctrine may be observed within both the structure of his thought and the method of its application. This gave him a highly developed, more circumspect and more defined outlook than that of his older contemporaries, for example Ibn Abu Layla (d. AH 148).[12]

Abu Ḥanīfa's methodology was reflected not only in his answering of actual cases but also in his inventing of hypothetical sample cases which he examined within the texts, deducing and applying the relevant reasoning that he found there. These hypothetical analogies of cases, *qiyās*, constituted a well-known tool that had been developed and utilised by Abu Ḥanīfa for legal deduction, and many scholars referred to him as the leader of analogy. Due to this remarkable tendency towards analogy, Abu Ḥanīfa was accused of lacking knowledge in the area of hadith – a questionable view in the light of the achievements of his students such as Abu Yūsuf and Muhammad b. al-Ḥasan, both of whom incorporated a considerable number of his narrations in their books of tradition. Some scholars rose to Abu Ḥanīfa's defence and responded to his criticism by collating all his narrations, *marwiyyāt*, of the Prophet's *aḥādīth*. Muhammad b. Maḥmūd Khawārizmi (d. AH 665) wrote such a book, which contained upwards of 800 pages.[13] It is something of an anomaly that Abu Ḥanīfa was well versed in the tradition, and yet such a negative claim had been made about him. It would, however, appear that he was less of a narrator than others of his contemporary scholars, a phenomenon that may be explained by the less traditionalist academic environment of Iraq, which contained many falsifiers of the *aḥādīth*. It is interesting that Abu Ḥanīfa left no documents that he himself had written, and all the information regarding his ideals and methodology has been gleaned from his students. Perhaps his Persian origins contributed to his individuality as an analytical lawyer, and he may have remained uninfluenced by Arab modes of thought.

The testimony of Shāfi'i corroborates this accreditation, maintaining that all scholars are dependent upon Abu Ḥanīfa for *fiqh*.[14] One may question what Shāfi'i meant by *fiqh* at this juncture; does he mean the analogy, close scrutiny and syllogistic understanding of the law? Or is he referring to *fiqh* in all its forms? No doubt Abu Ḥanīfa's famous students were totally dependent upon him for the development of their distinctive legal modes of thought and action. Continuous dialectic critical analyses between master and pupils would have ensured this.

Guidelines for the main aspects of Abu Ḥanīfa's methodology have been recorded in various historical texts, such as *Tārīkh Baghdad* and the *Intiqā'*.[15] His legal methodology can be summarised in the following statement:

> I would take the book of God and if I could not find an injunction therein, then I would refer to the Sunna of the Prophet. If I failed to discover an injunction in either of the main texts, then I would go to the words and statements, *aqwāl*, of the Prophet's companions. From these I would either take or leave evidence as I saw fit. I would not refer to anyone else. When I came to the *tabi'īn*[16] such as Ibrāhīm, Sha'bi, Ibn Sīrīn, Aṭā' and Sa'īd b. al-Musayyab, I would exercise my own opinion as they would do, since they are only men like me.[17]

One of the most distinctive disciples of Abu Ḥanīfa was Abu Yūsuf Ya'qūb b. Ibrāhīm al-Anṣāri al-Kūfi (d. 182/798), who is considered to be one of the founders of the Ḥanafi school. He is also known for his valuable exposition on the finance and budget of the state contained in his book *Al-Kharāj*,[18] a treatise on public finance, taxation, criminal justice and kindred subjects, which he wrote at the request of Hārūn al-Rashīd. The book was printed and edited a few times, but an *editio princeps* of the Arabic text was published in AH 1302 (French translation by E. Fagnan, Paris, 1921).[19]

For many years, Abu Yūsuf occupied the position of chief justice under the *'Abbāsi* dynasty, his time in office spanning the rule of Mahdi, Hādi and Hārūn al-Rashīd. No doubt he played a major role in the spread of the Ḥanafi school of thought, becoming an invaluable source for the practical lives of Muslims because he resorted to analogy and real-life cases (not just hypothetical ones). Abu Ḥanīfa produced another outstanding scholar, namely Muhammad b. Ḥasan al-Shaybāni (132–89/749–805), usually referred to as 'Muhammad' in classical legal texts. In Ḥanafi terminology, Abu Ḥanīfa and Abu Yūsuf were referred to as 'the two Shaykhs' if the former was in agreement with the latter on any particular issue. However, if Abu Yūsuf agreed with Muhammad and both disagreed with their master, their opinion was described as 'the view of the two companions'.[20] Al-Shaybāni's books are preserved, unlike those of Abu Yūsuf, which were all lost except *al-Kharāj*. Here, it would be useful to cite Chaumont:

> at that time, the very notion of a 'book', having a single and identified author, did not exist in erudite circles: a certain disciple would collect the teachings of one or another scholar which he eventually committed to writing, accompanied by his own embellishments or commentary; this compilation would then be handed down from disciple to disciple, each in turn adding his own commentary, until a final version came into being, and was attributed to an ancient authority.[21]

However, it is important to understand the historical development and various usages for the word *kitāb* in order to appreciate whether these works were seen by Muslim scholars as a single-author book or an annotation of 'legal views'. The word *kitāb* could have a diversity of meanings including letter or document. The marriage contract is still referred to in Arabic as *kitāb*. The concept of an annotated compilation was evidently known, since various compilations of Shaybāni's collections were divided by the scholars of the time into two categories according to the reliability of the compilers; thus we have:

1. Works narrated by reliable narrators, which are called *ẓāhir al-riwāya*. These include: *Al-Mabsūṭ*, *Al-Ziyyādāt*, *Al-Jāmi' al-Kabīr*, *Al-Jāmi' al-ṣaghīr*, *Al-Siyar al-kabīr* and *Al-Siyar al-ṣaghīr*.
2. Works related by less reliable narrators, which are called *al-nawādir*. These include: *Al-Kaysāniyyāt*, *Al-Hārūniyyāt*, *Al-Jurjāniyyāt*, *Al-Ruqqiyyāt* and *Ziyādat al-Ziyyādāt*.

The *ẓāhir al-riwāya* works were further collated and edited by Muhammad b. Ahmad Mirwāzi, also known as 'the martyred judge' (d. 344), into one volume entitled *Al-Kāfi*. This was annotated by Sarkhasi in the fifth century AH in a book entitled *Al-Mabsūṭ*, 'the comprehensive', which included the foundation of all cases, their evidence and analogy. In parts, it records some disagreement between scholars of the other competing schools such as Shāfiʿi and Mālik.[22] The dialectical interplay between the text and human activity is also evident in Mālik's ideas and writings.

Mālik b. Anas is the eponym of the Māliki school. The exact date of his birth is uncertain, but the hypotheses vary between the dates of AH 90 and 97. He died, at the age of about 85 after a short illness, in the year 179/796 in Medina.[23] The most influential of his teachers were Muhammad b. Shihāb al-Zuhri (d. 124/742)[24] and Rabiʿa b. Farrūkh, also nicknamed Rabiʿa 'the view-point' (d. 132 or 133), well known as a Medina scholar, who became an exponent of the Kufi school of individual legal methodology.

Miftāḥ al-Sa'āda has recorded an incident when Mālik refused to leave the Prophet's mosque on being asked by caliph Hārūn al-Rashīd to attend the court to teach his two sons. This request came during the period of *hajj*, when Mālik had come to Medina from Baghdad, and his reply reflects his view that know-ledge should be sought with the teacher in the mosque rather than the teacher taking the knowledge to the pupils. 'This knowledge came out from your household. You make it dignified if you wish and you may humiliate it if you wish ... knowledge should be walked to.' On hearing this, Rashīd sent his children humbly to study with Mālik in the Prophet's mosque.[25]

Mālik's emphasis on the norms and practices of ʿUmar and the people of Medina made his school a fundamental textual base of the Islamic legal fabric, which was in contrast to the analytical base of the Ḥanafi school. Mālik's scholastic aptitude can be best assessed by examining the content of the *Muwaṭṭa*, in which he reflects on 'the pre-emption of the legal life by religious and moral ideas'.[26] The *Muwaṭṭa*'s value, according to Schacht, 'could have gained popularity from among a number of similar works and does not stem only from recording the usual consensus of opinion in Medina, but from the fact that it was written in a language which seemed suitable for the layman to understand'.[27]

In writing the *Muwaṭṭa*, Mālik was responding to the request of Caliph ʿAbd al-Mālik b. Marwān, who asked him to compose a simplified text that would be accessible to the less specialised student. When he wrote the book, Mālik named it the *Muwaṭṭa* (the simplified) to reflect this objective. The value of the *Muwaṭṭa* was not only established by being easy reading but also was achieved by being a critical work of scholarship. Schacht states that 'the high estimation held by Mālik in all sources is justified by his strict criticism of *aḥādīth*'.[28] Mālik's distinct difference from Abu Ḥanīfa lay in his tendency to refrain from hypothetical *fiqh*, a methodology that echoes Zuhari's influence upon his mode of thinking. However, his employment of reason was also evident, and this could be ascribed to the fact that he was a student of Rabīʿa ('the viewpoint'). The strict textual methodology that Mālik employed is evidently influenced by the rich prophetic models available in Medina. Unlike Abu Ḥanīfa, Mālik never felt the need to devise cases and endeavour to answer them in a hypothetical way, due to the huge volume of cases that he encountered with large numbers of pilgrims who came to his town every year from all over the world.

Mālik himself did not clearly state the basis of his methodology as one uniform methodological approach towards legal knowledge; however, we can observe some references to his approach in the *Muwaṭṭa*, where he resorted to the practices, *'amal*, of the people of Medina rather than to their individual narrations, *khabar al-wāḥid*. Mālik perceived that the practices of the people were inherited from the preceding generations and were therefore somehow similar to sequential tradition, *Sunna mutawātira*. This tendency was rejected by both Shāfi'i and Abu Ḥanīfa's disciple Muhammad b. al-Ḥasan, who did not seem to subscribe to Mālik's observation that there is a continuous relationship between scholasticism and the dynamics of life within the inherited tradition of the Prophet. The social practice of early Medina society reflected such a relationship and provided a paradigm for the following understanding of Islamic law, particularly within the Māliki school. According to Qarāfi (d. 684/1285), who is a Māliki himself, Mālik's main sources of legal deduction are the Book, the Sunna, the consensus of the people of Medina, analogy, the statements of the Prophet's companions, *maṣlaḥa*, custom, *sadd al-dharā'i'*, *istiḥsān* and finally *istiṣḥāb*.[29]

The diversity of the sources of the Māliki school gave it a flexible leverage over other schools, particularly when it came to the employment of the principle of *maṣlaḥa*, which seems to have dominated the majority of cases for which there was no available relevant text. Mālik himself often founded his reason on *maṣlaḥa*, sometimes referring to this and analogy in preference to the traditions and individual narration, *khabar al-wāḥid*.

One particular case of Mālik resorting to the principle of public interest is inherent in his rejection of the hadith regarding the tying of the udders of camels and sheep, in order to convey a false impression to a prospective purchaser of the likely output of milk. Once the buyer had discovered the deception, his only recourse was to return the animal and receive only dates as recompense, or to keep it and persevere with a poor milker. Mālik's view was that this state of affairs violated public interest and that any faulty goods should be replaced with commodities similar to those required by the consumer. He also disputed a narrative in which the Prophet ordered the disposal of the contents of all cooking pots which contained meat from war booty. Mālik maintained that in certain circumstances, for example starvation of the people, this hadith did not serve the public interest.[30]

Mālik had a marked influence on many scholars, who learned from him and spread his school of thought to a different Muslim world. Abd al-Raḥmān b. Qāsim al-Miṣri (d. AH 197) accompanied Mālik for nearly twenty years; he documented his school and narrated the *Muwaṭṭa*. Māliki thought also spread to Spain via Abu al-Ḥasan al-Qurṭubi (d. AH 193).[31]

When we study Māliki texts, we can observe their difference from Ḥanafi literature in the fact that both imams and students composed them at various times and circumstances; this reflects the influence of environment on the legal writing of Islam. Schacht viewed this as important only as evidence 'of the law in the time of Mālik' and not of Mālik's individual activity.[32] Yet such a statement seems to have ignored the fact that Mālik, like most of the scholars of his time, was not attempting to write a full legal code for Muslims; rather, he was paving the way for scholars to discover suitable references to rising legal cases.

His work may also be valued as an important record for individual opinions on cases. Mālik's legal activity in the *Muwaṭṭa* may be observed in his careful selection of the narrations of the people of Hijāz, combined with the statements of the Prophet's companions and the legal dicta of the third generation of the *tābi'īn*.[33] It could be further argued that the value of Mālik's individual activity was portrayed in the full role that he played during his time as an accurate narrator and compiler of the 'prophetic living traditions', which could have been lost had it not been for him. Schacht criticises Mālik's order for the *Muwaṭṭa* in the following terms: as he was only concerned with the documentation of the Sunna and not with criticism of its form, he is exceedingly careless as far as order is concerned in his treatment of traditions.[34] Here, it would be useful to cite Al-Ḥāfidh b. Ḥajar's comments in discussing 'Umar b. Abd al-'Azīz's decree for the scholars to initiate the canonical documentation of Sunna. The reason why the tradition of the Prophet was not recorded in an orderly manner during the time of the Prophet's companions and the *tābi'īn* can be ascribed to two reasons: first, that there was a ban on the documentation of the tradition 'by the Prophet' to avoid mixing the tradition with the Qur'an; second, that they were not adapted to the methodology of writing because the individuals concerned were great memorisers.[35] The nature of the *Muwaṭṭa* as a source document and Mālik's character as an open-minded thinker were confirmed when Mālik refused to allow his book to be used as the sole official state reference by some of the 'Abbāsi caliphs, including Abu Ja'far al-Manṣūr and Hārūn al-Rashīd.

The other Māliki treatise, which is circuitously associated with Mālik, is more of a legal work than a mere collection of prophetic hadiths (as its title may allude to). The *Mudawwana* was probably initated by Asad b. al-Furāt (d. 212/827), one of Mālik's Qayrawāni[36] students, who died in Sicily after having contributed greatly to the spread of Māliki philosophy.[37] He had learnt the *Muwaṭṭa* from his teacher and travelled to Iraq, where he met the disciples of Abu Ḥanīfa Abu Yūsuf and Muhammad b. al-Ḥasan. He was undoubtedly influenced by these scholars and learnt the Ḥanafi *madhab* from them. Asad wished to discover Mālik's opinions on the new legal cases he had learnt. Unfortunately, Mālik died after Asad b. al-Furāt had travelled to Medina to seek his views, and consequently he went to Mālik's other students to discover their opinion. Abd Allah b. Wahb hesitated, then refused his request; but Ibn al-Qāsim accepted the challenge, and, as a result, Asad b. al-Furāt compiled a document which he entitled the *Asadiyya*. Then came Saḥnūn, a later student of Abd Allah b. Wahb and Ibn al-Qāsim, who showed a particular interest in perfecting what Asad had started. In the time of Sahnūn, many of the Qayrawāni masters, including Asad himself, were ultimately influenced by the Ḥanafi school of thought[38] and intended to bridge the gap between the textual traditional trend and the analytical stream of thought. Saḥnūn's edition for the *Asadiyya* subsequently returned him to his master, Ibn al-Qāsim. They worked on it together, producing the *Mudawwana*, which is considered to be one of the most important references compiled by Mālik's students on the subject of Māliki law in comparison with Ḥanafi law.[39]

It would be fair to state that Mālik's impact on his students and indeed on Islamic law stems from the fact that he represents a transitional phase in the human formation of the law. This is unlike the founder of the Shāfi'i school, who could be described as a scholar who changed the shape of Islamic law. According to Chaumont (quoting Al-'Abbādi), Shāfi'i's birth (AH 150) coincided with the death of Abu Ḥanīfa, even to the very day.[40] The exact place of his birth is uncertain; however, most biographers favour Ghazza Palestine, while other references maintain that he was born in 'Asqalān. Shāfi'i died in Egypt in AH 204. He was brought up in Mecca, studying under the famous scholar Muslim b. Khālid al-Zinji,[41] and he continued learning with him until he had licence to give *fatāwa* at the age of fifteen. Shāfi'i went to Medina, met Mālik and studied the *Muwaṭṭa* with him. He then travelled to Yemen in order to learn the *fiqh* of the great scholar Al-Awza'i from his students. He also studied the *fiqh* of Layth b. Sa'd (the top scholar of Egypt) from his student Yaḥya b. Ḥasan. In the year AH 184, Shāfi'i was brought to Baghdad accused of plotting against the 'Abāssis, an accusation from which he was later absolved. However, he decided to stay in Baghdad to learn from Muhammad b. Ḥasan Shaybāni, a close student of Abu Ḥanīfa. He then travelled to Mecca, having learned Iraqi knowledge of law, returning in AH 195 and staying for a further two years. His final journey was to Egypt (c. AH 199), where he resided until his death.

Shāfi'i can be seen as a distinctive scholar compared with other founder eponyms of Islamic law. His ability to structure the foundation and interior of law on the bases of prevalent theories and concepts apparently impressed Schacht, who named him 'the architect' of Islamic law, although this attribute has been questioned by Wael Hallaq.[42] This architectural metaphor was no doubt drawn from Shāfi'i's legal persona, which was a complex edifice of varied methodologies that he had acquired from his masters. This, coupled with an extremely sharp mind, enabled him to establish a strong bond between the prophetic *aḥādīth* and the law within a systematic methodology. He was able to produce a clear and independent Islamic methodology in understanding the law, an outstanding feat in view of the fact that the prevailing vision of law at that time was established on philosophy. His previously mentioned book *Al-Risāla*, 'Message', embodies the most important principles of Islamic law. His ability to learn and digest the *fiqh* of Mecca, and of Medina and Abu Ḥanīfa, equipped him with a new legal mentality; and, when he returned to Iraq for the second time in AH 195, Shāfi'i was clearly an individual with unique and flexible modes of thought. This flexibility may be best illustrated by his book *Ḥujja*, which represents his Iraqi views, a book he altered substantially in order to fit the new and different environment that he was to encounter on his arrival in Egypt. Shāfi'i was thus an adaptable scholar with two distinctive legal theories, the application of which was dependent upon environment and circumstance. Consequently, all schools of Islamic law were heavily influenced by his intricate structure of the law.

The foundation on which Shāfi'i established his ideas was the linking of the law with the traditions of the Prophet. This principle was subject to criticism from Goldziher, who contested the sequential relationship between *fiqh* and the prophetic traditions, *aḥādīth*, although Goldziher had no knowledge of the *Risāla* according to Chaumont.[43] Schacht has proposed that *aḥādīth* were fabricated at a later date to suit the demands of scholars, thus rendering them untraceable to the Prophet. Schacht justifies his theory by suggesting that early narrations were dispersed geographically in the form of 'living traditions' that had emerged within differing Islamic cities and, as such, may not be genuine. Several scholars such as M. 'Azmi have responded to this by offering reasons why the tradition used by early lawyers would be more likely to be authentic and not fabricated by later scholars. Using the text on which Schacht based his argument, 'Azmi presented different translations from those of Schacht and concluded that the term 'Sunna' should be defined as referring to the Prophetic tradition and not the prevalent tradition.[44] In his studies of early Muslim jurisprudence, Norman Calder maintained that hadith-based jurisprudence did not emerge in the early part of the ninth century with Shāfi'i, as Schacht had proposed, but was present throughout the ninth and into the early tenth century. He based his argument on examples of early judicial texts including the Māliki, as represented by the *Mudawwana* of Saḥnūn and the *Muwaṭṭa* of Mālik,[45] the Ḥanafi, as represented by the *Kitāb al-aṣl* or *Al-mabṣūṭ* by Muhammad b. al-Ḥasan al-Shaybāni and the *Kitāb al-kharāj* of Abu Yūsuf[46] and finally the Shāfi'i school, as represented by Shāfi'i's famous book *Al-Umm*[47] and *Muktaṣar al-muzani.*[48] Calder claimed that all displayed evidence of an 'organic growth', which indicates that a circle of later scholars would append the work of their predecessors.[49]

Although it is not the aim of our book to discuss in great detail such hypotheses, it would be pertinent to observe that the passages that were utilised do not seem to provide sufficient representation for the texts that the author aimed to examine, due to the fact that they are very small in size and sometimes contain errors of translation, such as translating the Arabic word *al-wazz*, geese, as 'ducks'.[50] The arguments contain few presumptions that are not explained. This is exemplified by statements such as the one made about a passage that the author did not include in the original translation he made, but to which he nonetheless referred later by stating: 'this fragment exists now incongruously, in the midst of authority statements. It was probably intended at one time to continue a dialogue section that deals with scepticality of water to animal purity.'[51] This passage seems to represent an account of a principle, which also makes a category distinction, which is contrary to Calder's assertion that the text which he examined only contains one statement of an account of law in the passage 1.5.b.[52] Furthermore, this partly omitted passage represents an important early reference to *istiḥsān* which Calder did not notice. The application of *istiḥsān* here is evident, since Mālik does not apply the direct analyses, *qiyās jali*, of chicken and geese to other domestic animals, which do not render water contaminated if they drink from it. He prefers classifying them among the carrion birds unless they are caged and cannot get to filth.

قال وسألنا مالكا عن الدجاج والإوز تشرب في الإناء أيتوضأ به قال لا إلا أن تكون مقصورة لا تصل إلى النتن وكذلك الطير التي تأكل الجيف.

Calder's argument that the *Muwaṭṭa* was partly composed after the *Mudawwana* is based on his observation that the *Mudawwana* contains 'an altogether superior version of one particular hadith relevant to water from a water hole'.[53] Then Calder wonders: 'Did the compilers of the *Mudawwana* have a copy of the *Muwaṭṭa* before them?' This argument seems in need of further support, bearing in mind that the initial composer of the *Mudawwana*, Asad b. al-Furāt, was a student of Mālik and learnt the *Muwaṭṭa* from him. So it is expected that the impact of the *Muwaṭṭa* is found in the *Mudawwana* and not the opposite. If Calder's hypothesis were correct, one would wonder whether the entire confusion was the product of the copyists or the authors of the original text of the *Mudawwana*. However, the points that Calder was making are interesting and represent a useful critique on the early forms of 'casuistic drafting' by a Western historian, who bases his critique on a contemporary logical analyses by utilising a concept of law which is entirely different from what he examines.

Shāfi'i's legal methodology, as gleaned from his works *Al-Risāla* and *Al-Umm*, can be summarised as follows. The prime steps to take in deducing a legal injunction (dictum) must be the referencing of the Book, the Sunna and *ijmā'*, the latter being employed to clarify the former.[54] Shāfiʿi recognised that the Sunna could be used to elaborate on the Qu'ran, even if the pertinent section had been narrated by a single individual, *khabar wāhid*, with the condition that the narrator is acknowledged as a reliable *thiqa* and trustworthy *'adl*. Shāfiʿi did not expect such a narration to be popular knowledge, *mashhūr*, if it was relevant to a widespread inappropriate public practice, *mā ta'ummu bihi al-balwa*; however, this knowledge is a requirement according to the Ḥanafi school. Furthermore, Shāfiʿi did not make it a condition for the accepted individual narration to be in compliance with the actions of the people of Medina, a clause that Mālik would have stipulated.[55] Shāfiʿi's requirement of an individual narration, prior to its legal utilisation, was that it should be transmitted in the proper manner, *ṣaḥīḥ al-sanad*. His attitude to weak hadith, *mursal*, was one of reticence; but, if a reputable first narrator had narrated such a hadith, then he would accept it. Shāfiʿi maintained that, after consulting the Book and Sunna, the next steps were to examine the *ijmāʿ* and the statements of the Prophet's companions and to prioritise them according to their compliance with Qur'an and Sunna[56] and, if still in doubt, to take the statements of orthodox caliphs in preference to other sources. If these measures failed to produce a satisfactory result, then he would resort to analogy, *qiyās*.[57]

Shāfiʿi's ideas and methodology did not only rearrange the cards of Islamic law; they were also an inspiration to the fourth most important jurist in Islamic law. Ahmad b. Ḥanbal, 'the Imam of Baghdad', was a celebrated theologian, jurist and traditionalist (164–241/780–855), and one of the most vigorous personalities of Islam, which he has profoundly influenced both in its historical development and in its modern revival.[58] He was born in Baghdad and studied with many distinguished scholars, such as the famous Abu Yūsuf (d. 182/798), and Shāfiʿi distant student, Abd al-Raḥmān b. Mahdi (AH 135–98). He was the eponym of the fourth school of Islamic law and was celebrated as a top scholar of his time due to his deep and independent knowledge of the Sunna. His most renowned work is *al-Musnad*,[59] a compilation of more than 40,000 hadith, which were collated from his lectures by his own son, Abd Allah. The methodology by which he deduced his legislative procedures relies heavily on the Book and Sunna, which surpass all other sources. From Ibn Ḥanbal's perspective, these texts overrule the individual views of any scholar, no matter how knowledgeable. A correct hadith could not be overturned by the *'amal*, actions of the people of Medina, or by analogy, or by the statements of the Prophet's companions, or even by consensus. In this ideal, he concurs with the view of Shāfiʿi. Subsequent to consultation of the text, Ibn Ḥanbal tended to resort to the *fatwa* (legal opinion) of the Prophet's companions, with the proviso that none had disagreed with such. On occasions where the companions had disputed certain issues, then he would refer to the texts and choose according to the preferred injunction that was closest to the matter in hand. It is interesting to note that he would refer to a weak hadith in preference to analogy, regarding such a narration as neither false nor emanating from an unreliable narrator, but rather giving this type of hadith a specific class of its own. Analogy as a source of reference was always a last resort for Ibn Ḥanbal, and was utilised only when all other channels of enquiry had been exhausted.[60]

At times, Ibn Ḥanbal was reluctant even to offer his opinion if he felt that the available evidence was conflicting. The reason for his unfaltering recognition of the views of the companions of the Prophet lay in his assertion that they, of all people, had practised the injunctions of the text in a more precise manner than other generations. In addition to this, just prior to his death, the Prophet himself had recommended referral to their views and practices as well as to his own. Ibn Ḥanbal's attitude to tradition and strict adherence to the text was inextricably linked to his doctrine of ethics, the latter maintaining that the objective of all action is the serving of God. To Ibn Ḥanbal, the concept of faith was inherent in words, deeds, intention and attachment to the Sunna.

He was constantly consulted on questions, *masā'il*, of all sorts relating to dogma, ethics or law. Although he may not have prohibited the writing down of his opinions as formally as certain traditions assert, it is certain that he warned his questioners against the danger of a codifying of his thought, which might then replace the principles of conduct traced by the Qur'an and the Sunna; he himself, in contrast to Shāfi'i, never sought to present it systematically as a body of doctrine. The fundamental purpose of his teaching is to be seen as a reaction against the codification of the law.[61] Goldziher refers to a widespread Ḥanbali following from the eighth to the fourteenth century which appeared in many parts of the Islamic world, particularly Iṣfahān, Rayy and Shahrazūr.[62]

The position of Ibn Ḥanbal regarding *kalām* (dialectical theology) was one of firm opposition and rejection, simply due to his perception of the employment of a non-Islamic methodology within this specific approach to knowledge. Ibn Jawzi reported that Ḥanbal had stated: 'Do not sit with people of *kalām*, even if they defend the Sunna'. In fact, this statement adequately sums up his view of the *Mu'tazila*, whose understanding of God and His relationship with humanity is defined through Hellenistic notions and a metaphorical interpretation of the anthropomorphic language that is used in connection with the Divine.

Ibn Ḥanbal's methodology of understanding Islamic law can perhaps be understood through his statement that faith incorporates both words and actions and that faith itself can both increase and decrease. All good deeds are integral parts of faith, whereas bad ones serve only to decrease the faith.[63] From this, we can identify his assertion of the strong link between faith and the practicalities of life. Further evidence of his rejection of *kalām* is apparent from a report of his reluctance to enter into any theological discussion that was not confined to the texts or the opinions of the companions of the Prophet and their followers. His understanding of hadiths appears to have been influenced by the various challenges faced by scholars of his era, particularly the theological challenges surrounding the creation of the Qur'an. The Jahmīs represent one of the most distinctive sects to practise the utilisation of polemics in their efforts to determine the theories regarding the nature of the Divine. Ibn Ḥanbal's son, Ṣāliḥ, reported his father to have classified the Jahmis into three groups. The first of these maintained that the Qur'an had been created; the second group acknowledged that the Book was the word of God; and the third theorised that the created part of the Qur'an was *lafẓ*, i.e. no more than what the human being was able to articulate on reading the text. Such was the complex theological environment within which Ibn Ḥanbal worked; his attitude to the law was doubtless influenced by this climate of controversy. This may go some way to explaining his tendency to focus on the Sunna, more so than on the law itself. He is reported to have stated that the fundamental principle of Sunna was to follow the companions and to avoid heresies, debates and arguments. Due to its lack of analogy and scope for metaphorical interpretation, Ḥanbal agreed that the Sunna could not always be totally comprehended by human rationality. He completely rejected any claim that the Qur'an was created, and he gave no credibility to those who declined to commit themselves either way regarding this debate.

The development of Ibn Ḥanbal's *Musnad* represents the culmination of work from a scholastic movement and documents, the hadiths of the Prophet's companions in a specific order that accords with their position in Islam, or indeed with their genealogy.[64] Abu Dawūd al-Ṭayālusi (AH 133– 204) is said to have been the first to compile such a document;[65] however, the *Musnad* has proved to be a much more detailed and comprehensive work. Ibn Ḥanbal's son is reported to have maintained that this compilation was actually extracted from around 700,000 hadiths.[66]

Ḥanbal was loath to record his legal thoughts, being apprehensive as to their validity; but his companions collated a number of his opinions, classifying these as different chapters of law. A scholar by the name of Muhammad b. Hārūn al-Khāl concentrated on all of Ḥanbal's narrations, entitling his work *Al-Jāmi'*, the container. 'Umar b. Abu Ali al-Hussain al-Khiraqi (d. 334/946) composed several books on the Ḥanbali school of thought, these being based upon the views of its founder. His most renowned was the abridged work *Mukhtaṣar al-Khiraqi*, which was annotated by Ibn Qudāma al-Maqdisi (d. 620/1223) in his famous book *Al-Mughni*. Subsequent to these publications, the Ḥanbali school was furthered intellectually by Ibn Taymiyya and his disciple Ibn al-Qayyim. Their methodology, however, differed from that of other Ḥanbalis in that both scholars referred to the original traditions and statements of the Prophet, rather than Ibn Ḥanbal's interpretation of these sources. Moreover,

Ibn al-Qayyim failed to mention Ibn Ḥanbal's recognition of consensus and the concept of public interest. It may be said that, with regard to consensus, Ibn Ḥanbal only approved of that which occurred during the era of the Prophet's companions, and he would use a different term for any consensus that took place after this time, namely an 'injunction with which no person disagreed with'. He is reported to have admitted the inevitability of analogy.[67] Such statement may have been the reason that led Ibn Taymiyya to focus on exploring the depth of analogy by utilising more complex attributes to describe the *'illa* or the common reasoning of similar cases.

Ḥanbal's respect for *maṣlaḥa mursala*, public interest not specified by the text, is evident from the Ḥanbali tendency to consider it analogous to that specified within the text. An important area of Ḥanbal's application of this may be found in his stance on public policy, whereby the ruler would give priority to the enforcement of actions that benefited the community as a whole, such as the punishment of alcohol-drinkers in the month of Ramadan, and the banishment of prostitutes to a land where they could not influence or harm others. Ibn Ḥanbal supplied a rich source of legislative deduction, and his subsequent school developed a range of cases that were able to represent a form of precedence, the fundamentals of which may be employed within an Islamic social structure. One example of this can be seen in the enforcement of a homeowner to accommodate a homeless person if his property is vacant. Ḥanbal also recognised *istiḥsān*, a concept that in simple terms indicates the making of an injunction for a case that differs from a similar one, due to the availability of a stronger textual evidence or consensus, or even to necessity.

A further source referred to by Ahmad b. Ḥanbal is *sadd al-dharā'i'* (the closing of the gates of evil); and the Ḥanbali school remains one of the strongest in its employment of this principle, which propounds the notion of prevention rather than cure. An example of this concept is apparent in the prohibition of the purchasing of commodities prior to their appearance in the market place. The principle in this case is to prevent the monopoly of certain goods and any resultant unfairness to the consumer. Ḥanbal also accepted the principle of *istiṣḥāb*, the approval of an injunction until the presence of a viable alternative be proven, such as in the consideration of all forms of contract to be legal and binding unless a relevant text that is prohibitive is found to exist. Currently the Ḥanbali School is very popular, particularly in Saudi Arabia, Kuwait and a large part of Syria, Iraq and the Gulf States.

The organisation of legal subject matter

Generally speaking, most books of Islamic law were compiled rather than organised in a classified text. However, there appear to be methodologies that may be ascribed to each school of thought, which represents a distinctive mode of compilation. It is clear that some legal topics are placed in differing order, depending on the particular school. For example, the chapter on 'transactions' precedes the one on 'marriage' according to the Shāfi'is and Ḥanbalis, whereas the Mālikis and Ḥanafis reverse this order. Furthermore, the actual contents of the subjects vary from one to another, the Mālikis, Shāfi'is and Ḥanbalis defining 'transactions' as only encompassing the contracts of sale, while the Ḥanafis take a much wider perspective and include all financial exchange (marriage, trusts, inheritance and so on) under this heading.

The schools also vary in their consideration of some particular topics, which may be viewed by some as relevant to the section on 'worship', but placed by others within 'transactions'. An example of this can be seen in the treatment of the subject of horse-racing, the Mālikis considering it to be ritualistic due to its connection with holy war, but the Ḥanbalis placing it under 'transactions' because it reflects the potential for financial gain.[68] Abu Sulaymān cites all the visions utilised by the four schools and offers an explanation of the relationship between one chapter and another. The reasons for these divisions lie in the varying influences absorbed from different academic points of view. Scholars would naturally propound those ideas that were relevant to their particular era and concentrate on the overt relationships within chapters, such as that between the topics of 'divorce' and of 'freeing the slave'.[69] Abu Sulaymān maintains that the organisation of legislative issues did not differ substantially between the Mālikis, Shāfi'is and Ḥanbalis, and he suggests that the Andulusian scholar Ibn Jawzi (d. AH 741) may have exerted influence here. He was a Māliki who divided law into two sections, 'worship' and 'transactions', and he classified the different subjects accordingly in his own work *Qawānīn al-aḥkām al-shar'iyya.*[70]

The question remains as to why these divisions continue to exist among the four main schools of law. The following shows the ways in which *fiqh* is divided:

The Ḥanafis	=	worship, transactions and penalties.
The Mālikis	=	worship, marriage, sale and judgements.
The Shāfi'is	=	worship, transactions, marriage, crimes and disputes.
The Ḥanbalis	=	worship, transactions, marriage, crimes, judgements and disputes.

Was this difference influenced by the methodology of each school in its quest to extract the injunction, or by the perceived definitions of these terms? The answers may lie in the fact that most of the scholars wrote down their notions as they were gleaned from practical cases, and these became the sources for their books, sometimes being listed according to the length of the chapter and sometimes being extracted from the footnotes or scripts that they had dictated to their students.[71] Bearing in mind all these factors, one may conclude that the culture of writing was perpetuated for the benefit of the scholar rather than the lay person, and accordingly the academic would have been expected to find the detail of the subject matter without consulting other scholastic references. The methodology of seeking knowledge at that time differed immensely from later years, in that it was solely dependent upon local references and required total absorption of these references, as opposed to the scanning of texts and the selecting of the main synopsis and concepts. Having said that, a further factor has contributed to the organisation of subject matter in the writings of the four schools. This was the way in which each school perceived the correlation between theology and law, which is confirmed by the fact that all schools place 'worship' at the top of their agenda.

Theology and law

The interaction between theology and law was particularly evident in both Abu Ḥanīfa and Mālik, the former often being quoted to have said that knowledge and theology are a more beneficial partnership than mere knowledge of the legal injunctions. Learning how to worship the Lord is better than the useless accumulation of academia. Abu Ḥanīfa perceived the law as a means of achieving the objectives of the creed; and one of the major issues of his era was the debate on *īmān*, faith, which he defined as belief in God and confirmation that He is the Lord. Abu Ḥanīfa maintained that those who pay lip service to God and do not believe in their hearts are in denial of the faith. Conversely, it is quite possible for someone to display apparent infidelity by not declaring an overt belief, yet God will know that there is true faith in his heart. Ultimately, the concept of *niyya*, 'intention', is utilised to evaluate whether or not a person is a believer, and this is generally the central tenet for identifying 'responsibility' within Islamic law. God knows and sees actual intention; therefore the relationship between theology and legislation is inextricably linked.[72]

The relationship between action and faith constitutes a further dimension to the legal thought process of Abu Ḥanīfa. He perceives that *'amal*, action, occurs as a result of a confirmation of faith, despite these being two differing concepts. One important conclusion he reaches is that sin does not necessarily distinguish an unbeliever from a believer. The perpetrator may be a believer who has committed a sin and as such will not be eternally in hell, the notion upheld by the *Khawārij* and *Mu'tazila*. Abu Ḥanīfa is quoted to have stated that the person who commits murder, the person who steals or commits any great sin, is not to be viewed automatically as a *kāfir*, unbeliever, and God will punish them according to their sins.[73] This idea may be understood on the grounds that the sinner accepts the existence of the Divine, but for some reason he has resorted to sin. In this case, Abu Ḥanīfa would resort to making the individual subject to law, *ergo*, a murderer may be killed, a thief may suffer amputation and a drinker of alcohol may be lashed. These actions would serve to purify the perpetrator from sin, rendering him clean after punishment.[74] At this juncture in the discussion, it is interesting to remark on the statement of a fornicator named *Mā'iz* who approached the Prophet subsequent to his misdemeanour and said: 'O Prophet of Allah, I have sinned. Purify me by punishment.' The crucial difference between the believing sinner and the non-believing sinner can be discerned when any illegitimate action is considered permissible, a perception that would take the sinner into the realm of an unbeliever. The Mālikis and various other Muslim scholars also hold this view.

Abu Ḥanīfa also maintains that no judgement should be passed on others, particularly in relation to matters that lie in the domain of God. It is fair to say that some have misinterpreted his words, erroneously considering him to have propounded the delaying of punishment, *irjā'*. Abu Ḥanīfa's defence of his notion lay in his conviction that a true believer would not remain unaffected by his sins, nor would he become complacent in the knowledge that he may not enter into hell. This further confirms his belief in the value of intention, not only within Islamic law, but also within theology.

The era of Mālik and Abu Ḥanīfa was rife with debate and conflicting theories. Very little, however, is recorded with reference to Mālik's involvement in polemics, and it is unlikely that he indulged in such debates as those that Abu Ḥanīfa was forced to confront. Mālik perceived faith as being inherent in both word and deed; and, from his perspective, the attributes of God stemmed only from an understanding of the text (beyond which he was loath to go). His understanding of legal injunctions resembles that of Abu Ḥanīfa, and the following example reflects his methodology of remaining close to tradition. A man once asked Mālik to interpret verse v: 20 of the Qur'an, which states: *Al-Raḥmānu 'ala al-'arsh istawā*, 'The Beneficent One, Who is established on the Throne'. The enquirer wished to know exactly how He had been established there. Mālik thought for a while and began to sweat, eventually replying: 'We know the meaning of the term "established", but we do not know the answer to "how?" To ask about this is heresy, but to believe it is a duty.'[75]

Finally, it could be stated that Islamic law has evolved through different phases since the early period of the Prophet until the end of the 'Abbasi period. However, the law seems to have remained basically unchanged since the fall of Baghdad in AD 1258 and the subsequent closing of the gate of legal individual opinion, *ijtihād*. Apart from the Ottoman period and its complex and controversial legal structure, Islamic law proper appears to have taken the individual organic form rather than the form of an organisational system. Despite the fact that many states claim to be Islamic, the strongest value of the law remains in the individual's commitment to it. It was the human unexplained tendency towards religion that kept the organic forms of Islamic law alive. Often, Islam propagates itself after lying dormant beneath such powers as the Atatürk (1881–1938) rule of government, communist Russia, the Shah of Iran and more recently the Baath government of Saddam Husain.

Notes

1 In Heliopolis, later called 'Ayn al-shām, a battle took place between the Arabs and the Byzantines in July 640, in which the Byzantines suffered a crushing defeat. The fall of Miṣr [Egypt] followed. *EI*[2], 'Miṣr', by F. Steppat vii: p. 146a. The Battle of Ajnadin on Jumada l 13/July 634 was the first major battle that led to the Muslim armies taking over the walls of Damascus in Muharram 14/635, abandoned by the Greek garrison *EI*[2], '*Shām*', by J. Lentin, lx: p. 281a.
2 See Glossary.
3 Al-Bilādi, *Mu'jam al-mā'ālim al-jughrāfiyya fi al-sīra*, Mecca, 1982, p. 44.
4 Ibid., 167.
5 Fifth Caliph of the Marwāni branch of the *Umawi* dynasty, who reigned from 99/717 to 101/720.
6 Zaydān, *Al-Madkhal*, p. 115.
7 Ibid.
8 Kūfa was built in AH 17 by 'Amr b. al-'Āṣ. It represented the rival intellectual town to Baṣra in both schools of grammar and law. Kūfa was also a permanent military establishment of the Arabs in Mesopotamia. It participated actively in the Islamic expansion into Iranian territory, and, throughout the first/seventh century, was a hotbed of intense political ferment. See Al-Bilādi, p. 267; *EI*[2], '*Kūfa*', by Hichem Djaït: vi, p. 345b.
9 One of the earliest great defenders of the use of individual opinion, *ra'i*.
10 *EI*[2], '*Fiqh*' by J. Schacht, i, p. 164; *EI*[2], '*Sharī'a*' by N. Calder, lx, p. 323.
11 *EI*[1] (1913–36). *EI*[2], '*Abu Ḥanīfa*', by J. Schacht, i, p. 123.
12 *EI*[2], '*Abu Ḥanīfa*', by J. Schacht, i, p. 123.
13 An *editio princeps* of *Marwiyyāt Abu Ḥanīfa* was published in Cairo in AH 1326.
14 Abu Zahra, *Tārīkh al-Madhāhib al-islāmiyya*, Cairo, 1987, 2, p. 374.
15 Ibid., p. 133, quoting *Al-Intiqā' fi faḍā'il al-a'ima al-thalātha al-fuqahā'*, by Yūsuf b. Abd al-Barr al-Nimri, and Al-Khaṭīb al-Baghdādi, *Tārīkh Baghdād*, Cairo, 1938, 13, p. 368.
16 Roughly meaning the following generation of scholars to the Prophet's companions.
17 Abu Zahra, *Tārīkh*, p. 375; Zaydān, *al-Madkhal*, pp. 132–3.
18 The word seems to have denoted 'tax' in both its general and its specific meaning.
19 *EI*[2], '*Abu Yūsuf*', by J. Schacht, i, p. 164.
20 Zaydān, *al-Madkhal*, p. 135.
21 *EI*[2], '*Al-Shaybānī*', by E. Chaumont, lx, p. 392b.
22 The book amounts to thirty volumes and was republished a few times. See the Beirut edition by Dār al-Ma'rifa, AH 1406.
23 *EI*[2], '*Mālik b. Anas*', by J. Schacht, vi, p. 262.
24 See above, Chapter 1.
25 Ibn Qayyim al-Jawziyya, *Miftāḥ dār al-sa'āda*, Riyāḍ, n.d., p. 86, quoted by Zaydān, *Al-Madkhal*, p. 136.

26 *EI*[2], '*Mālik b. Anas*', by J. Schacht, vi, p. 262.
27 Ibid.
28 Ibid.
29 Al-Qarāfi, *Anwār al-burūq fi aḥkām al-furūq*, 'Ālam al-kutub, Beirut, n. d., p. 1; Zaydān, *Al-Madkhal*, p. 136.
30 Al-Shāṭibi, *Al-Muwāfaqāt fi uṣūl al-ṣharā'a*, 4 vols, Cairo, 1975, 3, pp. 22–5.
31 Ibid, p. 165.
32 *EI*[2], '*Mālik b. Anas*', by J. Schacht, vi, p. 264.
33 This was quoted in *Tanwīr al-ḥawālik sharḥ 'alā muwaṭṭa' Mālik*, by Imām 'Ābd al-Raḥmān al-Suyūṭi, Beirut, n.d., 1, p. 5.
34 *EI*[2], '*Mālik b. Anas*', by J. Schacht, vi, p. 263.
35 Al-Suyūṭi, 1, p. 5.
36 Qayrawāni is the *nisba* of a person from Qayrawān, which is a town in central Tunisia. *Nisba* is one of the components of the medieval Arabic proper name. Its function is to express the relation of the individual to a group, a person, a place, a concept or a thing. See *EI*[2], '*nisba*', by '(Ed.)', viii, p. 53.
37 Zaydān, *Al-Madkhal*, pp. 139–40, *EI*[2], *Asad b. al-Furāt* b. Sinān Aba Abd Allah', by G. Marçais, i, p. 658a.
38 *EI*[2], '*Mālik b. Saḥnūn*', by M. Talbi, vii, p. 843.
39 Zaydān, *Al-Madkhal*, p. 140.
40 *EI*[2], '*Shāfi'i*', by E. Chaumont, ix, p. 181.
41 When Shāfi'i was a young literature enthusiast, he met Zunji (also known as Abu Khālid al-Makhzūmi). Zunji was the grand Shaykh and Mufti of Mecca. He managed to convince Shāfi'i that *fiqh* was better for him than literature. See *Al-Imām al-Shāfi'i* by Abd al-Ghani al-Diqr, Damascus, 1996, p. 55.
42 W. B. Hallaq, *International Journal of Middle Eastern Studies*, New York, 1993, republished in Variorum Collected Studies Series, *Law and Legal Theory in Classical and Medieval Islam*, Ashgate, 1994, pp. 587–605.
43 *EI*[2], '*Shāfi'i*', by E. Chaumont, ix, p. 181.
44 *EI*[2], '*Sharī'a*', by N. Calder and M. B. Hooker, vii, p. 321; see also M. M. Azmi, *Studies in Early Hadith Literature*, Beirut, 1968.
45 Norman Calder, *Studies in Early Muslim Jurisprudence*, Oxford, 1993, pp. 20–38.
46 Ibid., pp. 39–66.
47 Ibid., pp. 67–85.
48 Ibid., pp. 86–104.
49 Ibid., pp. 27– 245.
50 Ibid., p. 11.
51 Ibid.
52 Ibid., p. 4.
53 Ibid., p. 28.
54 Shāfi'i, *Al-Risāla*, ed. Ahmad Muhammad Shākir, Egypt, 1993, pp. 17–20, 64–82, 471.
55 Ibid., pp. 228, 370.
56 Ibid., pp. 465–71.
57 Ibid., pp. 476–86
58 *EI*[2], '*Ahmad b. Ḥanbal*', by H. Laoust, i, p. 272.
59 1st edn 1311/2893, followed by many editions. The best edition so far is by Ahmad

Muhammad Shākir, 1377–1400/1958–80.

60 Ibn Qayyim al-Jawziyya, *A'lām al-Muwaqqi'īn*, 1, pp. 24, 26; Zaydān, *Al-Madkhal*, 137.

61 *EI*[2], '*Ahmad b. Ḥanbal*', by H. Laoust, i, p. 272.

62 *EI*[1], '*Ahmad b. Ḥanbal*', by I. Goldziher, p. 189.

63 *Al-Musnad* by Ahmad b. Ḥanbal, ed. Ahmad Muhammad Shākir, Cairo, 1958, p. 75.

64 Muhammad Ajāj al-Khatīb, *Uṣūl al-ḥadīth*, Beirut, 1989, p. 183; Subḥi al-Ṣāliḥ, *'Ulum al-ḥadīth wa muṣūalaḥuhu*, Beirut, 1995, pp. 328–30.

65 A plain but useful edition was reproduced by Walīd al-Jiblāwi and published by Dār al-Ma'rifa, Beirut, in AH 1406, based on the edition of *Dā'irat al-Ma'arif al-'uthmaniyya*, published in Haydar Abad, India, in AH 1321.

66 Ahmad b. Ḥanbal, *Al-Musnad*, p. 23.

67 Abu Zahra, *Tārīkh*, 2, pp. 551, 553.

68 For more details, see Abd-al Wahab Abu Sulaymān, *Tartīb al-mawdhū'āt al-fiqhiyya* Mecca, 1988, pp. 7–8. This study is particularly interesting due to its focus on the structures of the subjects within the four schools and encourages one to examine why they have been so aligned.

69 Ibid., p. 90.

70 Ibid.

71 Ibid.

72 Al-'Ajami, *Al-Fuqahā' wa buḥūth al-'aqīda al-Islāmiyya*, Cairo, 1985, p. 89.

73 Ibid.

74 Ibid., p. 91.

75 Ibid., p. 171.

PART TWO

The law and its sources

3

The divine sources

Sharīʿa is a system of law unlike any other standard text-based legal system as understood in the West. To Schacht, *sharīʿa* 'is not law in the modern sense of the word any more than it is on account of its subject matter'.[1] Calder and Hooker maintain that *sharīʿa* 'designates the rules and regulations governing the lives of Muslims'.[2] Such definitions would be more complete if we add that *sharīʿa* covers all aspects of human existence, including life after death. It does not represent a set of theories and rules to be utilised within the limits of social government, but signifies a comprehensive way of life, which is similar to a path leading to water, as the word *sharīʿa* implies. The law is inextricably bound with the faith, following its route and regulating its orders and directives. One can safely say that *sharīʿa* proffers a legal path which a lawyer may follow in order to extract the rules that correspond to Islamic beliefs and values. Islamic law is understood via the employment of *fiqh*, a discipline that designates academic discussion and consideration for the divine law. However, it would be erroneous merely to consider *fiqh* as 'academic discussion', as such a representation could afford it a philosophical and polemic flavour that is contrary to its comprehensive nature. Despite this fact, Islamic law did utilise philosophical techniques and methods such as analogy.

The Qur'an presents the primary elements of legislation and contains, as Fārūqi states:

> what Muslims have always understood as the commanding imperative, the will of God. However, Muslims have recognized the imperatives and desiderata of the Qur'an as falling into different orders of rank or priority. Although they all belong to the divine will and are constitutive of it, Qur'anic values do not all enjoy the same degree of normativeness. Some are more fundamental and important than others. Some are direct and specific in what they demand of man; some are indirect, pointing to general directions. Some are explicit and comprehensible on first reading; others are implicit and have to be deduced from one or more Qur'anic premises.[3]

The traditions of the Prophet provide a paradigm for the way in which the Qur'anic prescriptions can be practised by human beings in their daily lives. Muhammad may be described as the corporal scripture, his words and actions making available the details that the written text could not.

Under the different conditions of Islam in Mecca and Medina, Muhammad was able to draw up the blueprints of a future life pattern for Muslims. When the man died, the living part of the scripture passed with him, and, for the first time, the companions of the Prophet had to walk a tightrope with no prophetic safety net. During the years 632–61, following the death of Muhammad, they managed to maintain their equilibrium on this narrow path by devising new instruments (such as consensus and analogy), with which to guarantee the security and accuracy of their decisions. As time passed, other methodologies emerged, coupled with a great emphasis on the accurate documentation of the tradition of the Prophet's hadith. Muslim scholars recognised the continuation of the prophetic safety mechanism, which remained in the form of the precedents he had set or their interpretation. The interpretive relationship between the views of the religious scholars and the Sunna and Qur'an was similar to the relationship between the Qur'an and Sunna during the early period of the Prophet's life, based on clarification and supplementation. However, the correlation could not remain static, since new situations and exposure to cultural diversity required corresponding legislation; this was duly implemented within both the spirit of the text and the prophetic understanding of public need and interest. The steps that the Prophet gave in utilising the Qur'anic verses to answer public needs were important guidelines that many scholars used later as methods to interpret both the Qur'an and Sunna to fit their local needs.

The primary sources (the Qur'an and Sunna)

Islamic law is by nature a text-based law. It focuses on the divine scriptures in order both to create the law and to confer its authority. The dependency of the law on the text is evidently significant in the formation of the law and its development. It can be observed, however, that this relationship is not a one-way process whereby the texts legislate and the law operates. It is a dialectical relationship whereby the text legislates and the law formulates. The formulation of the law can be clearly seen during the early period of Islam, in particular in the society of Medina linked with the idea of *'amal*, as Dutton maintains.[4] The *'amal* or common practice of Medina was in effect creating social tradition, Sunna, that became law. Although Islamic law is often seen as an echo of the Qur'anic concepts and textual principles, the legal process is more complex than just stating what the text has provided, since the law often creates a new legislation while calibrating the textual principles to fit the social eventualities. Despite the fact that the calibration process appears to be only an 'interpretation' of the text, the truth remains that it can provide new ideas that have not been stated in the text. We can also observe that the text itself leaves room for such interpretative legislation by being silent. This can be seen in many examples, such as the silence of the text regarding the exact form, colour or shape of women's dress, as well as the size of measuring vessels such as the *ṣāʿ*, which no doubt gave a privileged position to the *ṣāʿ* of Medina as the prophetic crucible of the law.

The Qur'an, or the Book, *al-Kitāb*, represents the most important source of Islamic law, being the ultimate word of the Divine. It is not seen by Muslims as purely a book of law, since it is a book that includes clarification of every matter. The word *al-Kitāb* indicates the significance of textual authority in the Islamic legal mind. It therefore also implies what was composed and given by God; this first source of Islamic law is to be respected more than any human-made law. However, the *kitāb*, like other written texts, raised the problem of understanding its real meaning, and this led to the birth of new branches of Islamic legal knowledge, such as *tafsīr*, or Qur'anic interpretation, and prudence of text, *fiqh*. Muslims believe that the Qur'an was secured by the divine will and that the accuracy of the Qur'an as a document can be affirmed on the grounds that it was presented and recorded by oral transmission as well as script. This belief is in contrast to that of many Western scholars, who contest the divine origin of the Qur'an in part or in its entirety.[5] For various practical and learning purposes, the Qur'anic injunctions were classified into themes and categories.

The following is a summary of what Muslim scholars usually consider to be the categories of legal injunctions or *aḥkām*[6] in the Qur'an. The first is relevant to the doctrine, such as belief in God, His messengers and the Day of Judgement. Next is the category which is relevant to human ethics. And finally, there is the category which is associated with the practical actions of the subjects of Islamic law. These categories are subdivided into injunctions, which are relevant to rituals or transactions.[7] The part which is relevant to transactions can be loosely classified within what is called, in modern legal terminology, the civil law.

These classifications do not always represent a clear-cut separation between law, ethics and theology, and dialectical interaction between these notions seems to be happening all the time. For example, it is often found that the texts which are relevant to legal injunctions are better understood by referring to the doctrinal texts, such as in the case of the application of the punishment for fornication which is stated in the Qur'an, with a note that confirms the divine decree for that punishment.[8] The texts which are relevant to ethics are also employed to clarify other injunctions, such as in the case of the Qur'anic rules and instructions required in a debt contract, which ends by stating that 'if you harm the witness, it shall be wickedness'.[9] The understanding of the position of the moral spirit of Islamic legislation, *rūḥ al-tashrīʿ al-islāmī*, is helpful in understanding how Islamic law functions in real life. In the case of debt, it is ethics that rule and not the materialistic relationship between the debtor and the person in debt. Therefore, if the person in debt cannot repay, then the debtor ought to grant him a further period until he can.[10] Such a concept could sound naive at a business level, yet Muslims argue that on the social level it is important in order to cement the individual relationship and to construct a stable social order.

The Qur'anic methodology in stating injunctions comes for the most part in three forms of expression: general, *kulli*, detailed, *tafṣīli* and synoptic, *mujmal*. The first includes the general rules and principles upon which the legal injunctions are based. This includes principles such as consultations,[11] justice,[12] individual responsibility,[13] and the principle of weighing the punishment according to the crime.[14] The second form is called *tafṣīli*, which provides the accurate details of the rule, sometimes even giving figures such as in the case of inheritance or divorce. The third form of injunctions, the synoptic, *mujmal*, is a form of language expression, which is stated in the framework of a requirement or rule that leaves its application to be highlighted by the prophetic model. An example of this is the prescription for prayer and other rituals such as zakah. Here, the Qur'an states only that such a ritual is a duty, leaving the detail of time, form and frequency to the Sunna of the Prophet.

The Sunna of the Prophet

The second source of Islamic law is the Sunna, or the tradition of the Prophet of Islam. The Sunna, as a general term, designates a norm or tradition, which is regularly acknowledged by a society or group of people. However, in the Islamic legal tradition, it became a term associated with all practices that have been ascribed to Muhammad, apart from the revelation of the Qur'an, in the form of words, actions, approvals or even silence. D. W. Brown maintains that the position of Sunna as the second 'root' of legislation was made on the instigation of Al-Shāfi'i.[15] However, the frequent use of words such as *Sunnat al-nabi* or *Sunnat Muhammad* would suggest a strong possibility that the position of Sunna was well in place long before Shāfi'i, and the role of the latter was merely to acknowledge that fact in a methodical way.[16]

Sunna is the second source of Islamic law after the Qur'an, because all the principles of Islam were revealed in a general form. The role of Muhammad was to carry the message and to elaborate on it. The legal authority of the Prophet was conferred by the Qur'an, which stated that obedience to him was part of obedience to God. The believers may not disagree with the injunctions and orders of the Prophet once his orders are clear.[17]

Categories of Sunna as legal interpretations for the meanings of the Qur'an

The Sunna's role as a legal interpreter for the meaning of the Qur'an is classified according to the clarity of verses, which are divided into four categories. The first is called *mujmal* or synoptic, which includes the Qur'anic verses with general principles that have no specified details. Examples of this are the verses which refer to prayer. The Qur'an ordered believers to pray, but it did not specify how prayer is to be performed. The Sunna's role here was to explain such verses, giving the details of prayer and how it is physically performed.

A second kind of verse is ambiguous, and the Sunna provided a clarification for these verses and words. For example, when the verse 'It is those who believe and confuse not their beliefs with wrong *ẓulm* that are truly in security, for they are under guidance'[18] was revealed, the companions of the Prophet understood the word *ẓulm* in the context that any 'wrong' committed by an individual could invalidate his belief. But the Prophet clarified that *ẓulm* here refers to polytheism, and he quoted a Qur'anic verse which states that polytheism is a grave sin.[19]

A third category of verse aims to clarify general words or concepts by specifying their exact meaning. These are terms such as 'You' in the following verse which speaks of inheritance distribution to people represented by the word 'you': 'God prescribes on you ...'[20] At this point, the Sunna maintained that this verse is specifically made for ordinary people. However, the Prophet's inheritances are treated differently, since they would become a gift to society.

A fourth kind of verse restricts an absolute meaning, *muṭlaq*. This is more relevant to the generality of small and individual items, unlike the second sort of verse in reference to *ẓulm*, which is relevant to a group of objects. Here, *muṭlaq* is relevant to specifying a part of a particular object. For example, the Qur'an maintains that the punishment for theft is to cut off the hand of the culprit if it is proved that he was acting not out of need but out of greed. The word 'hand' is a general concept, *muṭlaq*, which could denote in Arabic any part of the hand between the fingers and the shoulder. The Sunna specified that cutting should be just for the hand, from the palm to the wrist.

In addition to these Qur'anic forms of injunctions, the Sunna brought new dicta that were not previously observed, such as prohibiting the eating of the meat of domestic donkeys and predators with canine teeth or claws. Also, the Sunna prohibited a woman and her aunt from marrying the same man. At this point, it is interesting to pose the following question. Are these legal dicta and injunctions merely an interpretation of the existing Qur'anic legal rules, or did the Sunna literature create new injunctions and orders? Muslim scholars tried to justify the presence of new rules and aphorisms that had not been stated by the

Qur'an, some maintaining that the text permitted the Prophet to create these. Other scholars attempted to associate all the prophetic injunctions with verses from the Qur'an, the necessity of such an undertaking being arguable. The Qur'an in principle is not a book of law, but one of general instruction that provides legal theology based on what some contemporary Muslim scholars call the *tawhidic* principles of Islam blended with the practicalities of local culture.[21] Muhammad encountered various questions, and he used his own individual opinion to deal with issues as they arose. The notion of individual opinion was evidently rooted in the practices of the Prophet, which offered an analogy for later generations. However, there remains a distinction between the two types of analogy in that the decisions of the Prophet were confirmed or corrected by God through revelation. The history of Sunna records a few occasions where Muhammad's judgement was corrected by the Qur'an or even reproved.[22] Muhammad's opinions and actions often appeared to have been monitored by God as a guide, which contain a second level of divine directives. The practical directives of God's law were manifested in Muhammad's actions as a human being and thus include the influence of life skills and personal tastes. The entire Sunna does not signify legislation incumbent on Muslims to follow, yet despite this, many view the prophetic traditions as meritorious and worthy of imitation. However, Muslims are prohibited from following some practices that are considered as only relevant to the Prophet himself, such as fasting for longer than the accepted period of one day and marrying more than the specified number of four wives. The nature of Muhammad created a reflective dialectic relationship between a living individual and a divinely revealed text; this is repeated throughout the history of Islamic law between the 'reliable' older sources, local cultures and the understanding of scholars. Initially, the period of the orthodox caliphs was governed by legislative procedures that were guided by the Qur'an and Sunna, then the sources of that period gave direction to ensuing eras. This was particularly evident in the next source of Islamic law, the *ijmāʿ* or the consensus of scholars.

Ijmāʿ was seen by many Muslim lawyers to be 'almost divine'. However, the fact remains that, apart from the Qur'an and Sunna, all other sources of Islamic law are generally referred to as secondary sources. These secondary sources are mere 'tools' which were developed by various jurists in order to comprehend fully the instructions of the Qur'an and Sunna. Although some have become sources in their own right, perhaps it is only *ijmāʿ* which can be classified as a true secondary source and not a tool from which legislation can be derived. Even *ijmāʿ* was dependent on the Qur'an and Sunna for the deduction of *ḥukm* (legal injunction). Was *ijmāʿ* a new form of legislation that did not exist at the time of Muhammad? Or was it necessitated by the shifting and innovative events after his death? By looking at the commonly accepted definition of *ijmāʿ*,

we find that it designates a consensus of academic opinion on any legal issue that arose subsequent to the death of Muhammad. However, usage of the term *ijmāʿ* was in evidence in pre-Islamic Arabic society as reflected in its poetry, including the *Muʿallaqa* poem of Al-Ḥārith b. Ḥilliza al-Yaskuri.[23] It was often employed to signify 'the agreement to take an action'.[24] Technically, the word appears to have focused on the 'agreement' of the knowledgeable Muslim 'after the death of the Prophet', and this echoes the notion of the ever-changing social needs within the Muslim community, which necessitated such a measure.

The term *'ulamā' al-umma* (community scholars) was also introduced into the old Arabic idea of consensus, referring specifically to the community scholars of Islamic law. Needless to say, when the Muslim community was in its youth, following the death of Muhammad, they were the close companions of the Prophet, such as Abu Bakr, 'Umar, 'Uthman (r. 23–35/644–55) and Ali. The process of *ijmāʿ* probably took place following the posing of a question; a meeting would have been called, a statement posited, proofs given and questions asked on every possible variant scenario. At the conclusion of the debate, problems would have been solved, the argument tight and legislation possible.

A number of related questions arise in considering the actual application of *ijmāʿ*. For example, if one of the scholars did not agree with a particular view, then surely that would negate the notion of consensus. However, were the one in contention to be a less well-known companion, then would the disagreement be minimised? It would appear that most controversy was assuaged through the course of discussion. Zayd b. Thābit[25] is reported to have stated that if a man has sexual contact and does not ejaculate, then all he has to do in order to be clean for prayer is to wash his genitals and then make *wuḍu'* (ritual ablution of hands, face and feet). When the news of this opinion reached the Prince of the Believers, 'Umar, he was displeased, being aware that in this case the Qur'an required the full washing of the body. He called for Zayd and asked him for the basis of his opinion. Zayd replied that he had heard it from his uncles, Rifāʿa b. Rāfiʿ and Abu Ayyūb al-Anṣāri (d. 52?/672), reputable companions of the Prophet. 'Ā'isha (d. 58/678), the wife of the Prophet, was consulted in the debate. She commented on the issue thus: 'washing is required when the two genital parts exceed one another'. She supported her dictum with reference to the act of fornication that is established on the same basis, and exclaimed: 'How could such an act require stoning yet it does not require washing?' As a direct result of that discussion, 'Umar made the legal decision that washing is mandatory after sexual intercourse, with or without ejaculation.[26]

It can be observed here that consensus was reached following an initial disagreement. It could be argued that this example does not represent a consensus, since it is only based on the individual view given by 'Ā'isha. However, because the original argument was resolved by consulting 'Ā'isha, who based her knowledge on her experience with the Prophet, we have an example of the pattern of the dialectic reflection between the text and actual practice in the making of legal judgements. In many ways, this relationship between sources is similar to that of the Sunna and Qur'an in the interpretation of what is already known in order to understand that which is not.

The majority of Muslim scholars require absolute agreement before *ijmāʿ* attains validity as a binding source. Regarding this issue, there seem to be conflicting records on the value of *ijmāʿ*. Ibn Ḥazm (384?–456/994–1064) maintains that the person who does not accept proven *ijmāʿ* is considered to be an infidel, *kāfir* or apostate.[27] Despite this, he records an ambiguous statement made by Ahmad b. Ḥanbal (164–241/780–855) that could be understood either as a proof or as a rejection for *ijmāʿ*:

> Ibn Ḥazm narrated from Abd Allah the son of Ahmad that he heard his father saying: 'The man who claims [the occurrence of] an *ijmāʿ* is a liar'; how does he know that they did not disagree [after that]?

Despite its apparent errors of syntax, this statement should not be taken lightly, since it is recorded *verbatim* by many scholars.[28]

The supporters of *ijmāʿ* basically provide the following three grounds for its acceptability as a valid source of legislation. According to Āmidi (551–631/1156–1233) and Shāfiʿi, this Qur'anic verse offers the strongest evidence in support of *ijmāʿ*:[29]

> If anyone contends with the apostle even after the guidance has been plainly conveyed to him and follows a path other than that of the people of faith, we shall leave him in the path he has chosen and land him in Hell.[30]

Here it may be asked whether the text refers to *ijmāʿ* or to the acceptance of Islam in general, with the concept of *ijmāʿ* included in a way similar to that of any other moral practice enjoined by Islam. The historical background for the verse, as recorded by Abu Jaʿfar al-Naḥḥās (d. AH 338), does not support the idea of any form of consensus.[31] Sayyid Quṭb (1906–66) confirms this claim by stating that the verse is general and thus applicable to many examples.[32]

The second ground for the acceptance of *ijmāʿ* is stronger than the first. It is based on various hadiths cited by Āmidi,[33] which record the Prophet's confirmation that Muslims will not agree on that which is wrong,[34] and whatever is viewed by Muslims as correct is also correct in the eyes of God.[35] Āmidi also cites the view of those who rejected these hadiths on the grounds of their being weak due to having been narrated by single individuals, *āḥād*, and therefore not indicative of *yaqīn* (certainty). He refutes this criticism because he perceives the similar collective meanings of these traditions as being representative of their validity. Also, he observes that these hadiths were well known, *mashhūr*, during the time of the Prophet's companions, who did not reject them. A further question may be raised at this point regarding the agreement of Muslim scholars on errors of judgement. Was there no controversy surrounding the appointment of 'Uthmān as caliph instead of Ali, or the appointment of Mu'āwiya as the Prince of Believers? Could not these hadiths be taken to indicate the general meaning of agreement, such that Muslim *umma* would not agree to follow 'a stray faith'? The fact that these questions were challenged by scholars such as Āmidi indicates the strong controversy surrounding *ijmā'*. However, its strongest factor appears to lie in the requirement of total agreement among the available scholars.[36] If one person were to contest the issue, then no consensus would exist and the final decision becomes a form of individual opinion, *ra'i*.

This debate is clearly demonstrated in Shāfi'i's *Risāla*[37] when he maintains that *ijmā'* is a reliable legal source, *ḥujja*, so long as no one disagrees with it:

> I was told: 'your view is quite understandable with regard to the injunctions based on the Qur'an and the tradition of Muhammad which no Muslims disagree with. However, what is your proof for following what people, *al-nās*, agreed upon which has no text from God or a narration relating it to the Prophet?' Shāfi'i replied: 'If they agreed that it is referred to the Prophet, then what they said is acceptable, God willing. Whatever they have mentioned without referring it to the Prophet should not be ascribed to him specifically, since that might delude others and give them incorrect information. However, we follow what they the *nās* said, knowing that the tradition of the Prophet is not ambiguous to most of them. It might be to some of them, but we know that most of them, *'āmmatuhum*, would neither agree on something contrary to the tradition of the Prophet nor on a mistake.'

One may question whether Shāfi'i' intends the word *nās*[38] to be understood loosely as meaning the Muslim *umma* or whether he is referring to the Muslim scholars. No doubt the latter interpretation would fit the bill, since he accepts and relies on their narration of hadith. This alone goes some way to confirming that they are no ordinary scholars but must be acknowledged as reliable ones. It is also observed that Shāfi'i identifies two forms of *ijmā'*: an *ijmā'* that refers directly and specifically to the Qur'an or Sunna, and one which is not referenced yet remains acceptable to Shāfi'i because it is made by reliable companions of the Prophet, who acquired their knowledge directly from Muhammad.

When Shāfi'i was asked for proof, he referred the questioner to a hadith which states the following: 'May Allah bless a person who listens to what I say, memorises it, understands it and applies it … the heart of a Believer should not betray three matters: faithfulness of action for God, advice for the believers and being part of their group, *jamā'a*'.[39] Shāfi'i also drew on another hadith that was narrated by Ibn Sulaymān b. Yasār through his father, namely that the Prophet once said, 'he who would like to enjoy Paradise, let him be with the group. The devil is always with the individual and less with two persons …'[40] Shāfi'i was asked: 'What is the meaning of the instruction of the Prophet to join the group?'

He replied: 'There is nothing more than one meaning.' The questioner then asked: 'How can it only mean one thing?' Shāfi'i answered: 'The Muslim group is scattered in various lands, and it is physically impossible to be part of a group of individuals that is spread over the whole world ... therefore we cannot understand the word group as meaning a physical group.[41] The definition here relates to the mental unity of the group, with regard to being of one mind in what is allowed and prohibited.' Shāfi'i continued by maintaining that if someone says (and does) whatever the Muslim group says and does, then he is part of that group, but the person who disagrees is not.[42]

The consideration of *ijmāʻ* as a legal source fails to illuminate the reasons for affording it such a powerful position in the legal theory of Islam. This necessitates closer scrutiny into the historical backdrop for the formation of *ijmāʻ*. There is often emphasis on the prophetic statement that 'Muslims should remain part of one group' and 'the one who leaves the group will end in fire'. Also, it is observed that definitions of *ijmāʻ* include the phrase 'after his death'. Was the creation of the concept of *ijmāʻ* a question of establishing a legal device to assist in the interpreting of Islamic law after the death of the Prophet? Or were there also political circumstances that required the development of such a device? If this issue was placed on the agenda immediately 'after his death', then it would seem that the notion of consensus was implemented in order to address a specific incident. This could be supported by historical evidence of the major political upheaval that attended the dilemma of who was to lead the people after Muhammad's death.

The newness of the Muslim state created an urgent need for a leader who would be acceptable to all the companions of the Prophet and the leaders of the Arabic tribes. Any challenge to the authority of the new leader could be a potential threat to the entire social and political structure that had been established by the Prophet. Because there was a need for absolute agreement on the Prophet's successor, we can understand why the definition of *ijmāʻ* stipulated 'total' consensus. According to tribal customs and traditions of heredity, Ali was generally perceived as the natural successor to Muhammad since he was the closest relative, being both his son-in-law and his cousin. However, Islam had taken on new norms, and any post of public duty was regarded as a responsibility that ought to be assigned to the most suitable candidate. The elders of the community felt that there were more appropriate persons who were suited to the position, despite Ali's numerous qualifications. The choice was made swiftly in the *Saqīfa* place. 'Umar nominated Abu Bakr, and the agreement of the *umma* was granted. Ali hesitated in accepting the leadership of Abu Bakr, but finally conceded due to various personal and religious pressures. Perhaps Ali's giving of public allegiance to Abu Bakr was partly a result of his piety but also his realisation that consensus, in that instance, was vital to the upholding of social unity during such difficult circumstances. We may therefore conclude that the conditions for *ijmāʿ* were formulated on a political basis and not devised as a legal mechanism.

This conclusion could be further supported by the fact that the subject of *ijmāʿ* is discussed in detail in Juwayni's book on Islamic politics.[43] Juwayni discusses *ijmāʿ* while expounding the subject of appointing Muslim leaders; this is an indication that in the mind of Juwayni the issue was political rather than legal. He emphasises that *ijmāʿ* is not a proof, *ḥujja*, by itself, nor is it an autonomous legal mechanism.[44] Those meeting to form a consensus were not viewed as creators of an entirely independent ground for legal injunctions, since they needed to find a point upon which they agreed by referring to the available sources. One might argue against this claim by saying that in Islam it is difficult to separate theology from practice and law from politics, and this might be the reason why this mechanism remained in the legal mind of Islam and became a central source of the law. One might also argue that, if *ijmāʿ* was implemented by the Prophet's companions to decide on such an important issue, then the same treatment can be given to all other legal questions, and this then explains why the *ijmāʿ* becomes one of the most important sources of legislation after the Qur'an and Sunna. However, one can observe that the main weakness of *ijmāʿ* lies in its very strength, the concept of total agreement among the scholars. Abu Ḥāmid al-Ghazāli discusses *ijmāʿ* in terms of the problems that may occur when a community is asked to agree on certain matters. Ghazāli raises the point that 'such an agreement could be as impossible as seeing all the *umma* partaking in one action, such as the eating of dried grapes, *ẓabīb*, on the same day'. Ghazāli's defence here was: 'while there is no reason that makes the *umma* consume raisins simultaneously, yet, with regard to accepting the truth, they have a good motive because they are the community of the Truth'. Regarding the question of the improbability of consensus due to the fact that the *umma* could be scattered throughout many lands, Ghazāli suggests a way to overcome this difficulty and recommends a mechanism that he calls *mushāfaha*.[45] According to *mushāfaha*, Ghazāli maintains that individual scholars can be asked their opinion face to face, by travelling to see them. If *mushāfaha* is not feasible, the opinion of those who cannot be met individually can be gained by *tawātur*. *Tawātur* means narration by a large number of people who inform others of what has been witnessed. The tools of *mushāfaha* and *tawātur* are, according to Ghazāli, similar to certain *fatāwa* (legal decisions) issued by various schools of Islamic law. He states: 'we only know their opinions by *mushāfaha, tawātur* or by a combination of the two. For example, the view of the School of Shāfiʿi that marriage cannot take place without a guardian, *wali*, is known by *tawātur*'.[46]

Ijmā' and obtaining the view of *umma*

In defence of *ijmā'*, Ghazāli addresses the following question, which is relevant to obtaining the view of *umma*: 'How would we know the view of the whole group even if it is possible to know the view of one or two?' He replies: 'If it is possible to know the view of one, then the view of the second, up to ten or twenty, is also possible'. Ghazāli also deals with the possibility that some of those people, expected to form consensus, might not be readily available – for example, those who have been captured by the infidel, *kuffār*, or who are held in the lands of the Romans.[47] Nevertheless, he maintains: 'They have to be consulted', as the opinion of a captive person can be known and should be known, particularly if he is likely to disagree with the decision, a situation which renders the *ijmā'* invalid. 'How could the group be sure that the prisoner would not change his mind?' Ghazāli replies: 'The changing of his mind does not affect the *ijmā'* because change of view is not expected of all of the captives'.[48]

In addition to confirming the validity of *ijmā'*, Ghazāli also seems to be interested in proving the infallibility of the *umma*. He divides his argument into two parts, the first of which appeals to the Qur'anic verses that portray a balanced Muslim community, which can be a witness among humanity.[49] It seems that Ghazāli himself notes a generality within the verses that he cites in the first part of his proof. Therefore, to verify the claim that the Muslim community cannot make an error, he prepares a second argument that refers to other evidence from the Qur'an.[50] Ghazāli declares the second proof to be 'the stronger' because the subsequent prophetic statement supports it: 'My community never agrees on error'. Ghazāli clarifies that, from a terminological point of view, the second part reflects the more sound argument, but that it cannot exceed the strength of the proofs contained in the Book of Allah. Ghazāli demonstrates his powers of persuasion and logic here as he embarks on defending the truth of the last statement of the Prophet by utilising the *'ilm ḍarūri* (confirmed deduced knowledge), in which he refers to *akhbār mutafarriqa* (scattered narrations that confirm the validity of the Prophet's statement). He also utilises analogy, *istidlāl*, to deduce the correctness of these hadiths on the basis that they were well known by the Prophet's companions.

Ghazāli's discussion leaves little doubt that his definition of the *umma* does not encompass the entire Muslim community but only Muslim scholars, whose opinions were considered reliable and thus worthy of application. In his second chapter on *ijmā'*, he delineates the nature of the *mujmi'ūn*, those who may perform *consensus legis*. The *mujmi'ūn* are the *umma*, the community of Muhammad; this in the apparent *ẓāhir* includes any Muslim, yet it is clearly evident that the meaning includes only those who are expected to understand the legal case. Those who lack understanding of legislative concepts cannot participate, such as the uneducated or the scholars of *fiqh* who are not familiar with *uṣūl*, or vice versa. The contributors to *ijmāʿ* are scholars whose *fatwa* is accepted, and they can be treated as problem-solvers or among *ahl al-ḥal wa al-ʿaqd*. However, that would not exclude members of the public who are specialised in certain disciplines, and such persons may be consulted with no adverse effect to the validity of *ijmāʿ*.

Both Shāfiʿi and Ghazāli appear to imbue the term *umma* with similar definitions.[51] In the context of *ijmāʿ*, the usage of *umma* appears to indicate those individual and learned Muslim scholars who can take part in the formation of *ijmāʿ* as a source for Islamic law. This would also support our previous argument regarding Shāfiʿi's sense of the word *nās*; it could also prove useful in understanding the view that *ijmāʿ* can be twofold in that there may be one consensus among the scholars and another among the public, as Schacht, Wansbrough and Calder suggest.[52] Generally, it is a process that begins at the academic level and is then applied by the public; however, the inverse can occur whereby the public initiate the process and this can be either approved or rejected by the scholars.

Ijmāʿ today

It is necessary to acknowledge two forms of the consensus process, one of which is historical and the other contemporary. Historical *ijmāʿ* has been carefully documented and treated with great respect by various Muslim scholars, particularly when founded upon the unambiguous verses of the Qur'an and hadith.[53] Agreement in contemporary times is more easily achievable than it was during the period that witnessed the rapid and global spread of Islam, a phenomenon that occurred despite limited communication facilities. Today, modern technology and instant worldwide communication have facilitated the performing of Ghazāli's *mushāfaha*.

Currently, the notion of total agreement among all scholars can be treated with some leniency if we accept that the original stringent demand for absolute consensus had some political base. In this case, are we left with freedom and flexibility to permit the scholars of one country to make an independent *ijmāʿ*? If there were to arise a scenario that required *ijmāʿ*, discussion would commence, then conferences would be organised to which all Muslim scholars would be invited in order to contribute to the reaching of a decision. If any of the respected jurists were unable to attend, or failed to respond to the invitation, their opinions could be sought on an individual basis. Any resultant disagreement would indicate that it might not be perfect *ijmāʿ*.

A number of questions relating to contemporary *ijmāʿ* rise from the above discussion. How binding is it when an issue has been approved and agreed upon by all the scholars? Would it be as binding as the Qur'an and Sunna? Again, who selects the scholars themselves and confers the power of validity on the injunctions reached?

In essence, it could prove difficult, if not impossible, to achieve these ends without the existence of an official authority. Perhaps the best alternative to a full *ijmāʿ* would be the employment of the tacit or *ijmāʿ sukūti*, which takes place when one scholar pronounces an opinion on a certain matter and this remains uncontested. The Shāfiʿi school and some Mālikis rejected this form of tacit *ijmāʿ* on the ground that a silent person cannot be considered to have made a statement, since there may have been circumstances that prevented him from voicing an opinion or that simply resulted in him not hearing about it. In contrast, the majority of the Ḥanafi and Ḥanbali schools maintain that silent *ijmāʿ* is a justifiable ground for legislation; however, it would be considered less binding than a properly declared *ijmāʿ*.

The presence of this kind of *ijmāʿ* among other sources of Islamic law could be linked with the presence of the concept of silence, *sukūt*, as an important mode of will-manifestation. According to *EI*²,

> *Sukūt* refers to an individual's action of not actively expressing an opinion when involved in an action or contract that requires acceptance or rejection. This 'tacit' manifestation of will can only be clarified by circumstance. The concept is highlighted by the legal maxim that states 'no statement can be ascribed to a silent person, but silence when a need arises is a manifestation of will'. The 'value' of silence in Islamic law seems to place significant importance on the psychological 'state' of individuals performing contracts. This is best represented in the silence that is taken as acceptance, *riḍā*, in wedding ceremonies when a virgin bride is asked: 'do you take this man to be your husband?' This is based on the grounds that she is too embarrassed to say 'yes'. This contrasts with the previously married woman, who is expected explicitly to declare her will.[54]

In many ways, the silence of a scholar, under political pressure or some other form of impediment, can be seen as similar to that of a bride who is impeded by her embarrassment. The acceptance of the tacit methodology in the induction of *ijmāʿ* is interesting since it involves the utilisation of an uncertain approach by a supposedly high and almost divine source of Islamic law. This could explain the reason for the reservation of both Shāfiʿi and Māliki schools about it. Therefore it would appear that the silent *ijmāʿ* would be better placed not among this group of divine sources but amongst the next group of sources, the human sources that we will discuss in the next chapter. Needless to say, for some scholars, the same could be said about the entire concept of *ijmāʿ*.

Notes

1 *EI*[1], '*Sharī'a*', by J. Schacht, vol. 7, p. 321.
2 *EI*[2], '*Sharī'a*', by N. Calder and M. B. Hooker, vii, p. 321.
3 Fārūqi, *The Cultural Atlas of Islam*, London, 1986, p. 246.
4 Yasin Dutton, *The Origins of Islamic Law*, London, 1999, p. 3.
5 *EI*[2], '*Qur'an*', by J. D. Pearson, v, p. 400.
6 *Aḥkām* is the plural of *ḥukm*, which designates a decision or a view made after considering other facts.
7 Khallāf, *'Ilm uṣūl al-fiqh al-islāmi*, Cairo, 1986, pp. 32–6; Zaydān, *Al-Madkhal*, pp. 156–60.
8 Qur'an: xxiv: 59.
9 Qur'an: ii: 282.
10 Qur'an: ii: 280.
11 Qur'an: xiii: 59.
12 Qur'an: xvi: 90.
13 Qur'an: vi: 164.
14 Qur'an: xlii: 40.
15 *EI*[2], '*Sunna*', by D. W. Brown, ix, p. 878a.
16 See A. J. Wensinck and J. P. Mensing, *Concordance et indices de la tradition musulmane*, Leiden, 1943, 2, p. 557; also see above p. 4 where there is a reference made by Mu'ādh about obeying the Sunna of the prophet.
17 The Qur'an confirms Muhammad's authority to judge (Qur'an: iv: 65). There is a series of verses in the Qur'an which confirm the significance of complying with the Prophet – such as liii: 4, which maintains that his statements are not his own but revealed by God, and iv: 59, which indicates that in the case of disagreement in any matter then it is God and the Prophet who should be obeyed.
18 Qur'an: vi: 82.
19 Qur'an: xxxi: 13.
20 Qur'an: iv: 11.
21 Fārūqi, pp. 74–7.
22 Muhammad received reproof for permitting some Muslims to forgo joining the army in the battle of Tabūk (Qur'an: ix: 43) and for accepting a ransom for the captives of Badr (Qur'an: viii: 67).
23 Al-Shanqīṭi, *Al-Mu'allaqāt al-'ashra*, Cairo, 1993, p. 118.

اجمعوا أمرهم بليل فلما-------- أصبحوا أصبحت لهم ضوضاء

24 Ibn Manẓūr, *Lisān al-'Arab*, vol. 8, Beirut, n.d., pp. 8, 57.
25 The dates given for Zayd's death range from (42/662–3 to 56/675–6) *EI*[2] under 'Zayd b. Thābit'.
26 See Al-Zarkashi, *Al-Ijāba li īrād ma istadrakathu 'Āisha 'ala al-ṣaḥāba*, Beirut, 1970, p. 78.
27 Ibn Ḥazm, *Marātib al-ijmā'*, Beirut, n.d., p. 7.
28 These scholars include Ibn Taymiyya in *al-Muswadda*, al-Khaṭṭābi in *Al-Tamhīd*, Abu Ya'lā al-Farrā' in *Al-'Idda*, and finally Ibn Ḥazm in *Al-iḥkām fi uṣūl al-aḥkām*. See Abd Allah Muhammad al-'Alih, *Al-dirāsāt al-islāmiyya*, *The Arabic Journal of the*

Islamic Research Institute, Islamabad, 36, 3, July–September 2001, pp. 149–52.
29 Āmidi, *Al-Iḥkām fi uṣūl al-ahkām*, Beirut 1985, 1, p. 175.
30 Qur'an: iv: 115.
31 Naḥḥās informs us that this verse refers to an Arab named Bashīr b. Ubayriq who turned against Islam. See Muhammad Ali al-Ṣābūni, *Ma'āni al-Qur'an al-karīm*, 2nd edn, Mecca, 1988, p. 190.
32 Quṭb, *Fi ẓilāl al-Qur'an*, Cairo, 1980, pp. 2, 759.
33 Āmidi, 1, p. 186.
34 F. M. Denny informs us that perhaps the most fateful hadith on this topic is 'Truly my *umma* will never agree together on an error', cited by Wensinck, *Concordance*, only from the *Sunan of Ibn Māja, Fitan*, a *vox populi vox Dei* formulation that has played importantly in Sunni jurisprudence under the category of consensus or agreement, *ijmā'* as a source of *fiqh*. See *EI*[2], '*Umma*', by F. M. Denny x, p. 859b.
35 Āmidi, 1, p. 186.
36 Al-Samarqandi, (d. AH 539), *Mīzān al-'uṣūl fi nata'ij al-'uqūl*, ed. Zaki Muhammad Abd al-Barr, Qatar, 1994, p. 494.
37 Shāfi'i, *Al-Risāla*, pp. 471, 475.
38 Ghazāli too holds the opinion that *nās* (people) means the scholars; see p. 46 above.
39 Shāfi'i, *Al-Risāla*, pp. 401, 473.
40 Ibid., p. 472.
41 Ibid., p. 475.
42 Ibid.
43 Ibid., pp. 52–3.
44 Imām Al-Ḥarmayn Abu al-Ma'āli al-Juwayni, (AH 419–78). His book is entitled *Al-Ghiyāthi*, or *Ghiyāth al umam fi iltiyāth al-ẓulam*, Qatar, 1401.
45 A noun derived from the root *sh-f-h* which designates the oral narration or articulation of concepts.
46 Shāfi'i, *Al-Risāla*, p. 137.
47 Abu Ḥāmid al-Ghazāli, *Al-Mustaṣfā fi 'ilm al-uṣūl*, Beirut, 1993, p. 137.
48 Ibid., p. 138.
49 Qur'an: ii: 143.
50 Qur'an: vii: 181; see also iii: 103, xlii: 10, iv: 59, and iv: 115.
51 See above p. 46.
52 Norman Calder, *Stvdia Islamica*, Paris, Ex fasciculo lviii, p. 76.
53 *EI*[2], vol. 3.
54 *EI*[2], '*Sukūt*', by M. Izzi Dien, lx, p. 806a.

4

The human sources

Qiyās and *ijtihād*

In the previous chapter, it was demonstrated that Islamic law is part of a textually based faith system. However, a text cannot be sufficient to answer the new questions raised by ever-renewed human life and needs. Perhaps that is why Islamic legal texts provide for individual reasoning, *ijtihād*,[1] which is represented by analysis and other further sources of legislation that acknowledge the human mind and experience in the deduction of legal injunctions.

The theory of legal analyses in Islamic law was developed within the concept of *qiyās*. This encapsulates one of the important methods developed by Islamic law to deal with new cases and issues, the details of which were not explicitly covered by the Qur'an, Sunna and *ijmā'*. *Qiyās* is an Arabic word literally meaning 'measurement'. Technically it designates legal analogy or syllogism, which assimilates the injunction of one case and applies it to a similar one that has no specified injunction. A similarity between the two cases must exist initially, with regard to both their nature and their reason *'illa*. In defining *qiyās*, Bernand views it in a broad sense that can indicate both inductive and deductive reasoning.[2] This appears to complicate the definition and imbues *qiyās* with a much wider implication than is appropriate. Quite simply, it is a tool used by lawyers to compare cases. *Qiyās* itself does not employ the deductive or the inductive methodology, but is a mechanism used by either methodology to achieve a legal injunction. It is more naturally suited to the utilisation of inductive, *istinbāṭ*, than deductive, *istiqrā'*, reasoning. In the case of the former, one fact is derived from another, whereas in *istiqrā'*, a conclusion is deduced from an array of variables. The essence of Islamic 'legal' syllogism lies in the onus being on the application of one case to another rather than on referring to many to conclude one case.

Bernand recognises two forms of *qiyās* in the Islamic legal framework, namely *shar'i* (legal) and *'aqli* (rational).[3] Although this division is inherently correct, it should be pointed out that legal analogy is a form of rational analogy because both depend on the mind to analyse the relationship between any two cases.

Shāfi'i is responsible for the proper constituting of analogy, as a form of systematic reasoning more rigorous than a simple comparison of equivalent cases. He proceeds from the notion that every order given by God has a cause that is more general than the order itself.[4]

Islamic legal analogy is different from rational analogy because it is expected to conform with the Qur'an and Sunna in recognising the reality of life, whereas rational *qiyās* or what can be described as Greek syllogism is based solely on the activity of the mind to do so. Perhaps it would be appropriate to maintain that *qiyās* blends rational logic with the Islamic textual invariables' nature. A popular example of Islamic legal analogy can be found in the prohibition of alcohol.[5] The specific intoxicant prohibited by the Qur'an is named *khamr*, the generic designation for the alcoholic beverage made exclusively from grapes. In this case, the text indicates that prohibition is related specifically to the drinking of grape wine, and there is no mention of liquor made from barley or dates. However, because these wines have the same *ratio legis* or *'illa*, i.e. the causing of intoxication, an analogy between the three wines could be made. Consequently, all such brews would be accorded the same legal injunction as *khamr*, which is prohibition.

The rational dimension of *qiyās* is best portrayed by al-Ghazāli, whose logically based definition for *qiyās* is as follows: 'the utilisation of what is known as *ma'lūm*, to understand another *ma'lūm* so as to provide and confirm an injunction which is applicable to both of them'.[6] He describes the first case of *qiyās* as 'known *ma'lūm*' because the essence of the entire process of analogy lies in the establishment of total knowledge, *'ilm*. This seems logical, as it would be impossible to compare two elements if one of them were unidentified. Ghazāli goes on to describe the composites of *qiyās* and informs us that 'it requires *aṣl*, a base, and *far'*, a branch case which has no injunction, common reasoning and a subsequent new injunction'.[7] He does not require that both cases be present in the physical sense. Ghazāli's next comment is rather interesting and merits discussion: 'both [the known and unknown] could be purely rational concepts'.[8] Does Ghazāli make this statement in support of hypothetical jurisprudence, or is he merely emphasising the rational aspect of analogy? Could it be related to Ghazāli's well-known rational tendency? In fact, the answer may be found in a combination of all three hypotheses. The *ḥukm* (injunction) can be in the form of either the withholding, *nafi*, or the confirmation, *ithbāt*, of a person's rights or responsibilities. For example, the notion of the withholding of one's responsibility is inherent in the suspension of an individual's responsibility due to youth, while the confirmation of responsibility occurs for adults.

The Arabic terms that are used to describe *qiyās* vary as follows: *ilḥāq*, annexation, or *ta'diya*, extrapolation. Each of these terms basically has the same meaning, and that is the application of the injunction of the first case to the second case (or cases), all sharing the same *ratio legis* or *'illa* with the first.

Although *qiyās* appears to be a process which is undertaken by jurists, the scholars themselves do not actually 'create' a new injunction because such an injunction already exists in the used case. That is why it is imperative, in my opinion, to stress the fact that *qiyās* is not a source, *maṣdar*, as it is often described.[9] *Qiyās* appears to be purely a logical tool, employed by the jurist, in order to discover the relevant injunction. As such, its role is not to create the injunction but to discover the appropriate rulings that can be applied to a number of variables.

Requirements for *qiyās*

We stated earlier that the main distinguishing characteristic of Islamic legal analogy stems from the condition that it must be based on the Book or the tradition of the Prophet. *Ijmā'* too, like the previous sources, could be a basis on which the reason for *qiyās* is established. However, some Muslim scholars point out that often *ijmā'* is made purely on the agreement of scholars, and this does not represent a clear foundation upon which *qiyās* can be established.[10]

The process of *qiyās* examines the elements of shared reason and injunctions between two cases; but apparent similarity is insufficient cause for legal analogy. Both the original and the new case should share the reason on which the injunction is to be made, and the latter one should possess no previous ruling. The reason behind the original case must be clear and known, and if it is not stated then no analogy can take place. This is particularly true regarding rituals that have no apparent reasoning to explain their timing, numbers or formation, and therefore *qiyās* may not be applied. Because the notion of reasoning is central to *qiyās*, it cannot be used to create other rituals based on the divine command, the latter constituting the only reason that explains why morning prayer has two *rak'a* while evening prayer has four.

The traditional Muslim scholars of *uṣūl al-fiqh*, such as Āmidi, detailed a large number of requirements and conditions, *shurūṭ*, for each element of *qiyās*, including the original first case, the case that has no injunction, the *'illa* and the resulting injunction. Apart from the conditions of *'illa*, most of the conditions stated are *de facto* conditions which are spontaneously expected in such a legal procedure. An example of this is stating that *qiyās* should be dealing with a legal matter and not anything else such as a lexical one.[11] Moreover, if the 'injunction' of a case has been specifically restricted for that case, then it cannot be utilised in the process of legal analogy. For example, Muhammad enjoyed the sole privilege of being permitted to fast continuously day and night; therefore, in this case, any analogy between the Prophet and the ordinary man could not be valid, since all Muslims are expected to break their fast at sunset.

A further requirement for *qiyās* is that the reason or *ratio legis* in both cases should be identical. If the 'reason' is specifically for the circumstances of a case, it cannot be applied to any other. Permission to shorten prayer and break obligatory fasting is only given to the Muslim who is on a journey. The rational objective of this specification is the alleviation of human hardship, *raf' al-ḥaraj*. The course of fasting can also create hardship in a variety of circumstances, such as to the individual who undertakes manual labour; however, the text only specifies 'travelling' as the situation that allows shortening of prayer and breaking of fast. Because the stated *'illa* for the licence is journeying, no analogy can be made. Human judgement cannot be applied here, despite the rational objective of the legislation appearing to be the reduction of hardship.

This stringent requirement of *'illa* is currently being challenged by a few legal revivalist scholars, such as Ibn 'Ashūr,[12] Al-Raysūni and Ḥasan al-Turābi, who argue that there is a need to utilise 'public interest', *maṣlaḥa*, and 'objective of legislation', *maqāṣid*, in addition to the above *ratio legis* in order to apply *qiyās*. Accordingly, those who are involved in heavy manual labour, such as mining, are entitled to the same permission as those who are travelling. They maintain that there is a need to reconsider the background to *qiyās* and its requirements in order to construe the fundamental legal principles that led to the permission for their application to new cases. Necessary as this action is, it will require great care in the ascertaining of the actual objectives of Islamic law. Misconceptions regarding objectives of judgement could, in practice, lead to arbitrary injunctions with entirely different outcomes from those originally intended by the legislator, which are based on public interest.

In the following discussions we shall further highlight the notion of public interest *vis-à-vis* the factors surrounding *qiyās*. *Maṣlaḥa* represents the common good as the objective for legislation which is often stated in the Qur'an and the tradition of the Prophet. For instance, the Qur'an outlines the inherent negative consequences of intoxication as the reason for the prohibition of wine.[13] The Sunna justifies the shortening of public prayer on the grounds of helping any weak worshippers who are present.[14]

In support of the text, Islamic legislators deduce an injunction through analogy, basing it on the textually specified *'illa* rather than the rational wisdom, *ḥikma*, or apparent cause. The term *ḥikma* is utilised by Muslim legal 'analysts', but they refrain from focusing on its philosophical meaning as a lofty spiritual conception of the world, penetrating all knowledge within the grasp of man.[15] Rather, they prefer concentrating on whether or not the reason is associated with the text. A rational cause can be covert, *khafi*, unlike the overt textual declarations of the reasons for injunctions. The permission to break one's fast during a journey is intended to remove hardship. Hardship is an abstract concept and as such varies in definition and severity from one individual to another, therefore it cannot constitute a valid ground for the breaking of fast. The text fixed the injunction on travelling because it is a clearly overt and visible affair.

Islamic law makes the following provisions for the *'illa* on which *qiyās* can be based.[16] These provisions look at *'illa* as an abstract independent concept rather than as part of the requirement of *qiyās*, as stated earlier in this chapter.

First, the *'illa/ratio legis* has to contain a clear attribute. The potential for intoxication leads to the prohibition of alcohol, and in a similar vein there exists a scenario in criminal law whereby a person can receive a penalty for having the intention to commit murder. Because intention is covert, no one can be absolutely certain of its existence except the individual involved. Islamic law uses similar evidence to that used by conventional law as a means of identifying intention. If a weapon is found on the suspect, then there is a strong indication of the intention to kill.

A second requirement of the *'illa* is that it has to be ascertainable, *munẓabiṭ*. It must be precise and not vary according to individual circumstances. As we have seen, intoxication is the reason for the prohibition of alcohol. This *'illa* has a clear and identified reality. Intoxication generally causes the human mind to function in a less discerning manner, no matter who the consumer is or where he is from. The fact that alcohol tolerance varies from one individual to another is irrelevant here. What counts is the fact that the normal consequence of consuming alcohol is intoxication. The physical variation between alcoholic beverages is also irrelevant because intoxication can result no matter what type or quantity of intoxicant is being considered.

A third requirement for *'illa* is that it has to be commensurate to the injunction, *munāsib*. The term 'commensurate' signifies that the objective targeted by the spirit of the legislation will be achieved once the injunction is associated with the cause of the legislation. The execution of a deliberate murderer would represent an example of this concept, such a penalty being recognised by Islamic law as appropriate to the legislative objective of protecting the security of society. The prohibition of alcohol likewise indicates the aim of protecting the general populace from the potential threat of antisocial behaviour brought about by intoxication. In summary, the real purpose for legislating an injunction is to achieve the wisdom/purpose associated with that case. If the legislator's wisdom/purpose is clearly indicated in an injunction, the process of analogy will simply compare the two cases and deduce the correct injunction. But, because wisdom is not always apparent or easily identifiable, other attributes need to be utilised in order to understand what is considered suitable for analogy. The concept of reason proper, *'illa munāsiba*, has to be carefully considered before exercising *qiyās*. This involves the careful weighing up of what may be a misleading reason against a genuine one. For example, the race of the deliberate murderer or the colour or texture of wine would constitute unsuitable attributes to be utilised in executing the murderer or in the prohibition of other drinks that share these same characteristics, of *khamr*.

A fourth requirement for *'illa* or reason is that it has to be extendable. In other words, it should not be specifically for one particular injunction as remarked in the prohibition of intoxicants, wherein an extension can be effected from the textually specified grape wine to encompass any other alcoholic drink.

Qiyās, according to Shāfi'i, is not different from individual opinion, *ijtihād*. In fact, they are two names for one meaning[17] and Shāfi'i perceived all the terms and conditions of *ijtihād* in *qiyās*. When he was asked whether analogy could be based on the grounds of personal understanding, *iḥāṭa*,[18] Shāfi'i replied that understanding could be ascertained in different ways, one of these being the knowledge of both the apparent and the hidden. Shāfi'i maintains that personal knowledge may be based on the Qur'an, hadith or *ijmā'* and also on *ijtihād* utilising *qiyās*. In other words, he concludes that personal knowledge can be gained through the employment of analogy to reach for the truth.[19] Shāfi'i's statement here is interesting because he confirms that *qiyās* can be the truth, *ḥaqq*, in the mind of the person who is applying it *'inda qāyisihi*, but may not be the truth according to the minds of scholars in general.[20] His famous statement elucidates this point: 'our view is correct but is likely to be wrong, and the view of others is wrong but is likely to be correct'.

All the attributes relevant to *'illa*, i.e. the clarity of the argument, the specific nature of the reason, that it be commensurate with the injunction and that it be extendable, are basically designed by the scholars in order to ascertain their objectives in the legislative process. However, this poses a question as to whether or not wisdom can be accepted as a ground for legislation. Can we refer to wisdom to create new legislation? Perhaps we need to examine the 'clarity' of the purpose or wisdom of legislation; if it is apparent it may be treated as *'illa*, but if it is ambiguous and not easily discernible then it can be misleading if used as the main basis for *qiyās*.

In the modern period, the theory of *qiyās* is generally applied in the spirit of the Ḥanafis because of the major role accorded to personal effort by this school.[21] *Qiyās* could be a most important and effective tool for contemporary scholars in order to address needs and answer questions that have not previously been discussed in Islamic law. Muslim scholars who use both textual and rational procedures have already resolved many 'new' questions. They have analysed and allowed the utilisation of all modern technology on the grounds that earlier *'ulamā'* accepted various methodologies and technologies that were introduced to the Muslim community as they developed, such as transportation and communication. These have been justified on the grounds of analogy with previous similar practices, which were themselves, no doubt, based on various sources and principles to achieve *maṣlaḥa*, public interest.[22]

Istiḥsān, juristic preference

According to Wael Hallaq, consensus, *ijmā'*, or its binary opposite, 'disagreement', *khilāf*, acquired importance in Shāfi'i's legal theory mainly as a result of the different methods used by the jurists to interpret the texts, including the discussion and reasoning that it involved.[23] This fact is important in understanding not only the centrality of consensus and analogy in Shāfi'i's legal theory but also his attitude to the whole notion of interpretation of texts in Islamic law. Shāfi'i composed his book, *Al-Risāla*, in response to the inspiring questions sent to him by Abd al-Raḥmān b. Mahdi (AH 135–98) who was at that time a young scholar of hadith. Shāfi'i's main concern in writing his book was to establish an answer to the problem of how the text could be understood correctly. Another of his major objectives was to set up an Islamic methodology for legal judgement without straying from the Qur'an and Sunna. Evidently, Shāfi'i's concern with linking legal judgement to the text led him to reject the legal mechanisms which appear to be detached from it, such as *istiḥsān*.[24] He feared that, by going beyond the methodologically secure and generally recognised principles of legal interpretation, a scholar might compromise the divine element of *sharī'a*.

Istiḥsān is an Arabic verbal noun derived from the term *ḥasan*, good, which designates the preference of one object or idea over another. Technically it is associated with analogy, *qiyās*. In certain cases, it is found that it is preferable not to apply what seems to be the normal apparent analytical judgement but to revert to a less apparent analogy due to the existence of stronger evidence. An example of this notion is evident in the scenario where a person takes food because he has forgotten that he is supposed to be fasting. By analogy to a person who does this deliberately, the fasting of that individual would be void. However, there is another view that is preferred, *mustaḥsan*, one that takes into account the prophetic tradition which states that the act of fasting would remain valid if eating was a consequence of forgetfulness or error. Āmidi summarises the various definitions of *istiḥsān*, including those of Ḥalwāni, the Ḥanafi scholar, who highlights the relationship between *qiyās* and *istiḥsān*. He perceives *istiḥsān* as entailing the abandonment of a certain analogy in favour of one based on a stronger proof, for example on the Qur'an, Sunna, *ijmā'* or other legal sources.[25] The first analogy is called the overt, *qiyās jali*, whereas the *qiyās khafi* is covert. (It is concealed and unclear, but more relevant to the case in question.)

The basis upon which the preference is applied can be any other source of Islamic law, including the text, *ijmā'*, customs or even public interest and necessity. *Istiḥsān* that is based on custom reflects the richness of regional practice; and, for Muslims who reside outside the lands of Islam, it provides a source that could be employed to formulate new legal rulings of a differing nature from those previously applied. A classic example of such preference is the allowing of some kinds of religious endowments to be temporary, such as the endowment of books and food utensils. In this case, preference overturns the general principle whereby endowments, *waqf*, must be permanent. This is permissible due to the prevalent custom in certain societies, even though traditionally endowment is usually for immovable objects such as buildings. Preference can also be based on necessity, such as in the case of wells that become ritually impure[26] when an impurity comes into contact with their water; it is regarded by ordinary *qiyās* that 'all' the water therein becomes ritually impure. However, this determination is bound to cause serious public hardship since it will deprive the people of the use of their water. Therefore it was decided, for reasons of necessity, that only a certain amount of water should be removed and thrown away and the rest of the well water may be used. The notions of necessity and public interest lie in close proximity in these cases and are mostly based on necessity or custom and, when scrutinised, can be seen to be dependent on public need. The latter is considered when applying *'urf*, custom, in order to select one *qiyās* over another.

Shāfi'i's reservations about preference can be understood by looking at the following statement which Āmidi claims as having been ascribed to him:[27] 'he who practises *istiḥsān* is putting himself in the position of the divine legislator', because in Islam legislation is the right of God alone and because *istiḥsān* can be seen as a form of judgement based on personal desire. Although I could not trace Āmidi's statement about Shāfi'i in *Al-Umm* or *Al-Risāla*, there is little doubt that Shāfi'i was a strong opponent of the unfounded form of *istiḥsān*, which he describes as 'lustful action'.[28] To him, the rejection of one clear *qiyās* and preference for another that may be less clear would depend entirely on individual judgement. There is no doubt that, despite Shāfi'i's reservations about *istiḥsān*, he would accept a resulting injunction if it was clear that the injunction was based upon one of the valid sources that he accepted, such as the Qur'an or the Sunna.[29]

Āmidi, in his *Iḥkām*, provides us with a summary of the meaning of *istiḥsān* and its role.[30] He claims that Shāfi'i in effect practised *istiḥsān* in a few cases, including calculating *mut'a*[31] to be thirty dirhams, granting *shuf'a*[32] for a period of three days and not cutting off the right hand of a thief if he cheated the hangman and caused him to cut off his left one.[33] It can therefore be stated that Shāfi'i does not reject all kinds of *istiḥsān*, and we can observe that he identifies two kinds of preferences. The dutiful, *wājib istiḥsān*,[34] is based on a valid source such as the Qur'an and Sunna.[35] The other *istiḥsān* is one that he rejects because it is based purely on individual opinion. Shāfi'i criticises[36] the Ḥanafis' overuse of *istiḥsān* which did not seem appropriate to him. According to Abu Zahra, such a critique is not valid because the Ḥanafis also based *istiḥsān* on the sources of the Qur'an, Sunna, *ijmā'*, *qiyās* or necessity.[37] The main difference in opinion between the Ḥanafis and Shāfi'i on *istiḥsān* is the recognition of the form of *istiḥsān* which is being based on local customs, *'urf*. Shāfi'i does not consider *'urf* as a source of legislation, while the Ḥanafis do. It can be stated that Shāfi'i's criticism of the Ḥanafi *istiḥsān* as based on *'urf* is a natural consequence of the methodological difference between the two schools in the consideration of sources. It can also be stated that a recorded difference of opinion on the consideration of *istiḥsān* can exist within the same school. In the case of the *ṭarrār*, pickpocket, Al-Sarkhasi explains that, if the pickpocket lifts the object while it is kept inside a pocket in the sleeve of a garment, he becomes liable for the punishment of amputation. However, if the money is kept outside the sleeve, without adequate *ḥirz* or protection, then the thief is not liable for this punishment. Abu Yūsuf, the well-known Ḥanafi scholar, gave a different opinion on the basis of preference, *istiḥsān*, for amputation in all cases.[38]

When we consider Shāfi'i's criticism for *istiḥsān* as used by the Mālikis, then a further point arises. Mālikis base *istiḥsān* on public interest and on *qaṣd al-shāri'*, the intention of the divine legislator, which is a rather loose concept to comprehend. The *maṣlaḥa* which is referred to by the Mālikis is the undefined interest, *maṣlaḥa mursala*, which is not specified by the text. Abu Zahra supports this claim by stating that we know that *istiḥsān* for Mālikis meant undefined *maṣlaḥa*, because Mālik said: '*istiḥsān* is nine out of ten parts knowledge'; and, for Mālik, *maṣlaḥa* was part of such knowledge.[39]

We can observe that, despite Shāfi'i's criticism of *istiḥsān*, he still expected it to be used by scholars. This can be detected in his statement that, if a scholar speaks utilising *istiḥsān* without a confirmed source, *khabar lāzim* or *qiyās*, he will be closer to error than a person who speaks without knowledge.[40] This could be also the reason why he endeavoured to highlight its weaknesses in a chapter dedicated particularly to the critique of *istiḥsān*.[41]

Paret maintains that between *istiḥsān* and *istiṣlāḥ* there is a close proximity based on the preference of one injunction over another, whereby the usual method of deduction is to be excluded in the preparation of legal decisions. He further maintains that 'no one ever seems to have reached a lucid definition of their mutual relationship'.[42] In my opinion, such a definition has not been discovered because it is only important in so far as it defines the relationship between one secondary source and another. This relationship is often controlled by the methodological priorities of each school. The presence of the concept of necessity in the establishment of both the *istiḥsān* and *istiṣlāḥ* should not conceal the fact that they are two completely different sources – or mechanisms, to be more accurate. The first is devised to offset the missing gap in the theory of *qiyās*, while *istiṣlāḥ* is a concept which depends on public interest to provide a different and more appropriate answer for a case based on any source and not on *qiyās* only, as in the case of *istiḥsān*. Probably the main confusion between the two can be ascribed to the fact that both concepts did not remain within their original subject, and the two of them were employed by other sources to develop these other sources further and give them grounds of authority. A good example for this can be found in the custom or *'urf*, which is the next source that we will discuss; we find sometimes that one custom is preferred to another on the grounds of either *istiḥsān* or *istiṣlāḥ*, or referral to public interest and common sense.

The word *'urf* is lexically derived from a root which denotes knowledge. We have already stated in our discussions of the previous sources that custom is one of the sources in applying Islamic law within various societies and communities. *'Urf* is often defined as a practice which has been incorporated into the social life of a community and is known to be good and beneficial. Stewart maintains that *'urf* was not recognised as a source of Islamic law until the sixteenth century, when it gained something close to formal recognition, but before that time attempts were made to incorporate custom in the law without granting it formal recognition, particularly (but not only) by Ḥanafi jurists.[43]

However, various scholars, in citing the evidence for the acceptance of *'urf*, maintain that it is common knowledge that *'urf* is a ground for legislation because of the legal rule that states *al-'āda muḥakkama* – custom is referred to. Also, custom acts in contracts as one of its conditions.[44] Qarāfi, in defining *'urf*, referred to the Qur'an: vii: 199, which uses the word *'urf* as a ground for ruling by stating: 'and command with *'urf*.'[45] Zaydān points out that the word used for *'urf* in this verse refers to that which is good and not to custom. However, a careful examination of the above Qur'anic verse reveals that most of the interpreters who were consulted concluded that the Qur'an was referring to what is widely acknowledged as ethically and rationally 'good' in a society, or what is called *ma'rūf*.[46] The relationship between the two meanings (good and custom) in the word *'urf* is evident. Either word could be used to replace the other on the grounds that, for a practice to become custom, it should be seen as good by the society and in accord with the spirit of *sharī'a*. This relationship could be exactly why the Qur'anic verse used such a phrase as 'and enjoin with *'urf*', while instructing Muhammad in the affairs of his leadership.[47] Accordingly, there is no reason to deny *'urf* that appears to have probative validity on the ground of general interpretation of the text.

Both the Ḥanafi and Māliki schools refer to custom as a source for legislation whenever no text is available. The basis for that is the prophetic statement that 'Whatever Muslims see as good, it is good for Allah'.[48] However, if the custom contravenes the Qur'an or Sunna, then it would hold no legal value. Custom in Islamic law has many similarities to the same concept in conventional forms of law. It can be private, *khāṣ*, i.e. relevant to a profession or culture, or it can be general if it is accepted in wider society, such as the custom of entering the public baths without specifying the length of time spent there or the amount of water to be used. Such customs are approved in Islamic law because they do not violate its basic principles despite some possible minor inconsistency with the law. In the matter of public-bath use, there might be some element of ambiguity which may cause deception, *gharar*,[49] that Islam rejects in contracts. *Gharar* can occur in public-bath contracts when unspecified amounts of water and time are used by the customers. However, it is not possible to ban the use of public baths simply because of such a lack of clarity. Here we have a good example for applying *'urf* on the base of *istiṣlāḥ* or using public interest. The custom of paying a set fee for an unspecified service is a very common practice in numerous societies and can cause great hardship to the public if it is withdrawn. Again, it is the element of public interest which dictates that the law can accept a reasonable amount of vagueness regarding people's daily dealings in order to achieve the common good. The need to bathe is more important than the slight loss that might be incurred by the owner of the baths.

'Urf is defined, by Khallāf, as a social practice which is not in contradiction to the text.[50] An example of such a custom is evident regarding the gifts given to a bride at her wedding. These are considered as presents and are not included in the dowry. Among the people of Iraq, the dowry is deferred and not to be paid or asked for except in cases of separation by death or divorce.

'Urf could be a very useful source tool to be used in relation to Islamic questions raised by Muslims in lands distant from the original country of Islam. It could be of particular help to Muslim minorities living outside the Muslim world, so that they could utilise some of the common practices in societies that do not disagree with the basic principles and beliefs of Islam. A good example here is the one, cited by al-Imam Abu Isḥāq al-Shāṭibi (d. AH 790) and quoted by Zaydān, which states: 'The *'urf* which can be considered in certain parts of the world as wrong, yet is not considered wrong in other parts, is the uncovering of men's heads'.[51] In the East, respectable people consider this to be a shameful act. However, it is not shameful in the Western parts of the Muslim world. In the East, a man who does not wear a head-cover can be rendered unfit to give a creditable testimony in courts of law, whereas in the West a man with an uncovered head has no significance. The same applies when it comes to financial matters that have been specified by the Qur'an. The amount of material support that a man is expected to give his wife may vary according to the standard of living in various societies.

All the sources that we have discussed thus far were affirmative sources that formulate the legal injunction for an action after it occurs in a reactive mode of instruction. The source that will be discussed next is the only proactive source, which aims to prevent what is prohibited before it occurs.

Sadd al-dharā'i'

This is a term of Islamic law, literally meaning 'closing off the means that can lead to evil'. The concept is based on the *sharī'a*'s tendency to prevent evil, *dar' al-mafāsid*, and a legal maxim states that it has preference over achieving good. It is viewed as a continuation of *maṣlaḥa mursala* and is often included in books of law as an alternative legal source.[52] Some scholars, including Muhammad Abu Zahra and Zuḥayli,[53] following in Shāṭibi's footsteps, tried to study it from a positive angle by focusing on the *dharī'a* alone. This approach, however, would appear to deprive the source of an essential dimension in favour of a preconceived proviso to prevent a prohibited action. As Ibn al-Qayyim states in his *I'lām al-muwaqqi'ūn*, 'when objectives cannot be reached without certain means, these means become a part of these objectives and are therefore treated as the objectives themselves'.[54] However, the merit of Shāṭibi's approach towards *sadd al-dharā'i'* is that he places it in a philosophical legal perspective, by focusing on 'the means or *dharī'a*' rather than seeing it as an alternative autonomous source. Accordingly, it is an external element that could influence the *ijtihād* or the effort that a scholar would exert to find the appropriate legal injunction for a case.

In fact, *sadd al-dharā'i'* preconceives the circumstances of the future outcome of an injunction of a case.[55] Shāṭibi terms the future outcomes of the actions of individuals *ma'ālāt af'āl al-mukallafīn*. These must be taken into account when considering the injunction of a case. It is interesting to observe that the scholars who do not recognise an injunction based on *dharā'i'* would still consider these 'outcomes', but they would be based on public interest, *maṣlaḥa*.[56] A contract of sale, where payment is deferred, affords an example of this. The legitimacy of such a contract would be dependent on its outcome. If it leads to a masked contract that results in payment of usury by reselling the same item to the original vendor for a higher price after a designated period of time, then it would not be permitted. However, if there is no hidden illegal intention, then it is permitted. Schacht seems to confuse the concept of legal trickery with the concept of *sadd al-dharā'i'* in assuming that the contract of sale described above must be a credit contract,[57] whereas it could well be a genuine contract of sale that does not intend to mask a credit contract.

In addition to the concept of *sadd al-dharā'i'*, Shāṭibi includes as sources other concepts that could influence the outcome of an injunction, such as legal 'trickery' which entails the manipulation of concepts, *ḥiyal*, the consideration of academic disagreement, *khilāf*, the legal preference, *istiḥsān* and the establishment of legal interest.[58] *Ḥiyal* is another mechanism which was based on the notion of the future outcome of a person's actions. Schacht explains that it denotes the use of legal means for extra-legal ends, ends that could not, whether they themselves were legal or illegal, be achieved directly with the means provided by the *sharīʿa*. Schacht also maintains that the Ḥanafis, on their part, while they state that *ḥiyal* which cause prejudice to another are forbidden, are not really concerned with the moral evaluation of *ḥiyal* in detail, and they take their legal validity for granted.[59]

Shāṭibi sheds some light on the unethical element of legal manipulation which apparently leads to evasion of the law. He states that those who allowed *ḥiyal*, such as Abu Ḥanīfa, only permitted it in the practice of certain cases that achieved the public interest without aiming to violate the law. It would only be valid if it were based on individual cases, *ʿala ḥukm al-infirād*. On that basis, it is permitted to donate part of one's wealth before the time of zakah-payment is due in order to avoid paying it.[60] Such a donation is allowed since it will achieve not only the interest of the donor and the benefactor but also that of the community. Qur'anic economic philosophy propounds the redistribution of wealth in society rather than allowing it to be concentrated in the hands of the few. This aims to achieve better public welfare.[61] At this point, it has to be stated that we are dealing with the delicate area of the literal wording of the law versus legal ethics, which represents a major challenge to any legal system.

The concept of *murāʿāt al-khilāf*, or disagreement of scholars, also stems from the notion of *ma'āl al-afʿāl*. Accordingly, if a woman marries without permission from her guardian, this would be considered to be technically void, *fāsid*, from a Māliki perspective, yet quite accepted by the Ḥanafi school. In order to avoid grave injustice in this case, the Māliki judgement is lenient and the marriage would be considered valid, particularly with reference to its consequences, such as inheritance and parenthood.

The notion of *istiḥsān* discussed earlier is also seen by Shāṭibi to be governed by the actual intention of the legislator, which influences the outcome of the injunction. The example of loan, *qarḍ*, that he cites here is interesting, although it does seem slightly bizarre. Shāṭibi maintains that the loan contract is in fact a *riba* contract, but it was legitimised in order to remove hardship by the consideration of future outcomes of the contract. This example seems to have little to do with *istiḥsān*, since the reason for allowing loans in Islamic law is based purely on the text.[62]

Finally, it is useful to remember while discussing *sadd al-dharā'iʿ* that the nature of the concept comes from its converse nature, which stops at the gate that could lead to a reprehensible action. The opposite concept to *sadd al-dharā'iʿ* is *fatḥ al-dharā'iʿ*, which designates the opining of the means to good actions thus leading to good results.[63] This is only a reflection of the idea of *sadd al-dharā'iʿ* and seems to be an unnecessary legal mechanism the purpose of which can be achieved through many other legal means, including *maṣlaḥa*.

Notes

1 *Ijtihād*, literally 'exerting oneself', is the technical term in Islamic law, first, for the use of individual reasoning in general, and later, in a restricted meaning, for the use of the method of reasoning by analogy. *See EI*[2], 'Idjtihād', by J. Schacht , iii, p. 1026a.
2 *EI*[2], '*Kiyās*', by M. Bernand, v, p. 238b.
3 Ibid.
4 *EI*[2], '*Manṭiq*', by R. Arnaldez, vi, p. 442.
5 Qur'an: v: 90 states: 'prohibited to you are intoxicants and gambling, (dedication of) stones, and (divination by) arrows.
6 Ghazāli, *Mustaṣfā*, p. 280.
7 Ibid.
8 Ibid.
9 See Al-Zarqa, *Al-Madkhal al-fiqhi al-'ām*, Damascus, 1968, 2, p. 60; Abu Zahra, *Uṣūl al-fiqh*, Cairo?, 1958, p. 4; Zuḥayli, *Uṣūl al-fiqh al-islāmi*, Damascus, 1988, 1, p. 600.
10 Āmidi, 3, p. 174; and Ghazāli, *Mustaṣfā*, p. 328.
11 Āmidi, 3, pp. 173–264.
12 See Chapter 5.
13 Qur'an: v: 90.
14 The prophetic hadith states: 'he who leads the prayer, let him make it light because among the public there are the ill, the weak and the needy'.
15 *EI*[2], '*Ḥikma*', by A. M. Goichon, iii, p. 377.
16 Zaydān, *Al-Wajīz fi uṣūl al-fiqh*, Baghdad, 1987, pp. 204–8; Zuḥayli, *Uṣūl al-fiqh*, 1, pp. 246–9.
17 Shāfi'i, *Al-Risāla*, p. 477.
18 The word *iḥāṭa* is used in the Qur'an: ii: 255: 'Nor shall they compass aught of His knowledge except as He wills'.
19 Shāfi'i, *Al-Risāla*, p. 478.
20 Ibid., p. 479.
21 *EI*[2], '*Qiyās*', by M. Bernand, v, p. 238..
22 For further detail on public interest, see Chapter 5.
23 Hallaq, *History*, p. 22.
24 *Al-Risāla*, pp. 25, 503–8.
25 Āmidi, 4, pp. 392–3; Zaydān, *Al-Wajīz*, p. 230.
26 Hallaq, *History*, p. 109.
27 Āmidi, 4, p. 390.
28 *Al-Risāla*, p. 507.
29 Abu Zahra, *Uṣūl al-fiqh*, p. 270.
30 Āmidi, 4, p. 391.
31 See Glossary.
32 See Glossary, *EI*[2], '*Shuf'a*', by M. Izzi Dien, lx, p. 494a.
33 Āmidi, 4, p. 391.
34 Shāfi'i, *Al-Umm*, Beirut, 1983, 7, p. 313.
35 Shāfi'i, *Al-Risāla*, p. 25.
36 Ibid., pp. 503–60.
37 Abu Zahra, *Uṣūl al-fiqh*, p. 272.
38 *EI*[2], '*Ṭarrār*', by M. Izzi Dien, x, p. 304a.

39 Abu Zahra, ibid.
40 Shāfi'i, *Al-Risāla*, p. 505.
41 Shāfi'i, *Al Umm*, 4, pp. 307–23.
42 *EI*^{2}, '*Istiḥsān*', by R. Paret, iv, p. 255.
43 *EI*^{2}, '*Urf*', by F. H. Stewart, x, p. 887.
44 Zaydān, *Al-Wajīz*, p. 254; Zarqa, *Al-Madkhal*, 2, pp. 833–8.
45 Zaydān, ibid.
46 Abu Bakr Muhammad b. al-'Arabi (AH 468–543) summarises the various interpretations for the meaning of the word *'urf* in Qur'an: vii: 199. These are basically four: *'urf* is 'what is well-known *ma'rūf*', 'the testimony of belief in God', 'what is well-known about religion' and 'all the goods *maḥāsin* which are not rejected by the public *nās* and are approved by laws *sharā'i*''. Ibn al-'Arabi's own view on *'urf* is also general: it is that which 'does not violate the Sunna and the book': *Aḥkām al-Qur'ān*, pp. 823–5. See also Muhammad b. Abd Allah b. Muslim b. Qutayba (AH 213–76), *Ta'wīl mushkil al-Qur'ān*, Cairo, 1973, p. 4; Nāṣir al-Dīn Abd Allah b. 'Umar al-Bayḍawi, *Tafsīr al-Bayḍāwi*, Beirut, 1982, p. 232 ; Abu Bakr Ahmad b. 'Ali al-Jaṣṣāṣ, *Aḥkām al-Qur'ān*, Beirut, n.d., 3, p. 38.
47 Qur'an: vii: 199.
48 Abu Zahra, *Uṣūl al-fiqh*, p. 273.
49 *Gharar* is an Arabic word which indicates unclear risk; see *EI*^{2}, '*Taghrīr*, by M. Izzi Dien, x, p. 93a.
50 Khallāf, p. 89.
51 Zaydān, *Uṣūl al-fiqh*, pp. 257–8.
52 *EI*^{2}, '*Sadd al-dharā'i*'', by M. Izzi Dien, viii, p. 718b.
53 Zuḥayli, *Uṣūl al-fiqh*, 2, pp. 902, 921; Abu Zahra, *Uṣūl al-fiqh*, p. 287.
54 See n. 52 above.
55 Shāṭibi, 4, p. 194.
56 Ibid., p. 200; see also Zuḥayli, 2, p. 921.
57 *EI*^{2}, '*Ḥiyal*', by J. Schacht, iii, p. 510b.
58 Shāṭibi, 4, pp. 194–211.
59 *EI*^{2}, '*Ḥiyal*', by J. Schacht, iii, p. 510b.
60 Shāṭibi, 4, p. 202.
61 Qur'an: lix: 7.
62 Qur'an: ii, 275.
63 Zuḥayli in defining *fatḥ al-dharā'i'* states that it is to apply *dharīa* if it achieves a public interest: *Uṣūl al-fiqh*, 2, p. 903.

PART THREE

The source-tuners

5

Public interest and the source of law

The concept of public welfare and interest in Islamic law occupies a central position in the formation of legal opinion and the interpretation of the legal texts. It acts as a 'key tuner' that harmonises all sources of the law.[1] Lexically, public welfare is included under the Arabic word *maṣlaḥa*, which is derived from the root *ṣ-l-ḥ* designating construction, restoration of good and the removal of harm or corruption. The concept is termed 'public interest' here as a basic working term, although it carries with it a wider sense than just serving the public, since it includes every cause and effect that contributes to the betterment of life and faith in Islam.

To ascertain the divine textual authority, Muslim scholars often speak of three forms of *maṣlaḥa*: that which is *mu'tabra* or recognised by the text, that which is *mulghāt* or rejected by the text, and finally *maṣlaḥa mursala* or the interest that the text did not discuss.[2] This includes any public interest that falls within the objectives of Islamic law without being found in a known designated legal source reference, be it the text or otherwise. The objective of 'public interest' comprises the benefits of both individuals and groups according to the principles of Islamic law.

The notion of public interest has become a centre of controversy between two groups of Muslim lawyers. The reformists identify it as a concept upon which the basic understanding of Islamic law should be established and, accordingly, suggest that the deduction of injunctions should be realigned to fit with the notion of *maṣlaḥa* rather than the strict rules of *uṣūl al-fiqh*. The other traditional schools of thought hold that, as a foundation for understanding the law, *maṣlaḥa* as a concept must be treated with caution, since it may be used as a tool of misinterpretation in the achieving of the interest of the individual over that of the public. They suggest that, although Islamic law acknowledges public interest as a guide to understanding legal objectives and application, it could easily lead to major errors of judgement if utilised by those who are not well versed in Islamic law. The position of law, *vis-à-vis* human needs, is based on regulation and not on any realignment of law with a view to accommodating the specific wishes of the individual, despite the fact that Islamic law is intended to achieve human interest.[3]

Abd al-Raḥmān summarises the traditional school's view on this issue by maintaining that legal evolution in Islam does not indicate the alteration of law as a system; rather, it means that boundaries are set and parameters defined for the process of human evolution within the legal system, including habits, customs and other aspects of life.[4] The main question that needs to be answered in the debate between the traditionalists and the reformists is: what extent of flexible interpretation of the text does the philosophy of Islamic law accept in the application of law? This question has been raised not only by recent scholars such as the late Ṭāhir b. 'Āshūr of Tunisia (AH 1297–1379/AD 1879–1973), Turābi and Raysūni but also by earlier deeply traditionalist scholars such as Shāshi (d. AH 365) in his book *Maḥāsin al-sharī'a*, which roughly translates as 'the sagacious merits of the *sharī'a*'.[5] To support his theory of human interest within the law, Shāshi based his argument on the hypothesis that God did not disclose reasons for all His actions and rulings; therefore a large number of legislative measures are left to the interpretation of humans on the grounds of their understanding. Shāshi maintains that 'the wise creator would only wish good for his creatures and he would run their lives according to the noble policy which was based on their mind and nature – welfare, mind and nature representing the attributes of God'.[6]

The argument that Shāshi provides in supporting this claim is analogical and is a response to those who claim the presence of reason, *'illa*, in all matters:

> Let them consider noble kings; do they inform their subjects of all that they know, or do they reveal all their plans and policies leaving out none of the details – no matter how small?[7]

Shāshi maintains that this scenario is more than unlikely and goes on to equate the principle here with the intentions of God, the minutiae of which He does not elaborate to His people but which suffice to achieve wisdom and social welfare. Shāshi claims that this principle echoes the aforementioned sentiment that, once the wise ruler declares his objective of public interest and welfare, this should suffice with no further elaboration necessary. Any explanation of meaning and motivation behind the laws on which welfare is established becomes inappropriate. This notion is also applicable when the wise Causer changes rules, and rituals are altered on the grounds of human welfare.[8] Here, Shāshi appears to submit that a reliable and wise Causer must be accepted as having sagacious and proper reason for any alterations that may occur.

Shāshi identifies two kinds of reasons, *'illa*: the general, which he labels *maṣlaḥa*, and the private, which he calls *khāṣṣa*. As we have seen, the former is constructed upon the foundation that God's actions are the result of His prior knowledge that these will perpetuate public welfare. Therefore, any matter that may not be understood as relating to this public interest is part of the unseen, divine knowledge. On the other hand, *khāṣṣa* is the specific form of *'illa* that is referred to by scholars of analogy, *qiyās*.[9] By combining the two, Shāshi theorises that we will have greater understanding of the knowledge of what is unconcealed for human understanding, *al-shay' al-khafi*. He continues to maintain that God established the affairs of humans and other creatures on his inspiration to them of their general meaning, rather than on specific details and descriptions.

Evidence of this may be found in all matters and situations. For example, if we see two men, one with less hair than the other, we might discover the reason for the variation by studying their natures and habits, *ṭibā'*.[10] Also if we observe one brown-skinned man and another who is red-skinned, we may comprehend the reason for this difference once we have studied their natures, *ṭibā'*. However, if we wish to delve further into some observations that are similar in detail, we might fail. For example, attempts to judge the exact number of hairs in the beards of two men merely by looking at them would doubtless produce differing results. Since each individual has a different perception of what is observed, one observer may perceive 1,000 hairs and another 1,001, and so on. This notion may be extended to answer the question of why certain numbers, for example seven, are attributed to so many things, and it may be surmised that these are symbolic representations which suggest definition and amount when neither can be rationalised.[11]

In conclusion, Shāshi maintains that the deduction of general objectives and principles of law can only take place within the general legal methodology and not in individual cases, *furū'*, due to the possibility that the latter may be of unknown meaning, *majhūl al-ma'āni*.[12] Finally, it may be observed that, although Shāshi's main aim in the formulation of his theory was to refute the Ismā'īlīs' claim that the key objectives of *sharī'a* are not what is apparent, *ẓāhir*, he unintentionally initiated an important analysis for the consideration of *maṣlaḥa* in *uṣūl al-fiqh*. The presence of Shāshi's views within the deep *uṣūli* school proves that such a school pays great attention to the objectives of the law and not only to its structure, as claimed by the main critics of the discipline.

A later scholar, Abu Isḥāq al-Shāṭibi (d. AH 790), represents one of the most important scholars to focus on the principle of *maṣlaḥa*. Shāṭibi provided a ground for the recent scholars such as Ibn 'Āshūr to initiate a debate that could cast doubts on the strict adherence to principles of Islamic jurisprudence. In his book *Al-Muwāfaqāt*, he maintains that Islamic law contains objectives upon which detailed interpretation may be founded. He studied and carefully analysed the Qu'ran and the tradition of the Prophet to produce a unique methodology pertaining to the understanding of Islamic law, i.e. the methodology of *maqāṣid*, 'objectives of law'. He theorises that *sharī'a* was enacted with the purpose of achieving *maṣlaḥa* and that the objectives of the individual can be found in every detail therein.

Shāṭibi views the issue of *maqāṣid* as a foundation for the understanding of legal texts. His ideology was perceived by many as an alternative to the theory of Islamic jurisprudence, the latter resorting to the text in order to deduce the legal injunction. The notion of objectives, on the other hand, moves outside the text, and the deducing of the objectives of the legislator may employ other means, such as human understanding of these objectives.[13] The *Muwāfaqāt* commences by maintaining that *sharī'a* was created for the sake of human welfare, both for present and future generations. This no doubt echoes the views of the *Mu'tazila* and later theologians, with the exception of Rāzi (d. AH 606), who maintained that the injunction of the Divine was open neither to question nor to quest for reasons behind it.[14]

Prior to discussing the topics relevant to the purpose of *sharī'a*, Shāṭibi provides an argument to show that *sharī'a* has aims and purposes. These aims are divided in accordance with the purpose of the legislator or the individual. The aims of the legislator are further categorised into four in order to highlight his purpose. The four categories that he provides here do not seem to serve a legal function since they appear as answers to theological questions which prevailed during his era. It can be observed that they are not logical since they do not appear to have separate conceptual divisions. The first category is entitled 'the aim of the legislator for conceiving the law', *qaṣd al-shāri'fi waḍ' al-sharī'a*. This category appears to address the theological question 'why did God make *sharī'a*?' This was answered mainly under the same heading and continued into the other remaining two categories. Shāṭibi more or less claims that the aim of the legislator was to achieve public interest for the faith and world, *maṣāliḥ al-dīn wa al-dunya*.

The second category, entitled *qaṣd al-shāri'fi waḍ' al-sharī'a li al-ifhām*, assumes that *sharī'a* was formulated to clarify God's instructions to people, *ifhām*; and Shāṭibi then discusses the point further. This is not a further conceptual category for the first category but obviously states an answer to the question that it seems to pose: 'why did God make *sharī'a*?' The answer is implicit in the title (of the second category), i.e. to clarify God's order to people, *ifhām*. The third category follows the same idea and assumes that the intention of *sharī'a* was to make people responsible and continues to highlight the subject further. The fourth category appears to be an answer to a different theological question, i.e. 'why did God make the individual responsible for the law?'

According to Shāṭibi, the main objective of *sharī'a* is to achieve the reason for the divine creation and to clarify God's rulings for His people. The second point is rejected by some scholars, such as Raysūni, who asserts that clarification is not an objective but a mean of understanding the objective, and that Shāṭibi was incorrect to include the section relevant to legal clarification, *qaṣd al-shāri' lil ifhām* among the objectives of the law.[15] However, it appears that Shāṭibi's view is justified. He seems to have deliberately included the point of clarification in the objective of the legislator in order to establish it as an integral part of the law, which places responsibility on the capability of the individual. (Therefore, when hardship occurs, responsibility is removed.) The question remains as to why Shāṭibi compromised methodological logic to achieve this when he could have reached the same conclusion by classifying the aims under different headings. Shāṭibi here seems to be providing a legal annotation for the law to make sure that it will not be misinterpreted.

Ibn ʻĀshūr[16] represents one of the important figures in modern Islamic scholarship; he emphasises *maṣlaḥa* as a concept upon which the understanding of Islamic law could be established as an alternative for *uṣūl al-fiqh*. Ibn ʻĀshūr was the Grand Shaykh of the Zayṭūna mosque in Tunisia, and this afforded him a distinctive position of authority among Muslim scholars. His philosophical approach was reflected in all his studies, including Qur'anic interpretation, *tafsīr*, wherein he utilises a rational methodology. He argues that classical Muslim interpreters focused on the literal meaning in their consideration of the 'general objectives of the Qur'an'. The reasons for revelations, in his view, were overused by interpreters in extracting the meanings of the Qur'an. To Ibn ʻĀshūr, this is contrary to the art of interpretation as a process of the exploration of meaning and general objectives of what the text includes.[17] However, recent research[18] indicates that Ibn ʻĀshūr, in his *tafsīr*, is evidently influenced by the *Muʻtazili* school of *tafsīr*, particularly that of Zamakhshari (467/1075–538/1144). His inclination towards accepting popular narration ascribed to Jewish anecdotes, *Isrāʻīliyyāt*, is one of the strong criticisms directed against his rational methodology.[19]

The same sceptical approach to interpretation is found in Ibn ʻĀshūr's approach to various Islamic disciplines. To him, the Arabic language should be understood within its historical context and ought to develop alongside the intellectual development of the community that utilises it. The language declined with the decline of the Arabic world, particularly in the fifth century AH when the focus of the scholar concentrated on Arabic structure rather than its use. The same claims and criticisms that ʻĀshūr makes on *tafsīr* and the Arabic language are repeated in his approach to Islamic law and jurisprudence. This reflected his position as a modern pioneer in the understanding of Islamic jurisprudence, looking through the lens of the objectives of the law rather than moulding the law to serve the rules and principles made for its application by humans. He maintains that the reason for the improvisation of Islamic jurisprudence was to search for the objectives of *sharīʻa*. However, during the process of the historical development of Islamic jurisprudence, these objectives were overlooked by many scholars, who failed to record them within a separate section deserving of attention. *Maṣlaḥa* was one of the major subject areas that Islamic jurisprudence was unable to recognise as the main objective of Islamic law and treat as a separate issue. This omission has led to a fundamental drawback in the science of Islamic jurisprudence. He maintains that the rules of Islamic jurisprudence were extracted from individual legal cases and did not evolve at the same time and pace as the law, because they were documented two centuries after Islamic law.[20] In addition, he provides a critique for the principles of Islamic jurisprudence which were given a status of certainty, despite most being doubtful due to their bases in unsound sources and references.[21] He maintains that even Shāṭibi, in his *Muwāfaqāt*, could not prove the certainty of these principles, but he does not offer a reason for such a conclusion. However, Shāṭibi's argument appears sound, as he bases it on the same 'objectives' line of reasoning as Ibn 'Āshūr.[22]

Ibn 'Āshūr divides his book into three parts. The main argument for his *maqāṣid* theory is included in the first part. Like Shāṭibi, he provides Qur'anic evidence to prove that *sharī'a* does have objectives.[23] He also discusses the need for the lawyer to know the cause of injunction by understanding its reason, searching for any contradictions in the evidence that he possesses, analysing that which has no injunction in order to supply one, and finally reducing the number of non-rational ritualistic injunctions. This can be difficult to achieve, since a ritualistic injunction by definition indicates an injunction that has no rational basis, such as the time for prayers.[24]

The methods by which the cause of an injunction can be determined are at the centre of Ibn 'Āshūr's argument. To ascertain the cause of any legal injunction, Ibn 'Āshūr suggests three paths from which the injunction may be deduced: the *sharī'a*, the Qurān and the sequential Sunna, *Sunna mutwātira*.

The first path looks into the legal precedents of *sharī'a* and its sources. The legal precedents that Ibn 'Āshūr uses are the precedents that have known reasons: for example, the prohibition of *gharar*[25] in all-exchanging contracts. This prohibition is deduced by examining various contracts which are prohibited because of inherent *gharar*, such as the prohibition of exchange of that which is not measurable for that which is measurable, *makīl*, and the prohibition of exchanging dry dates for fresh ones. The prohibition related to these contracts is established due to the potential for deception that could result from not knowing the quantity of one of the exchanged commodities. Once it is established that deception is the objective that prohibits the contract, then any similar contract would be prohibited.[26]

According to Ibn 'Āshūr's first path, the deduction of legal injunction may also be reached through contemplating the sources, *adillat al-aḥkām*, that share the same reason, *'illa*. These *'illas* can be promoted to the position of a legal objective, *maqṣad al-shāri'*. The example that Ibn 'Āshūr provides here is the prohibition of selling food before it is received, based on the reason, *'illa*, of encouraging the ready availability of food in the market. The same *'illa* is shared by two other injunctions that aim to make food readily available in the market; the first prohibits the sale of edible commodities in exchange for other such commodities that are to be delivered in the future. The second prohibits the monopoly, *iḥtikār*, of food. All three examples share the same *'illa* that food should be made readily available in the market. According to Ibn 'Āshūr, this reason, 'the availability in the market', should be promoted from the status of a reason to the status of an objective to be applicable to all similar forms of injunctions.[27] Ibn 'Āshūr further comments that 'availability in the market' is relevant only to certain kinds of trade contracts; however, in other types, the goods are not expected to be readily available, such as in partnership, *sharika*, which accepts that food does not have to be readily available and thus does not have to be an objective.[28] Ibn 'Āshūr seems to be missing the point here that the kind of reason he is deducing is not based on a certain *qaṭ'i*, indication, that highlights the objective of the legislator. The deduction of such a 'shared reason' could be based on pure speculation, which, according to Islamic legal philosophy, represents the view of one human jurist whose judgement could be fallible. Even if the jurist is correct, we have to remember that the details of individual reasons can change according to cases and may be altered from one time to another and be influenced by the custom, *'urf*, of the region. Finally, the ascription of an objective to a certain matter or concept is a divine matter according to Islamic law, and this would lead to the question of whether such assertions could be given easily on a basis which contains speculation.

The second path for the deduction of the causes of injunctions from *sharī'a* is to know the legal objectives through the clear indications, *adilla*, of the Qur'an, as normally used in Arabic. An example of a verse that contains a very clear indicator of a Qur'anic objective is ii: 183, 'fasting was prescribed for you', which would literally mean 'fasting has been scribed [written] upon you'. Ibn 'Āshūr says that the meaning here is very clear and that the word 'scribed' did not mean that the Qur'an is written, but rather meant that it was made as a command for you. He says that 'this kind of injunction leaves little doubt about the meaning of the text' and that 'only this kind of "clear" interpretation can be used in deducing an objective of an injunction'. It is observed here that Ibn 'Āshūr is using the same interpretative methodology as a conventional jurisprudent. He seems to realise his weakness by maintaining 'can we not see *alā tara*'; then he cites examples of verses that are termed *qāṭ'iyyat al-dilāla* by the classical *uṣūli* scholars. He states: 'can we not see that the meaning of these verses is beyond doubt?'[29] Although Ibn 'Āshūr does not use the same terms as the *uṣūlis* to describe these verses, as he does not call them 'the verses of *qaṭ'iyy al-dilāla*', 'firm meaning', but rather *wāḍiḥ al-dilāla*, 'the verses of clear meaning', the fact remains that he is employing the same classification with slightly modified tautology.

The third path is that of Sunna, which is transmitted by a large number of narrators, *mutawātir*.[30] Ibn 'Āshūr accepts only the Sunna which has been directly experienced by the Prophet's companions. This can be in the form of either meaning, *ma'nawi*, or actions, *'amali*.[31]

In addition to the previous three methods, Ibn 'Āshūr suggests one further path which he terms the 'path of the forebears, *salaf*'. He states that he did not include this argument among the previous three methods that support the deduction of legal objectives, because there are insufficient statements from the *salaf* to confirm the existence of such objectives. He states that, although some of the *salaf* confirmed the presence of such objectives, these confirmations constituted mere individual opinions that cannot be tested as a proof, *ḥujja*, to support the argument. Despite this, he adds that it can be observed that their collective views and practice can conclude the presence of legal objectives.[32] This is evident to him because these *salaf*, in most cases, would search for the legal objectives and induce their injunctions while considering the objectives. Ibn 'Āshūr provides six examples, none of which seem to offer clear statements of primary legal objectives that can be utilised for independent deduction.

Ibn 'Āshūr's first example refers to the view of Al-Layth b. Sa'd on the prohibition of land-letting, which he bases on the Prophetic statement that 'He who has a land should plant it, donate it to his brother to plant or keep it fallow for himself'.[33] This is probably the strongest indication that Ibn 'Āshūr cites in support of his argument for using the legal objectives of *sharī'a* in the deduction of injunctions. Ibn 'Āshūr concludes that it is likely that Layth's reason for the prohibition of land-letting is that it (letting) could lead to other contracts which are illegal.

The second example has almost no indication of any objective other than being a personal view expressed by one scholar. In this reference, Ibn Mas'ūd is cited as objecting to Khabbāb b. Arrat, who wore a gold ring. Khabbāb responded to this criticism as follows: 'you will never see it on my hand again'. Here, Ibn 'Āshūr does not detail the objective that Ibn Abbās, Khabbāb and the scholars have considered in the injunction. The third example cited by Ibn 'Āshūr refers to the hadith narrated by Mālik in the *Muwaṭṭa*, regarding the option of the two contractors of a sale to cancel the contract so long as they have not departed. Ibn 'Āshūr maintains that the meaning of 'departed' here is not physical departure from the place where they made their contract, but rather it means verbal disagreement and departure from the will to carry on the contract. This conclusion, he claims, is made on the grounds of the objective of Islamic law which aims to reinforce the binding nature of all contracts. The fourth example refers to Shāṭibi, who maintains that a legal statement of an individual, *khabar al-wāḥid*, would not be taken into legal account if it were to disagree with one legal principle, *qā'ida min qawā'id al-shar'* – according to Abu

Ḥanīfa, but not Shāfiʿi. However, Mālik confirms that it would be accounted for if it were supported by another rule. On this ground, Mālik rejected the hadith that permits the selling of milk-producing animals if their udders were tied beforehand, because it departed from the general principle of Islamic law.

Ibn ʿĀshūr's fifth example refers to Mālik's interpretation of a statement made by ʿUmar on the death of his son: 'I would have perfumed him had I not been in the status of *Iḥrām*[34] for Hajj'. Mālik concluded that the aim of perfuming the deceased is to benefit the friends and relatives and not the deceased himself. Ibn ʿĀshūr maintains that this injunction is an example for deducing a general rule of *sharīʿa*. The final example he gives, to prove the priority of the objectives and aims over narration, is based on the response of the Prophet's wives to the case of Sālim, who was adopted before Islam by one of the Prophet's companions named Abu Ḥudhayfa. When the Qur'an cancelled the system of adoption, Abu Ḥudhayfa's wife informed the Prophet that the new law was causing her practical hardship, *ḥaraj*. She said that Sālim was like a son to her; she always removed her head-cover in front of him, and they only had one room to live in. 'What should we do, O Prophet of Allah?' she asked. The Prophet replied: 'Breast-feed him five times, then he will be prohibited to you (he would be as a son by milk)'. Ibn ʿĀshūr continued to state[35] that, while ʿĀ'isha tried to use this hadith in practice, all the other wives of the Prophet rejected it, apparently on the grounds of *maqāṣid*, objectives of the law, maintaining that this decision was an isolated permission given by the Prophet to one individual.[36]

In his discourse, Ibn ʿĀshūr maintains that the objectives of Islamic law have a paramount position, which cannot be disregarded by reference to legal words only. He denies that Shāfiʿi could have made a statement such as 'if any hadith is correct, then I will take it as my conviction', claiming that such a statement would no doubt be falsely attributed to Shāfiʿi. Ibn ʿĀshūr maintains that Shāfiʿi's legal deduction and use of objectives go against such a case, unless he meant by 'a correct hadith', one which is perfectly clear in its indication. He also denies that Ahmad Ibn Ḥanbal stated that 'a weak hadith is better than analogy'. Here, Ibn ʿĀshūr maintains that he could not have made such a statement and that this was falsely attributed to Ibn Ḥanbal because, if analogy can accept error, then a weak hadith can accept a lie.[37] Ibn ʿĀshūr's argument here appears to be weak due to the fact that he does not provide enough evidence to prove that these statements are falsely attributed to Shāfiʿi and Ibn Ḥanbal.

To Ibn ʿĀshūr, the prophetic personality has many attributes that provide sources for understanding the meaning of his words and actions. To achieve this understanding, it is imperative to consider the capacity in which the Prophet was acting. Ibn ʿĀshūr informs us that the Prophet acted in three capacities:

those of judge, preacher and leader. Ibn 'Āshūr provides examples of these and maintains that rulings made by the Prophet in his various capacities should not be confused and that each ruling should be applied only within that capacity and its context. This argument can pose the question of how to identify the actual capacity in which the Prophet made his dicta, particularly when they occurred simultaneously as he acted as judge, legislator and leader, this being the case in most of his judgements. There are many traditions that were referred to after his death by the closest of his companions, and these needed deep consideration before reaching a decision on how to interpret them. To resolve this, Ibn 'Āshūr suggests twelve capacities which he terms *ḥālāt* and maintains that when he was guided to them he was greatly relieved.[38] He further states that a scholar ought to use all available evidence and indications to find the *ḥāla* that is associated with every prophetic dictum. In my opinion, such consideration could be useful when cases are clear-cut, such as the examples provided by Ibn 'Āshūr, but the basic question remains regarding how to discover the actual intention of the legislator in Islamic law, which is an intensively text-based law. The main problem associated with this type of legislation is the identification of the difference between various kinds of rules which seem to fit a variety of conditions and circumstances. Also, the Prophet often responded in different capacities to different circumstances. Let us re-examine the above-cited case of Sālim in some detail.

Mālik narrated in the *Muwaṭṭa'* that

> Abu Ḥudhayfa adopted Sālim [before Islam]; he would treat him like his own son, when God revealed: 'name them after their fathers'.[39] Abu Ḥudhayfa's wife came to the Prophet and asked his opinion, since Sālim was to her like a son. He would be permitted to see her while she was not fully dressed, as this was unavoidable because they had only one room. The Prophet responded by saying: 'breast-feed him five times, then he will be prohibited to you (he would be your son by milk)'. 'Ā'isha took that prophetic dictum and applied it herself.[40] ... She would order her sister to wet-nurse the boys who would need to visit her frequently when they grew up. The other wives of the Prophet refused to do the same, maintaining that his dictum was specifically for the case of Sālim.[41]

Many questions are raised here, other than criticism of the correctness of this tradition, the most important being: what is the actual nature of the case upon which the Prophet was passing judgement here? Does it only relate to Sālim, as the wives of the Prophet said, or is it a general one, as 'Ā'isha seemed to understand it? And, if we accept Ibn 'Āshūr's previous ideas, then what were the Prophet's capacities when he passed this judgement? The Prophet appears not to have acted as a lawyer, but more as a Prophet who was interpreting the divine new order during a period of transition. This dictum was specific to the time when the entire legal system was being formulated. The breast-feeding of boy children was a temporary measure to resolve a social problem which arose when the adoption system was cancelled, creating a barrier between the boys and their adoptive mothers and aunts. Although only 'Ā'isha seems to have been criticised for taking advantage of the dictum, Hafṣa too is reported to have used the same dictum in the case of the young 'Ābdullah b. Sa'ad, when she requested her sister Umm Kulthūm to breast-feed him ten times.[42] The question remains as to why the other wives of the Prophet refused to accept the practice. It could be argued here that the Prophet's dictum was based purely on a personal matter and that the choice was left to the individual at the time to make a decision. While some wives of the Prophet rejected the practice, 'Ā'isha used it in terms of the words of the law and spirit, bearing in mind that she was the mother of believers and operating at a time which was not very far from that of the revelation. Such a practice became unacceptable at a different time. That is why 'Umar and Abd Allah b. Mas'ūd insist that such a physical maternal relationship can only be valid in early childhood.[43]

The above discussion was intended to provide a summary for what was considered as important to the understanding of the methodology of the reformists' theory as represented by Ibn 'Āshūr. His book's second and third parts that include the classification of objectives and the descriptive part of the ethics of *sharī'a* were not included, since in my opinion they represent a repetition of what other scholars of Islamic law have discussed in many other works.

The final question that would be useful to answer at the conclusion of this chapter is: which way would be the best for the future of Islamic law? To abandon the principles of *uṣūl* is undoubtedly a very simplistic approach which was not the real aim of Shāṭibi and Ibn 'Āshūr. However, it is imperative to acknowledge the importance of 'noting' the actual aim of the legislation while looking for the legal injunction that fits different cases. This could be achieved by applying Shāshi's earlier suggestion of combining the two, which could give greater understanding of the knowledge of what is unconcealed. Islamic law is a complex and comprehensive system of law that requires a combination of both methodologies and vision to achieve its best results. There is no doubt that Islamic law suffered from rigidity and dryness caused by the 'freezing' of the objectives of the law for the benefit of applying rules and principles that only aim to convey the 'Islamically correct' aim of the legislator. But who knows what that aim is? It is ironic to note that this symptom is found in any other law, be it religious or human-made. Perhaps it is an indication that Islamic law is becoming similar to other human-based legal systems and not just a phenomenon so different from them.

Notes

1 See Chapter 4: *Qiyās*; *Istiḥsān*; *Mubāḥ*; *Sabab*.
2 Abu Zahra, *Uṣūl*, pp. 278–80; Zaydān, *Al-Wajīz*, pp. 236–44.
3 Al-Būṭi, *Ḍawābiṭ al-maṣlaḥa fi al-sharī'a al-islāmiyya*, Beirut, 1982, pp. 14–15.
4 Jalāl al-Dīn Abd al-Raḥmān, *Al-Maṣlaḥa al-mursala wa makānatuhā fi al-tashrī'*, Cairo, 1983, pp. 32, 103, 117.
5 See Chapter 7, p. 104.
6 Introduction to Shāshi's manuscript, folio 13b.
7 Ibid.
8 Ibid.
9 Shāshi, folio 4a.
10 The term *ṭibā'*, 'natures', seems to be used by the author with reference to some form of scientific discipline.
11 Shāshi, folio 4a–b.
12 Shāshi, folio 4a.
13 Shāṭibi, 2, p. 5.
14 Ahmed Raysūni, *Naẓariyyāt al-maqāṣid 'inda al-imām al-Shāṭibi*, Virginia, 1995, p. 144.
15 Ibid., p. 295.
16 See p. 70.
17 Ibn 'Āshūr, *Maqāṣid al-Sharī'a*, ed. Muhammad al-Ṭāhir al-Mīsāwi, Amman, 1999, pp. 50–3.
18 The major part of the methodology of Ibn 'Āshūr's *tafsīr* was systematically examined by Dr Haya Thāmir Miftāḥ al-Ali in her well-researched book, *Al-Shaykh Ibn 'Āshūr wa manhajuhu fi tafsīrih al-taḥrīr wa al-tanwīr*, Qatar, 1994.
19 Al-Ali, pp. 254, 275.
20 Ibn 'Āshūr, p. 180.
21 Ibid., p. 121.
22 Shāṭibi maintains that Islamic jurisprudence is certain, *qaṭ'i*, and not doubtful, *ẓanni*, because it is based on the general principles of *Sharī'a*, *kulliyyāt al-Sharī'a*, and anything of this kind is certain. Shāṭibi, *Muwāfaqāt*, Cairo, 1975, pp. 1, 136.
23 Qur'an: v: 6, ii: 179, v: 91, iv: 3, ii: 205.
24 Ibn 'Āshūr, pp. 131–5.
25 *Gharar* designates deception which could occur due to the nature of the contract, the commodity or the contracting individual. The last is called *taghrīr*, a term in Islamic law normally meaning 'deception'. The Ḥanafis divide *taghrīr* into *qawli*, verbal, and *fi'li*, positive action of fraudulence, which takes place by deceiving the purchaser by misrepresenting the commodity's appearance or nature. See *EI*[2], '*Taghrīr*' by M. Izzi Dien, x, p. 93.
26 Ibn 'Āshūr, pp. 137–8.
27 Ibid., p. 138.
28 Ibid.
29 Ibid., p. 139.
30 Ibid.
31 Ibid., pp. 139–40.

32 Ibid., p. 142.
33 See Ahmad b. Ḥajar al-Āsqalāni, *Fatḥ al-bāri fi sharḥ ṣaḥīḥ al-Bukhāri*, Cairo, n.d., vol. 5, p. 10.
34 During Ḥajj, a Muslim assumes *Iḥrām* by refraining from hair-cutting, perfuming and other practices.
35 Ibn ʻĀshūr, pp. 45–6.
36 *Muwaṭṭa Mālik*, narrated by Yaḥya al-Laythi, Beirut, 1987, p. 416; Al-Suyūṭi, *Tanwīr al-ḥawālik, sharḥ ʻala muwaṭṭa' Mālik*, 3 vols, Beirut, n.d., 2, p. 116.
37 Ibn ʻĀshūr, p. 148.
38 Ibid., p. 160.
39 Qur'an: xxxiii: 5.
40 Evidently ʻĀ'isha used this dictum long after the Prophet's death.
41 *Muwaṭṭa Mālik*, narrated by Laythi; Al-Suyūṭi, *Tanwīr al-ḥawālik*, 2, p. 116.
42 *Muwaṭṭa Mālik*, ibid., 2, p. 114.
43 Ibid.

6

Ḍarūra, necessity

A discussion of the sources from which legal injunctions can be deduced would not be complete without the exploration of the principle of 'necessity', which represents a further 'key tuner' that plays a central role in Islamic law by filling in the gaps left by the legal sources and by addressing the implications of necessity caused by unexpected conditions. In Arabic, necessity is termed *ḍarūra*. This word is derived from the lexical root *ḍarar* that signifies 'harm' or 'damage'. According to Ibn Manẓūr, *ḍarar* denotes the dire state of hardship.[1] In a loose legal context, *ḍarūra* designates both the state of necessity and its cause, *sabab*, which justifies altering a legal injunction on the ground, of avoiding imminent harm.

The Qur'anic common meaning for legal necessity is observed in a few words repeatedly used in various verses.[2] Some of these refer to the individuals who are compelled under necessity, while the other verses speak of the subject matter of necessity, including necessity as a legal status. Other usages within the Qur'anic verses refer to the meaning of *ḍarar*, harm, and no discussion or specific definition of necessity can be found. Traditional Muslim lawyers tend towards this idea of 'no definition' and appear to focus on the practical impact of harm rather than necessity as a defined and independent concept. Such a concept seems to be treated in the Qur'an as something to be clearly understood by individuals during the time of revelation. The hadith, however, provides more of a detailed concept on various occasions. The most distinctive statement that the Prophet made regarding necessity is recorded by Imam Mālik in his *Muwaṭṭa'*. The hadith states: 'No harm to be caused and no harm to be retaliated'.[3] The Ottoman *Majalla*[4] included this hadith under section 19 with the same group of legal maxims relevant to necessity.[5] This is apparently a strong indication that such a concept is based on that hadith.

As regards the traditional legal scholars, it may be observed that they follow the Qur'anic tendency of discussing the concept of necessity from the angle of 'a compelled person'. However, Muslim scholars speak of the compelled person without identifying his/her attributes. The methodology of definition by example is common among Arabic writers in general and not only among legal writers.

This could be ascribed to the metaphorical nature of the Arabic language and culture. However, this methodology seems to be deliberate on occasions, with a view to avoiding the hypothetical definition which could deviate from the meaning of the text in order to serve non-existent cases.[6] Shāfiʿi highlights the concept of necessity by providing the following statement which offers a practical example of it: 'it is the status of someone in a place where there is no food, or any supplies to satisfy the pangs of hunger, leading him to be expecting death or illness'. For Shāfiʿi, the status of necessity is established by the weakness caused by hunger, when a person begins to feel unwell or expects to faint while walking or riding, thus preventing that individual from reaching his destination.[7]

The avoidance of hypothetical and preconceived theorisation in Islamic law contributed to the development of legal disagreement, *khilāf*, which could only be resolved by accepting such a disagreement as a default of the system and a sign of its individual diversity. One example of this is the disagreement between Ahmad Ibn Ḥanbal and Ibn Qudāma, who belonged to the same school of law. The subject of the disagreement was the location of *ḍarūra*. According to Ahmad, the status of *ḍarūra*, that justifies violating the law, is governed by the location of its occurrence. Accordingly, it can only be granted if the need arises in uninhabited areas. Therefore, prohibited food may not be consumed in towns on the pretext of necessity. The reason Ahmad gives here is that a person cannot be 'desperate' in a town because he can ask for the help of others, a situation quite different from that of a person in an isolated area. The question which follows here is: what would happen if the need for food became life-threatening in the town, and no one provided such help? In discussing necessity in towns, Ibn Qudāma answers this question by providing the exact opposite view from that of Ahmad. He tries to justify Ahmad's view, maintaining that whatever he said could be understood to be referring to the common situation when *ḥalāl* food is available in towns.[8] It is interesting to notice that Ibn Qudāma, in answering this question, presented a generic definition for the concept of necessity that allows the breach of law. It is what Ibn Qudāma calls the permitting necessity, *al-ḍarūra al-mubīḥa*. A permitting necessity is a kind of necessity without which damage, *talaf*, will take place if the prohibited food is not consumed.[9] As regards the scope of necessity, Ibn Qudāma disagrees with the school's master since he views *ḍarūra* as a recognised matter, *amr muʿtabar*, only on the grounds of the real presence of danger and not on the grounds of pure surmise, *maẓanna*. Therefore *ḍarūra* can occur not only in places where it is normally expected such as the desert, but also in unexpected places such as towns when food is scarce for any reason. In such conditions, the violation of prohibition is justified. Here we can make two observations: first, that *ḍarūra* may not only be present during a time of emergency such as war or famine, but can also exist during normal times. Second, 'necessity', to Ibn Qudāma, is a legally recognised matter, *amr mu'tabar*. The concept of 'recognition' or *i'tibār* is the same concept used in Islamic law to identify the form of public interest which is acknowledged by the law, *maṣlaḥa mu'tabara*. This similarity in terms clearly reflects the close proximity of *maṣlaḥa* and *ḍarūra* and the area within which they both operate.

One may ask: how can a case of necessity be recognised legally? In answer, Ibn Qudāma accepts the *ḍarūra*, recognition on the basis of human judgement.[10] This raises the question of whether he is accepting human rationale as a ground for *i'tibār*, recognition of *ḍarūra*, or whether he is referring only to what is 'permitted' by the text as being left to individual discretion on personal and daily issues. There seems to be little doubt that he is actually referring to human reasoning that can differentiate between what is speculative, *maẓanna*, and what is real, *haqīqī*. This is manifested by the following statement:

> Necessity is a recognised matter according to the presence of the reality [of such a matter] and it is based not only on doubt, but whenever necessity exists it can permit what is prohibited, whether there is doubt or not.[11]

الضرورة أمر معتبر بوجود حقيقته لا يكتفى فيه المظنة بل متى وجدت الضرورة أباحت سواء وجدت المظنة أو لم توجد .

It might be useful at this juncture to point out that this reveals an unusual preference for rational interpretation by a famous scholar of the Ḥanbali school, which is renowned for its close textual interpretation.

Another point worth discussing is the deciding factor that could justify the violating of the law on the grounds of *ḍarūra*. The writings of lawyers on *ḍarūra* differ on whether it is the fear of 'perishing' or the fear of 'harm'. The role of human reason appears to be crucial here to assess the establishment of the eminence of such fear in order to make a judgement to violate the law.

In today's complex world, Muslim lawyers search for legal grounds on which Islamic law can be better equipped to deal with new social demands and needs. The definition of necessity is one of the legal challenges with which Muslim lawyers have to deal. Al-Zuḥayli maintains that necessity occurs when a state of danger or extreme hardship so affects a human being that he is led to be certain that serious harm, *ḍarar*, will be inflicted on his life, body, honour, mind, property or whatever is associated with these objectives.[12] Mubārak refutes Zuḥayli's definition of *ḍarūra* on the grounds that it includes the consequence that justifies the violation of the law. Mubārak suggests that *ḍarūra*, should be defined in an abstract format, and accordingly it is 'the fear of perishing' or a harm that threatens any objective that Islamic law stands for, such as the human soul. However, this abstract definition could be understood to include self-induced hardship, which is not accepted by Islamic law as a justifiable reason to violate the law.[13]

Zuḥayli also argues that, when necessity occurs, it becomes permissible to do what is normally prohibited by the law and for the sufferer to delay or neglect an obligatory command to avoid harm and yet still be considered a law-abiding individual.[14] The *ḍarūra* is not thought to disagree with the legal sources such as the Qur'an, Sunna and *ijmā'*, because the sources are only valid when there is a freedom of individual choice between what is allowed and what is prohibited, such as water and wine. Also, *ḍarūra* is seen as a temporary measure that derives its authority from the text.[15] – that is, provided that certain conditions are maintained. These are: that the nature of the prohibited object which is allowed on the grounds of necessity remains morally unaltered. It remains *khabīth*, wicked, not *ṭayyib*, good. This subtle classification of all elements of life in Islam is incorporated in its law as the *custos morum* to guard the social ethics against possible erosion that can be caused by the claims of necessity. Accordingly, an individual might commit a prohibited act but remain uncomfortable about it. Ghazāli confirms this classification of acts in discussing the subject of what is *muḥarram*, prohibited:

> If a dictum is made that what is prohibited is allowed for the poor, then this dictum is only made under the compulsion of need, *ḥāja*. A situation of this kind is similar to allowing the consumption of alcohol or pig meat on the grounds of necessity, and therefore it would not alter the nature of what is *ḥarām* to become good, *ṭayyib*.[16]

In other words, Ghazāli's view is that the status of *ḍarūra* is an exception to the general rule; what is prohibited remains as such, and it does not become permanent.[17] Zuḥayli observes that all the definitions of *ḍarūra* focus on food and therefore fail to provide the comprehensive meaning needed for such a concept.[18] Despite all that Mubārak claims about Zuḥayli's definition, it would seem that the latter offers good potential to be a benchmark for the future legislation of Islamic law.

The notion of *ḍarūra* can provide a useful tool for Islamic law to deal with the fluctuating issues of contemporary society. This is particularly true when it is operating outside an Islamic state, which provides the environment for its application. Here we are not referring to the suspension of *ḥudūd* in Islamic society, without the presence of an Islamic organisation or state; the law can only operate in an organic form that has been adapted to fit the needs of the individual, such as when a small family cannot raise the finances required for purchasing a house. The mortgage system is the alternative to which many individuals must resort; and some Muslim scholars, such as Yūsuf al-Qaraḍāwi and other members of the European Council of *fiqh*,[19] are giving legal decisions that the mortgage system is allowed for the purchase of the first home only. It is important to note here the effect of *ḍarūra* in creating different shades of *fiqh* or legal understanding of the law which make references to particular groups of people or circumstances, such as women, *fiqh al-nisā'* or minorities, *fiqh al-aqalliyyāt*. Abd Allah Ibn Bayya and Faiṣal Mawlawi, two well-known members of the Muslim Council of Europe, refer to the concept of *ḍarūra* that justifies what is normally not allowed in applying Islamic law in the West. They go to the extent of accepting the notion of 'need, *hāja*'[20] to make a legal injunction redundant.[21]

Islamic law also recognises that necessity can be based on the view of the expert of a particular profession. A medical necessity may exist which justifies a doctor's decision to amputate a limb or to treat a patient under a 'hardship' condition, such as that of war. Here the ultimate decision lies with the doctor, and the law does not expect from him/her more than a correct professional judgement in balancing human life against medical action.

The interplay between *ḍarūra* and *maṣlaḥa*

The injunctions of necessity are often based on the principle of *maṣlaḥa*, public interest, as the deciding factor when considering what is harmful and what is not. From the point of view of scope[22] it is important to note that the principle of *ḍarūra* is temporary, whereas the principle of *maṣlaḥa* is permanent. Accordingly, when the 'status of harm' ends, then all rulings must return to normal. We should also point out that, while necessity leads to public interest, the opposite is not always true. Examples of this are the building of public highways and bridges, which can clearly be seen as being in the public interest but may not be deemed to be necessary by environmental groups or public fund-holders. However, *ḍarūra* has more scope than *maṣlaḥa*, since it can be referred to in times and circumstances that appear unsuitable for the latter, such as the time or place of emergency. The interplay between *maṣlaḥa* and *ḍarūra* could hold the key to understanding the actual position that *maṣlaḥa* occupies *vis-à-vis* the primary sources of Islamic law, such as the Qur'an, Sunna and *ijmā'*.

This was the focal point for the challenging debate initiated by Najm al-Dīn al-Ṭūfi (657/1276–716/1316) which made him well known among the early modernists, such as Rashīd Ridha, who published Ṭūfi's text in his journal *Al-Manār*.[23] Ṭūfi proposed that the position of *maṣlaḥa* among the legal sources of Islamic law has preference over all sources, including the Qur'an, Sunna and *ijmā'*. The fundamental ground upon which he based his theory is his interpretation of the previously cited[24] prophetic statement that maintains: 'No harm to be caused and no harm to be retaliated', *lā ḍarara wa la ḍirār*.[25] He observes that the word 'harm' in this statement refers to public interest and that it should always be given priority even if it disagrees with the text. His argument is based on four hypotheses.

First, the Qur'an, Sunna and *ijmāʿ* can be ambiguous sources in achieving human welfare because of variant interpretations. Therefore their interpretation needs to be guided by their supreme objective, which is the achievement of public good and interest. If they appear to disagree with it, public interest should be given priority over them by the texts' own commands. Ṭūfi argues that the commands of God are based on objectives that aim to serve the individuals and are not intended simply for the benefit of God.[26] In the case of *ijmāʿ*, *maṣlaḥa* precedes it because unlike *ijmāʿ* it is approved by all scholars, including those who rejected *ijmāʿ*.[27]

The second part of his argument is that *maṣlaḥa* is an independent source which is not bound by the texts. The kind of public interest that Ṭūfi has in mind is different from what other scholars have accepted.[28] It derives its authority from the recognition awarded to it by human rationale only as guided by customs and human experience.

Third, the scope for Ṭūfi's rational *maṣlaḥa* is *muʿāmalāt*, transactions, and *ʿādāt*, customs. *ʿIbādāt*, rituals, do not fall under *maṣlaḥa*. He maintains that 'rituals are the strict rightful dues to God alone'.[29] According to Ṭūfi, humans are unable to ascertain the size, place and time of God's dues, therefore it has to be dealt with as God would wish. This could throw a new light on the view of Ṭūfi in the sense that human beings can recognise their interest and what is good or harmful more than the law can. This could open the gate for personal 'opting out' of the legal decision in favour of their interest. But did Ṭūfi really want to give *maṣlaḥa* priority over the law? Maybe not entirely, since he saw it only as a means to achieve its objectives because '*maṣlaḥa* is the pinnacle objective of the law, *quṭb maqṣūd al-sharīʿa*'.[30] Finally, *maṣlaḥa* is valid even when there is a textual decision and it can contradict the text's decision as well as the consensus of scholars.

All those who have discussed Ṭūfi and his theory of *maṣlaḥa*[31] seem not to have observed that what he is actually proposing is to base *maṣlaḥa* on that same ground upon which the principles of *ḍarar* and *ḍarūra* are based. In my opinion, it would be more appropriate to recognise the situations in which public interest becomes necessity, *ḍarūra*, which is an acceptable ground for suspending all sources. It is an unnecessary legal detour to refer to *maṣlaḥa* on the grounds of *ḍarūra* simply to give *maṣlaḥa* its legal legitimacy. This creates a clash of authority between the primary sources and a secondary source, when the primary sources (Qur'an and Sunna) are suspended on the base of a secondary source (the *maṣlaḥa*) that derives its legitimacy from the very sources that it is suspending.

Ṭūfi's theory of *maṣlaḥa* can be better understood by recognising the *ḍarar* and *ḍarūra* factors in the structure of his theory, which bring it close to the temporary concept of necessity rather than *maṣlaḥa*. This is based on the following five reasons. First, the most important hadith that Ṭūfi uses is clearly referring to *ḍarar* and *ḍarūra* by the nature of the hadith and its wording. In fact, the same hadith is often used by lawyers to justify other sources such as *sadd al-dharā'i'*.

Second, Ṭūfi states that the consideration of public welfare interacts with the understanding of the primary sources by *bayān* and *takhṣīṣ*, clarification and specification, not by *ifti'āt*[32] and *ta'ṭīl*, suspension and denial. Such a statement can only be understood if his thesis is applicable only in certain and specific cases, when harm to individuals is expected. The suspension of primary sources is only a temporary measure, which is valid in the case of *ḍarūra*.

Third, when we deconstruct the theory of *maṣlaḥa*, as Ṭūfi suggests, we find that the examples that he cites support his preference of *maṣlaḥa* over the primary sources based on a blend of two legal textures. These are the philosophy of avoiding harm to the public and the *modus operandi* of the principles of jurisprudence. The latter utilises two legal mechanisms created by Islamic jurisprudence, namely *istiḥsān*, or legal preference[33] and the concept of *ḍarar*, which justify the direct rejection of the text or *ijmā'*. In both cases, the concept of *ḍarar* is the main factor that dominates the operation of the law.

Fourth, although *maṣlaḥa* is respected by the text and other primary sources, there is no indication that it is the ultimate objective of legislation. The verses and hadiths might suggest a distinctive value for human welfare, but this value carries less legal weight against the divine primary sources, except in the case of *ḍarūra*.

Fifth, and finally, when Ṭūfi discusses the sources of the law, he describes the text, *naṣṣ*, and *ijmā'* as the strongest of evidence. Yet he maintains that, when these sources disagree with *maṣlaḥa*, the latter should be given preference over them, not by false claims or rejection of text and *ijmā'*, but because *naṣṣ* and *ijmā'* could not mean harm, *mafsada*. However, if the result of their judgement causes harm, then the essence of their objective, *madlūl*, should be explored. This could lead to two possibilities: first, that harm is meant, and in such a case it can be interpreted as an exception to the rule that prohibits inflicting harm or retaliating with harm, *lā ḍarara wa la ḍirāir*, such as in the cases punishing the criminals, which inevitably causes them harm. Second, the meaning has a specific definition, *dalīl khāṣ*, which is only applicable to a certain case. However, if there is no *dalīl khāṣ* that justifies taking such a harm, then we have to restrict it by the meaning of the hadith that indicates that no harm is to be inflicted and no harm to be retaliated.[34] This statement leaves little doubt that Ṭūfi's theory is nothing but an application of *ḍarura*'s theory and has little to do with *maṣlaḥa*.

The interplay between *maṣlaḥa* and *ḍarūra* can be further understood by looking at what Ghazāli writes in his *Mustaṣfā*. He maintains that *maṣlaḥa* means the preservation of the aim of the law, *maqṣūd al-shar'*, which includes the preservation of human faith, souls, minds, offspring and property. The preservation of these objectives is the highest priority of *ḍarūrāt*.[35]

As an example of an action that can be taken on the grounds of public interest which is justified by necessity, Jamīl Mubārak refers to Ghazāli's view on taxation in his book *Shifā' al-ghalīl.*[36] For Ghazāli, the proscription of levying taxes becomes justifiable in the case of the just ruler defending the nation's land when the public treasury does not hold sufficient funds to provide for emergencies, such as in the case of war. Islamic law stipulates the following four conditions when taxes are levied on the ground of necessity.

The first condition is that the ruler must be just in order to prevent the misuse of such a privilege. Ruling governments have been known, in the history of Muslim societies, to drain the public of their money to line their own purses. The second condition is that the taxes should not be levied in a way that could in itself cause more hardship. The third condition is that it should be the only way to raise public funds for a purpose that achieves the public interest. If taxation can be avoided by borrowing from the public, then so be it. The fourth condition is that all funds which are raised by taxes on the grounds of necessity must go only to the government.[37]

These conditions could raise some questions relevant to application and authority, such as who decides on the presence of these conditions, and who can give a ruler or his government the status of a justice, particularly when such a decision involves political circumstances. However, these questions may not always be relevant since there are many clear cases that can be decided upon by the individuals themselves, such as in the case of famine or war where the sources of life become scarce or unavailable. In such circumstances, an individual is allowed to eat what is prohibited, *ḥarām*,[38] to ward off death by hunger.

Such an example presents a case where public interest and necessity overlap, giving the individual a full option to decide on the course of action to take. Needless to say, the individual action would then be based purely on a personal judgement, which would not suspend the individual's legal responsibility. The exercise of such an 'individual authority' is valid in many Muslim countries today, particularly those that suffer from famine or war such as in Africa or Iraq. It could also be a justifiable measure even when such conditions are not present, but where there exist valid driving circumstances that permit the violation of the Islamic rules. Muslims who live outside Islamic countries, where they cannot find *ḥalāl* food, might be allowed such permission and may eat whatever is available. However, such a decision has to be taken with great care in order to avoid habitual consumption of unlawful food.

Ḍarūra based on *maṣlaḥa* are the grounds on which Islamic law justifies shooting Muslim captives who have been used by the enemy as a human shield, *turs*. Ghazāli maintains that

> in such a situation the balance needs to be drawn between two objectives. One supreme objective is the defence of Islamic land, whereas the second is the preservation

> of the life of a few individuals. Giving a preference to either of the two options is not indicated by text or analogy. Therefore it would be fair to refer to other clear indications, *dalalāt*, which leave little doubt that the protection of the boundaries of Islam and the souls of all Muslims is more important than the protection of a specific individual at a certain time, who is likely to be killed by the enemy anyway.[39]

Due to the close proximity of the two concepts, *maṣlaḥa* and the objectives of Islamic law are often classified in a misleading manner that could lead the reader to conclude that they are identical. Public interest is classified according to its significance to human needs, thus it is divided into three categories: the essential, *ḍarūriyya*, the necessary, *ḥājiyya*, and *taḥsīniyya*, the embellishing interest. Mubārak maintains that Ghazāli was one of the scholars who conceived such a classification. However, it can be argued that the objectives of Islamic law according to Ghazāli are different from the concept of public interest.[40]

A careful examination of the *Mustaṣfā* reveals that Ghazāli was quite clear in maintaining that 'interests' are only concepts that were developed to achieve the objective, *maqṣūd*, of Islamic law.[41] In other words, public interests are tri-laterally divided by considering the proximity of the interest to the objective of the law and not to human needs. To view *maṣlaḥa* in this way reduces its ambiguous relationship with necessity and helps the lawyer to refer to it in practical cases. When a lawyer makes a legal decision, he needs to achieve a balance between public interest and the necessities that could clash with it. The following are two general principles often used as guidelines during such a process.

First, a preference for necessity over public interest can only be valid when a priority between two interests is established. For instance, drinking alcohol, which is prohibited by the text on the grounds of public interest, can be allowed if there is certainty that drinking is the only option available to avoid human death from thirst. The same reasoning applies in the cases of loss of lives in war, the destroying of a house in order to prevent the spread of fire to other houses, or the destruction of houses in order to build a dam that would prevent water from flooding a town.

Second, when necessity contradicts a legal principle, it is not valid unless supported by a valid ground which justifies such an action. The destruction of a house by fire is justified because the firemen need to stop the spread of the flames on the grounds of public interest. Such destruction should not be based on fictitious public interest, *maṣlaḥa wahmiyya*, and false claims which have no benefit for the public. Needless to say, the ascertaining of what comprises a necessity can only be validated by recourse to Islamic law. Finally, it can be relevant to bear in mind that 'necessity' only provides a temporary licence, *rukhṣa*. This justifies the exception of a certain case from the general rule or principles. This permission for a case to be treated differently is no longer valid once the reason for such permission expires.

From the above discussion, there remain many unanswered questions, such as who decides on what is necessary and how a decision can be made. Can Muslim people cooperate with an outside force to achieve justice in their land? If not, then can international organisations such as the UN be legitimised by Islamic law to sanction an invasion of a Muslim country on the grounds of necessity? These questions appear pressing in the current political climate of countries such as Iraq. Without careful involvement of the law accepted by the Muslim masses in such countries, the political situation can only become increasingly more complex and lead the already suffering world into further disorder.

Notes

1 Ibn Manẓūr.

2 Qur'an: ii: 173, v: 3, vi: 145, xvl: 115, vi: 119.

3 The exact wording of the hadith is: *lā ḍarar wa lā ḍirār*. See *Muwaṭṭa'al imām Mālik, riwāyat Yaḥya b. Yaḥya al-Laythi*, Beirut, 1987, p. 529; see also *Sunan Ibn Māja*, Istanbul, 1972, 2, p. 784.

4 The term refers in its best-known application to the civil code in force in the Ottoman Empire, and briefly in the Turkish republic, from 1285/1869 to 1926. *EI*[2], v, p. 1,010.

5 Al-Bustāni, *Majallat al-aḥkām al-'adliyya*, 3rd edn/reprint of the Istanbul original edition published AH 1304–5, Beirut, n.d., 1, pp. 29–31.

6 This tendency seems also to have been affected by the inclination of the Qur'an and hadith, that individuals should try to use their own judgment and not expect answers for all life's details (Qur'an: ii: 67–72); also O you who believe do not ask about matters that when revealed to you it will not please you. The Prophet's hadith states: 'Do not ask me when I choose to be silent', *dharūnī mā taraktukum*.

7 Shāfi'i, *Al-Umm*, 2, p. 276.

8 Ibn Qudāma, *Al-Mughni*, 14 vols, Beirut, 1984, 11, p. 75.

9 Ibid., p. 76.

10 Ibid., p. 75.

11 Ibid., p. 76.

12 Al-Zuḥayli, *Naẓariyat al-ḍarūra al-shar'iyya*, Beirut 1995, pp. 67–8.

13 Self-induced hardship may be represented by the example of practising hard sports such as mountaineering or the rigorous practice of rituals such as fasting for long periods.

14 Al-Zuḥayli, ibid., p. 68.

15 He has explained to you in detail what is forbidden to you except under compulsion (ibid., vol. 1, p. 119).

16 Al-Ghazāli, Abu Ḥāmid, *Iḥyā' 'ulūm al dīn*, 1st edn, Beirut, n.d., 2, pp. 92, 99.

17 *Maṣlaḥa*, according to Muhammad al-Ṭāhir b. 'Āshūr, is an attribute for individuals' actions that lead always or most probably to the good of individuals and groups. See *Maqāṣid al-Sharī'a*, ed. Muhammad al-Ṭāhir al-Maysāwi, Amman, 1999, p. 203.

18 Zuḥayli, ibid., p. 67.

19 See Chapter 10.

20 See Glossary.
21 This view was stated in a television interview on the Iqra channel on 19 December 2003. It is based on the view of the Ḥanafi school, which accepts all forms of contracts if the ground of *ḍarūra* is proven.
22 Scope here means the suitability of application from the point of view of time, place and legal base, which is often called in Arabic laws *sarayān al-Sharī'a*. See Hans Where, *The Hans Where Dictionary of Modern Written Arabic*, ed. J. M. Cowan, London, 1974, under *sarayān*.
23 *EI*[2], 'Al-Ṭūfi', by W. P. Heinrichs, x, p. 588a.
24 See n. 3 in this chapter.
25 Muṣṭafa Zayd, *Al-Maṣlaḥa fi al-tashrī' al-islāmi*, 2nd edn, Cairo, 1964, p. 207.
26 Here, Ṭūfi is criticised because he misunderstood or misinterpreted the texts in order to prove his point. For example, Qur'an: x: 57, 'O people, there has come direction from your Lord, a healing for the diseases in your hearts and, for those who believe, a guidance and a mercy'. This example proves the opposite to his claim, since it states that it guides people to the truth. This would contradict the statement that the human who is guided supersedes the text that guides. For Ṭūfi's view, see Zayd, p. 212; for its refutation, see the discussion *Naẓariyyat al-maṣlaḥa fi al-Fiqh al-Islāmi* by Ḥusain Ḥāmid Ḥassān, Cairo, 1981, p. 544.
27 Zayd, p. 227, Ḥassan, pp. 546, 547.
28 Zayd, p. 35.
29 Ṭūfi's treatise in Muṣṭafa Zayd, *Al-maṣlaḥa fi al-tashrī' al-islāmi*, p. 213.
30 Ibid.
31 Zayd, pp. 113–27; Al-Būṭi, *Ḍawābiṭ*, p. 178.
32 Ibn Manẓūr, 2, p. 70.
33 See earlier discussion of *istiḥsān*.
34 Zayd, p. 209–10.
35 Ghazāli, *Mustaṣfā*, p. 174.
36 Mubārak, *Naẓariyyat al-ḍarūra al-shar'iyya*, Cairo, 1988, p. 214.
37 Ibid., p. 215.
38 *Ḥarām* includes all prohibited food, whether legally prohibited or non-ritualistic.
39 Ghazāli, *Mustaṣfā*, pp. 176–80.
40 Mubārak, pp. 212, 223.
41 Ghazāli, *Mustaṣfā*, pp. 174–5.

PART FOUR

The legal mechanisms for understanding the law

7

Islamic jurisprudence, *uṣūl al-fiqh*

This chapter aims to highlight the perception of Islamic jurisprudence as a distinct legal discipline within the Islamic theory of knowledge. *Uṣūl* is an Arabic word, indicating the plural form of *aṣl*, which designates the origin or root of a matter or object. Often the expression *uṣūl* is used in Arabic in reference to the rules that govern a specific topic or discipline. Thus *uṣūl al-lugha* governs language, and *uṣūl al-ḥisāb* governs mathematics. In law, *uṣūl* is utilised to denote the principles and methodologies upon which injunctions can be deduced from the legal sources. According to Abu Zahra, *uṣūl al-fiqh* is a scale which is used to ascertain the legal judgement of the human mind.[1] The word *fiqh* linguistically designates understanding or comprehension in general terms which could involve any aspect of knowledge. In law, it is the discipline of knowledge that focuses on the understanding of Islamic legal injunctions that rules the acts of the people, who are responsible to the law.[2] Because the law only deals with the practical injunctions of the individual, dogmatic and behavioural injunctions are not included in this definition.[3] The result of *fiqh* is called 'the branches', *furū' al-fiqh*, which is parallel to *uṣūl al-fiqh*, the roots of the law, designating the standards and norms of the *fiqh*. The difference between the branches and the roots is given by the *Encyclopaedia of Islam*:

> works on *furū'* set out the norms of the law, in greater or lesser detail, and with varying quantities of justificatory argument. Works on *uṣūl* identify and classify the sources of the law, expound a methodology whereby these give rise to norms, and present a structure of authority which distinguishes the qualified jurist from the layman.[4]

Ghazāli summarises the difference between *fiqh* and *uṣūl* by maintaining that *fiqh* focuses on the action of the individual in relation to legal orders, *khīṭāb al-shar'*, whereas *uṣūl* focuses on the areas of knowledge (such as hadith) in order to discover that area's indications for various meanings, whether through the understanding of words or definition. A scholar of *uṣūl al-fiqh* must know how to implement the process of deducing injunctions, *aḥkām* (sing. *ḥukm*), from the available sources. Ghazāli maintains that it is imperative to consider the injunctions first, then the sources of their divisions and the means of deducing the injunction from these sources.[5] A legal injunction, *ḥukm*, is defined by Muslim scholars as the legislator's statement, relevant to the actions of individuals.

The division of these injunctions into categories is evidently influenced by the Islamic doctrine that perceives human actions as causes for divine punishment or reward in proportion to the amount of action.[6] Accordingly, three 'will-based' categories of injunctions are found in the writings of Islamic law. These categories oscillate between allowing and banning an action or leaving it optional. The injunctions are sometimes specifically given in the form of 'do' and 'do not do' instruction, while on other occasions they simply describe a cause or condition which determines the legality of an act. It is observed that, while there is a distinct relevance in the inherent nature of the first two, the third criterion, the 'causational', suggests a somewhat different philosophical basis, since it represents an injunction which is triggered by a cause or a reason.[7] For the purpose of practical legal application, these trilateral divisions are further broken down into five levels or qualifications, as Schacht would call them.[8] They include *wājib* dutiful, *mandūb* preferable, *ḥarām* forbidden, *makrūh* abominable, and *mubāḥ* permissible.[9]

Wājib is derived from an Arabic root which refers to an action that indicates an obligation or responsibility. Often this term occurs in textual sources in an imperative formula to 'do' that particular action, for example 'establish worship and ward off [evil]'.[10] The affirmative form is also employed, whereby formulae indicating that God 'enjoins' or 'orders' are used, for example 'Lo Allah enjoineth justice and kindness ... He exhorteth you in order that ye may take heed'.[11] On other occasions, the term 'prescribed' is utilised, for example 'fasting has been prescribed upon you',[12] and also in the prophetic tradition, which maintains that 'God has prescribed charity on everything; when killing [an animal for food], perfect your killing. Slaughter well by sharpening your knife. Let your beast of burden have comfort ...'[13]

A further form of *wājib* is implicit in the commanding formula: 'it has been made as a duty upon you'.[14] In addition, there is another form of *wājib*, which is based on the concept that God has a right to have people do a particular action such as performing hajj.[15] In this case, the duty is unequivocally owed to God. This definition of duty is also found in the prophetic tradition. The perfect form is also employed in the Qur'an to indicate an action which is enjoined by God.[16] Another form of *wājib* is worded as a warning, or threat, indicating that disobedience will be punished.[17]

All these forms of discourse, of providing injunctions and imperatives, are considered as *wājib*, an incumbent injunction that highlights what the Divine expects the individual to perform. Muslim scholars have elaborated upon the classification of these forms of injunction, categorising them with regard to their restrictions by time, space or circumstances. This has created a plethora of *wājibs* that are often intermingled, sometimes confused and overlapping and only identifiable once the source and the inherent spirit of legislation is referenced. To resolve the problem, the Ḥanafi school created a stronger subsection of the *wājib*, which they termed *farḍ*.

Juynboll maintains:

> the Ḥanafi school makes a distinction between *farḍ* and *wājib*, applying the first term to those religious duties which are explicitly mentioned in the proof texts (Qur'an and Sunna) as such, or *ijmā'*, and the second to those the obligatory character of which has been deduced by reasoning. This distinction is not made by the other schools, and as a norm for action *farḍ* and *wājib* are equally binding.[18]

This statement is somehow general and needs adjustment, since the distinction that Ḥanafis make is based on the certainty of the source and not on the source itself. The Ḥanafis consider as a *farḍ* all the injunctions that are proven on the basis of a certain source that has no form of doubt to it, that is, *dalīl thābit lā shubhata fīh*.[19] This would obviously preclude all kinds of Sunna, namely *Sunna ḍa'īfa* or weak Sunna, which Juynboll's general statement could be understood to mean. Finally, it would seem that the meaning of the word *wājib*, at least in the Ḥanafi context, is closer to the English term 'dutiful' than the 'obligatory' that Schacht prefers. This claim is supported by looking at the various usages of the word in Arabic, such as using the term *wājib* for 'home work'.

The second category, *mandūb*, refers to 'that which is preferable'. Technically, this term designates that which has been requested by the legislator but does not carry compulsion. Āmidi provides an interesting guideline for *mandūb*: 'it is an act, the performance of which is considered preferable to its non-performance. The person who adheres to *mandūb* would be worthy of praise, yet one who ignores such would incur no reprimand or punishment.'[20] *Mandūb* normally appears in the form of an order that is not compulsory: a Qur'anic example refers to debt using the imperative form, 'write it'.[21] This is followed by another verse which states: 'if any one of you entrust another with a pledge – let the trustee restore that pledge to the owner. Let him fear Allah.'[22] This implies that the initial imperative is not intended as compulsory, but that the answering of the request would be meritorious. The *mandūb* is also found in a straightforward formula that defines its meritorious nature, particularly with reference to voluntary ritual and practice, as seen in the Prophetic statement: 'the person who comes to this house [of God] and commits no vulgar words or acts will return home as if he was born again'. Here, vulgarity is not forbidden, but the person who refrains from such words and deeds is offered a restored innocence and purity.[23] This kind of injunction is given a variety of titles, such as the preferred, voluntary or just Sunna. It often appears to come into differing categories, depending on its proximity to the tradition of the Prophet. If the Prophet practised a meritorious action regularly or suggested its practice, then it is called confirmed, *mu'akkad*. His personal practice of the extra prayer before morning prayer is an example of this. If an action is not practised regularly, such as voluntary fasting or minor pilgrimage in the month of Ramadan, then it is referred to as 'not confirmed', *ghayr mu'akkad*. All prophetic actions that have no ritualistic dimension come under the heading of the customary tradition, *Sunnan al-'ādāt*. These would include prophetic practices that formed part of his personal attributes, the following of which would constitute meritorious practice.

The third category, *ḥarām*, represents the opposite of the first, and it includes all that has been prohibited, such as 'the taking of usury'.[24] The format in which this type of injunction is normally expressed can vary. Some direct prohibition, *nahi ṣarīḥ*, is in evidence,[25] but there exists also a form of rebuke against a person who might commit a prohibited act. Certain chapters reveal a form of 'don't do',[26] while other chapters order the perpetrator to 'refrain from doing'.[27] Sometimes the injunction appears with an order 'not to do', and the resultant punishment is specified for those who violate the order. An example of the latter may be observed in the case of the adulterer.[28] Often, books of Islamic law pertaining to prohibition cover issues that warrant direct prohibition, for example, polytheism and theft, or matters that are prohibited due to their links with the aforementioned – for example, trading before the call for Friday prayer, prohibited originally because this would coincide with the time of prayer. Āmidi prefers to call this category the banned, *maḥẓūr*,[29] which to him is synonymous with the word *ḥarām*. However, the introduction of the banned concept here could be helpful in identifying the difference between an action or object which is intrinsically 'bad', and prohibited by the law, and one which is not intrinsically bad yet is prohibited by law.

The fourth category, *makrūh*, abominable, represents a minor form of the prohibited, not dissimilar in amplitude to the *mandūb*, which is a minor form of *wājib*. *Makrūh* refers to an object or action from which the legislator has requested the actor to refrain. However, if this request is unheeded, there is no resultant punishment, but compliance with the request will reap reward. An example of *makrūh* is the eating of garlic by one who intends to attend the mosque or socialise with others. The consumption of garlic itself is not prohibited, but it is abominable in the latter case.

Āmidi explains that both *makrūh* and *mandūb* 'could' also be prohibited and dutiful actions, according to some scholars. However, his opinion is that only the *makrūh* could mean that which is prohibited. This distinction between the two is based on some prophetic traditions that specifically indicate the presence of that which is *mandūb*.[30] However, there seems to be no reason why the same principle is extended to *makrūh*, since the two concepts are diametrically opposed.

The final category, *mubāḥ*, indicates that which is allowed, whereby individuals have the option of 'doing' or 'not doing such an action'.[31] Most objects and actions that are pertinent to general human existence fall into this category, since the rule is that everything is allowed unless there is a text that prohibits it.[32] Āmidi says that all Muslim scholars agree that *mubāḥ* is a form of the legal injunction applicable to people. He also cites the view of some *Mu'tazila* who deny the qualification of a legal injunction to be applicable to *mubāḥ*, contending that allowance exists even before the law. Āmidi refutes such a claim on the grounds that what is allowed can only be such in *sharī'a* when practised by people as part of their compliance to the command of the legislator, *khiṭāb al-shāri'*.[33]

These five dimensions of injunctions are set in Islamic law and appear to lie in an inverted parabolic curve which ranges from the prohibited to the enjoined. The types of injunction that lie centrally tend to be closely related to one another. Many of them can change position on the curve, according to circumstance and *maṣlaḥa*, public interest, which is one such topic that can alter action and its injunction from one category to another. An example of this may be cited as follows: eating and drinking are allowed, but excess of either would be abominable.[34] The same principle applies to the following cases: some leisure activities are allowed, but if pursuit of play leads to loss of ritual then this will be prohibited; the breaking of fast is allowed during the making of a journey, yet if someone opts to continue the fast, this is allowed, *mubāḥ*; however, if such an action would be to the detriment of health, then it would be prohibited, *ḥarām*. When considering these divisions, it is useful to bear in mind that the format of classifications of legal injunctions has varied according to the angle from which these injunctions are perceived.

The five divisions of *ḥukm* are often followed by further classifications, *al-ḥukm al-waḍ'i* and *al-ḥukm al-taklīfi*, which designate conditional injunctions and proscribed injunctions respectively. The former, the *ḥukm al-waḍ'i*, does not take into account human ability and will to act, unlike *al-ḥukm al-taklīfi* which is focused on the individual, as implied by the word *taklīf*, duty. The *waḍ'i* explains conditions and procedures required when certain actions are to be undertaken. In practice, *waḍ'i* injunction arises as a consequence of another cause, *sabab*, such as that timing is a consequential injunction to prayer; or again, the condition that two witnesses are required is a consequence to an intended marriage contract.[35] The latter classification, *ḥukm al-taklīfi*, covers injunctions that are overtly proscribed by the texts in the form of 'do' or 'don't do'. The conditional injunction, *ḥukm al-waḍ'i*, is identified by Ghazāli's *Mustaṣfā*,[36] Shāṭibi in *Muwāfaqāt*[37] and Āmidi's *Iḥkām*.[38] It arises as a consequence of the text, which declares an object or a matter to be either a reason or condition for its prohibition, permissibility, ability, advisability or its recognition as deserving of merit. This *waḍ'i*, injunction, is divided into *sabab* cause/reason, *sharṭ* condition, *māni'* prevention, *ṣiḥḥa* correctness or *buṭlān* falsehood, and finally *rukhṣa* permission. It would appear that *sharṭ* and *māni'* could be viewed as the negative element of *sabab* and *sharṭ*; if the cause did not occur, then there would be no reason for prevention. Differences between the preceding terms are rather subtle; we will therefore highlight the terms which have not been discussed before.

Sabab, cause, is a constant that leads to the injunction, normally accompanying it but not necessarily creating it. It is often defined as the designation given by the lawmaker for an injunction.[39] In other words, *sabab* indicates the circumstances for an injunction, like the breaking of fast during a journey. When a person is travelling, he/she would be in a situation that provides a reason, *sabab*, that justifies eating during the fasting season. The schools of law are divided in their opinions about *sabab*. The Shāfi'i and Ḥanafi, like the modern Germanic school of law, concentrate on the apparent will. In contrast, the Māliki and Ḥanbali schools and the Shī'a focus on the actual intention, *niyya*, a tendency similar to that in Roman law. In contemporary Islamic civil application, the importance of *sabab* can perhaps be well understood from the UAE Civil Code definition of it as 'the direct purpose aimed at by the contract'.[40]

There is close proximity between *sabab* and *'illa*, the latter being the *ratio legis* that accompanies the injunction. *Sabab* need not be the rational justification for certain injunctions, such as the association of prayer with certain times of the day. *'Illa*, on the other hand, is the clear justification for an injunction upon which the jurist can build further injunctions. The difference between the two can be so close that sometimes they overlap and no difference between the two is found. It can be maintained that every *'illa* is a *sabab*, but not every *sabab* is *'illa*: for example, the reason for the prohibition of alcohol is that alcohol causes intoxication, so there is a clear *'illa* for the defined result. The reason why hajj must be performed on a certain date cannot be based on reason, therefore this injunction is *sabab* only, but not *'illa*, like intoxication, the concept of which humans understand, due to its likelihood of causing harm to others.

The classical divisions of *sabab* include *ḥikma*, which is a complex Qur'anic term that communicates a diversity of meanings, including wisdom, knowledge and acumen. Ḥikma often mixes with *maṣlaḥa* and is seen as an unclear form of *sabab*, which varies according to circumstance.[41]

Sharṭ, condition, can also be seen as a form of *sabab*, which tends to be an external matter that can occur without the legal action; however, without such an action it is void. An example of *sharṭ* is found in the case of a divorce pronouncement, which would be void without the existence of marital status, but naturally marital status could exist without divorce. Also in the case of zakah-payment, there is a requirement that one year should lapse before the zakah is due.[42]

Rukhṣa designates a permission to perform or not to perform an injunction. It has two conflicting definitions in works of Islamic jurisprudence. The conflicting opinions rise from the dispute over whether *rukhṣa* is a part of *ḥukm al-taklīfi* or *ḥukm al-waḍ'i*, which designates conditional injunctions and proscribed injunctions (see above).[43] However, it does not really seem to fit either of them, and jurists probably formulated *rukhṣa* in order to fill a gap between the dual classifications. *Rukhṣa* applies to both the *ḥukm* and designates the permission given by the legislator for an individual to choose whether or not to perform an action, despite the presence of an injunction against it: for example, eating that which is prohibited when absolute necessity occurs.[44]

Māni', is an Arabic verbal noun which designates the reason for prevention. Legally it is a concept or a status that nullifies an injunction, despite the availability of all validating causes and circumstances. An example of *māni'* is found in the case of a son who would be prevented from inheriting from a father whom he had murdered.[45] *Māni'* appears to be more factual evidence and circumstances that confirm the non-validity of injunctions, and so is somewhat different from the other attributes that we discussed earlier (*ḥalāl*, *ḥarām* and so on) that reside in the essence of the injunction itself. This can also be said of *sharṭ* and maybe *ṣiḥḥa* and *buṭlān*. In my opinion, these ought to be classified differently from the previous attributes of injunctions and perhaps labelled as the external attributes of injunctions.

Ṣiḥḥa, correctness, and its opposite *buṭlān*, incorrectness or falsehood, influence the validity of the injunction and are rendered as part of the conditional injunctions. The legislator appears to create these circumstances or conditions in order to validate or nullify an injunction. If the condition required is available, then action will be valid and correct; otherwise it will be void. An example of that is hajj, which is expected to be performed within certain conditions to make it valid. Like *sharṭ*, this is an external attribute to the injunction. In my opinion, both ought to be classified separately from the attributes of the legal injunctions, which describe their internal nature.[46]

Various descriptive divisions for legal injunctions that do not involve the ability of the individual, *qudrat al-mukkallaf*, can be found in works on *uṣūl al-fiqh* that examine the attribute of the injunction itself, *waṣf al-ḥukm*. One early example of this division is cited by 'Alā' al-Dīn Abu Bakr Muhammad b. Ahmad al-Samarqandi (d. AH 539) and is in many ways similar to the previous division that classifies legal injunctions under dutiful, meritorious, prohibited and so on.[47] He further divides these into subdivisions according to perspectives which seemed important in his time. While these divisions have little legal value, they are important for the history of law since they reflect the political and theological currents that can influence the structuring of Islamic law. For instance, Samarqandi's division of injunctions into *ḥasan* and *qabīḥ* has clearly been the result of a theological debate on the subject of human actions and reflects his Maturīdis affiliation.[48] He further divides *ḥasan* and *qabīḥ* according to human nature, rationale and according to *sharī'a*, maintaining that the three divisions do not always agree with each other.[49] He emphasises the concept of ascertaining the distinctiveness of various divisions in such a way that their meanings should not influence the meaning of the other.[50] Accordingly, the prohibition of an object does not mean the abstract allowance of that which is opposite to what is prohibited: for example, the dictum that requires a person to abstain from alcohol does not necessitate the drinking of water, if it is not needed.

The subjects of law

The individuals who are subject to the law are termed *maḥkūm 'alayh*. This concerns how the law perceives the individual and whether the individual is seen as only a subject of the law or whether the law exists to serve the individual. As a starting point, the conditions that qualify the individual to be a subject of the law may clarify the relationship between the individual and law.

An individual is qualified to be subject to the law if he/she can fulfil the following conditions:

1. Comprehension, *fahm*, of the imposed legal injunction.[51]
2. The competency to fulfil the legal obligation, *ahliyya*, with regard to the above.

An individual who is unable to understand the rules of the law is not viewed as a responsible subject of the law, *mukallaf*. The Prophet stated that there would be no responsibility attached to 'a sleeping person until he wakes, a child until puberty is reached and a deranged person until sanity is regained'. Thus, the cognitive powers of the individual are the deciding factor that indicate whether or not the individual is able to fulfil the first condition. However, the responsibility imposed on children, the deranged and so on, such as paying zakah, *nafaqa*, maintenance, and liability, is not perceived as the violation of the previous diminished-responsibility principle. These individuals continue to be subject to public duty in a similar manner to ordinary members of society, and their guardians are expected to act on their behalf.[52] An individual whose mental health had deteriorated to the point of insanity would still be expected to pay alimony to his wife, because he had undertaken the contract while still *compos mentis*.

The *ahliyya* is also termed *dhimma* by the Muslim jurist and presents a 'legal persona' that is given for every individual, whether young, old, insane or ill. The *ahliyya* may be subdivided into competency of rights, *ahliyyat wujūb*, and competency of duties or actions, *ahliyyat adā'*. The former designates the capacity of the individual to receive rights and perform duties.[53] *Ahliyya* is further divided according to competency of action; *adā'* represents the legal acts of the individual, be it in the form of words or actions. This establishes the acceptability of contracts and leads to injunctions that are relevant to them. This is equally applicable to the individual who violates the law, the perpetrator being responsible for his actions. The law exists as a regulating mechanism to govern the individual. It aims to establish duties and responsibilities according to the notion of individual and public interest and not according to the rules of governments, who might aim to achieve the objectives of the ruling elite. The establishment of individual legal 'status', *ahliyya*, in Islamic law does not nullify the consideration of the law, even when impediments arise that nullify the ability of the individual. Such impediments that restrict rights and ability are identified to protect the individual from the consequences of unwilling actions.[54] Accordingly, a deranged person or a minor still own what is termed an incomplete *ahliyya*.

According to Ghazāli, injunctions are like fruit, each possessing an individual attribute, *ṣifa*, and intrinsic reality, *ḥaqīqa*, which are the results of the planting process, *istithmār*. The fruits are consumed as an end product and have 'means' for their consumption. This metaphorical fruit is made up of incumbency, prohibition, preference, abomination, allowance, good and bad and so on. The producers of the fruit are the sources, i.e. the Qur'an, Sunna and consensus, and the means of consumption are the ways in which the sources are understood directly, implicitly or otherwise.[55] The consumer is symbolic of the scholar who must digest the contents and ultimately offer judgement in the light of the opinions he deems best. In my published opinion, Ghazāli's methodology in discovering the limit, *ḥadd*, of objects aids in the understanding of the specific roles of the various sources of Islamic law. Accordingly, it is crucial to make a careful epistemological distinction between the various sources by exploring the difference between terms such as *maṣdar*, source, and *dalīl*, guide, the former referring purely to the Qur'an, Sunna and *ijmā'*, consensus, and the latter incorporating *qiyās*, *istiḥsān* and other mechanical means that are employed to deduce legal injunctions. The word *maṣdar* conveys the meaning of a reservoir of rulings that can be used for legislation, unlike *dalīl*, which represents tools and instruments of legislation.[56] Employment of the term *dalīl* would probably offer a better indication of the function and position of the sources of Islamic law, so that confusion is minimised between the dynamic sources for the injunction, which include Qur'an, Sunna and *ijmā'*, and those that are only tools used by scholars to embark on an injunction. This epistemological vagueness could be ascribed to the fact that all these concepts and their rules were clear in the scholars' minds but not articulated in their writings.

To draw a distinction between sources according to their roles further illustrates their value in the legislative deduction. An example of this can be clearly seen in the multi-faceted role of *maṣlaḥa*, public interest. *Maṣlaḥa* often acts not only as a *maṣdar* or a *dalīl* for other sources, but sometimes presents itself as a *sabab* that leads to their application. For example, *maṣlaḥa* would be a *maṣdar* when it clarifies a primary injunction; it would be a *dalīl* if a secondary injunction such as *qiyās* were based on it; and it would be a *sabab* when it explains the actual circumstances that justify the strict application of the meaning of text, such as in the case of breaking of fast during a journey on the grounds of hardship. Hardship, in this example, represents public interest posing as a *sabab* that provides the circumstances of the injunction.

The apparent confusion in terminology used by various Muslim academics may be ascribed to such reasons as the lack of clear epistemology on which a distinction between the notions of probability and certainty is founded. Hallaq attributes this problem to a lack of relevant written works in the third and fourth centuries. Hallaq maintains that 'we have virtually no works from these periods, yet this is not as a result of lack of developing legal theory, but rather due to the historical fact that such works simply failed to reach us'.[57] He goes on to say that, when considering the level of advancement in the fifth and sixth centuries AH, we can deduce that legal theory had continued its development despite this dearth of available legal texts. Hallaq claims that the textual nature of law gave rise to the development of methodology, epistemology and some form of cohesion within presented texts of the fifth century AH; these reflect the earlier period from which we have extensive records of legal theory.[58] Hallaq goes on to proffer three reasons for the importance of this era in the development of Islamic law: first, major problems regarding legal theory were addressed during this period, efforts which laid the foundation for further more detailed analyses; second, the fifth century witnessed an almost unprecedented proliferation of works; third, various highly influential works were produced by some of the most brilliant legal theorists, whose creativity was to have a major impact on the development of Islamic legal theory. Hallaq seems to be unaware of a manuscript compiled in AH 365 by Al-Qaffāl al-Shāshi.[59] This work provides a clear indication not only of the gradual development of legal theory but also of the presence of systematic modes of thought, which were built on the methodology and research of previous scholars such as Shāfi'i.

On the relationship between *maṣlaḥa* and *qiyās*, Hallaq maintains that most works on Islamic theory do not treat *maṣlaḥa* as an independent topic but consider it within that of 'suitability' under the subheading of analogy, and not devoting to it an independent section or chapter. Its inclusion there is due to the 'suitability' nature of *maṣlaḥa*, which designates it as an extension of *qiyās*. He also maintains that some later authors included discussion of this matter in a chapter designated *istidlāl*, which usually covers all sorts of inferences that do not belong to *qiyās*.[60] This statement can mislead us into making an assumption that *maṣlaḥa* is seen by Muslim scholars as only part of *qiyās*. *Maṣlaḥa* in fact is part of all the sources of Islamic law which are used as a guide in deducing legal injunction: even the ultimate source of sources, the Qur'an, refers to *maṣlaḥa* as a guide and philosophy in deducing an injunction. The Qur'an cites a few examples in which certain actions are justified on the grounds of both public and individual interest.[61] All other sources also utilise *maṣlaḥa* in their legal deduction. The reason why *maṣlaḥa* appears more clearly in the *qiyās* section is due not to the fact that *maṣlaḥa* is part of *qiyās* but to the fact that *qiyās* itself is a dangerous human tool to play with.

Shāshi, in his book *Maḥāsin al-sharī'a*, provides us with elaborate examples of the methodology on which scholars of that period would construct their thoughts and ideas. Direct textual derivation was obviously an important and fundamental methodology in Muslim legal writings. Furthermore, his work demonstrates acceptance of the classification of sources, as it is quite noticeable that he utilises the texts in the order of their hierarchical status. Shāshi also acknowledges the principle of *'āda*, custom, as one of the acceptable means of managing social structures. In addition, he emphasises the value of human rationality,[62] which is intrinsically personal and thus unique to each individual. Our main concern here is to examine elements that represent the level of structure that Hallaq accepts in establishing the standard of legal theory in different centuries, i.e. epistemology, definition of and distinction between probabilities, and legal language within these categories. Shāshi provides us with such elements throughout his text. These are clearly reflected in the introductory chapter, particularly[63] where he discusses the commonality of injunctions. He maintains that many are based on a general meaning that is common to most people, although this may be lacking in certain instances where the individuals in question do not fall under such injunctions. Many of these injunctions were applied to the Arabs who had been initially targeted by the call to Islam, but nevertheless they remain applicable to others and may be interpreted more broadly to encompass synonymous circumstances. Shāshi maintains that messengers (legislators) were given wisdom and a sense of interest in order to establish *sharā'i'* (plural of *sharī'a*). These legislative systems frequently contain public interests that may not be overtly revealed to the layman, unlike the Divine or those who are divinely inspired.[64] Elements of definition and classification are evident in Shāshi's work when he discusses *'ibāda*, rituals, maintaining that these are divided into different categories: those that are voluntary and those that are prescribed textually. Shāshi also provides us with another concept of worship whereby further divisions of *'ibāda* are applicable, such as bodily worship (*'ibādat al-abdān*) via pilgrimage and prayer. Some *'ibāda* are a requirement for introducing other forms of worship, such as purity, which is a prerequisite for prayer.[65]

Shāshi introduces the notion of an injunction that takes into account the geographic location of the situation. A cited example of this is the use of stones for personal hygiene, which Shāshi suggests may be altered to account for differing environments, where elements available for cleanliness may not be the same as those available to the Arab peoples. He maintains that the original recipients of the Message were either *aṣl* (model) or *far'* (followers), and that this concept was imperative if the message of Islam was not to be restricted purely to the land of the Prophet.[66] On Shāshi's part, this displays a flexibility of observation regarding the objectives of Islamic law that predates scholars such as Shāṭibi, who is cited by Hallaq.[67]

According to Shāshi, the importance of other injunctions is based on their meanings, which are often highlighted by the legislator. The prohibition of alcohol is an example of this, whereby drink is perceived as a tool with which the devil may create animosity between people, thus preventing them from remembrance of God and prayer. Shāshi's dialogue on the ruler's responsibility offers an important early legal insight into the ruler's role. He perceives the ruler as being responsible for the protection of the public, maintaining that an integral part of rulership must sometimes include the prevention of the public from falling into minor offences, even if they seem harmless, in order to avoid the possibility of graver sins. Shāshi states that 'this is in accordance with the principles of honourable polity, *siyāsa fāḍila*, which is portrayed in the following example: the grazing of land that is on the periphery of a protected zone is allowed; however, this should be prevented in order to avoid the possibility of straying onto ground that is *ḥarām*'.[68]

Shāshi's discussions leaves little doubt that he was providing a further step to his Shāfi'i school by establishing a plethora of abstract legal theories to set up reasons for the legal injunctions. The reason why Shāshi took such an initiative was to refute the Ismā'īli theology that maintains that God only legislates according to a rationally understood reason and whatever is not understood by the mind, such as the numbers of prayers and amounts of zakah, can be viewed as symbolic of what God intended.[69]

At this juncture, it is interesting to examine Hallaq's critique of the work of Shāfi'i regarding the notion of what constitutes a theory and how close he was to such a concept. Hallaq maintains that 'the *Risāla* does not offer exposition of a legal theory proper'.[70] This suggests that Hallaq evidently seeks abstract ideas that constitute a theory, and a methodological construction of that theory in a logical sense that would create a cemented fabric according to his definition. It seems that, in Shāfiʿi's opinion, a theory represents only a hypothesis that does not stand by itself, and perhaps he was loath to present a cut-and-dried notion which had the potential of being either right or wrong. A divine inscription of law cannot be categorised or indeed constructed, like theorisation. This probably explains Hallaq's statement that 'the all-inclusiveness of revelation means, in Shāfiʿi's view, not only that positive law must ultimately rest on the divine texts, but also the methods by which that law is discovered must rest on these same texts'.[71] Also, in considering Shāfiʿi's situation, one must bear in mind the fact that he deliberately avoided philosophical epistemology and vision in seeking to discover the 'truth' of the divine text.

With regard to Shāfiʿi's having been described as a 'master architect' of Islamic jurisprudence, perhaps we need to rephrase this judgement and say that he was a 'master archivist'. When he wrote the *Risāla*, he neither discovered nor structured the science of Islamic jurisprudence; and, as Hallaq maintains, the term *uṣūl* did not occur in his writings. According to Dr Nashami, the fact that Muslim scholars followed Shāfiʿi's rules does not make him the designer of those rules.[72] Indeed, all the principles that Hallaq claims repeatedly as being central to the *Risāla* must be derived from the revealed scripture. He maintains that Sunna is a binding source of law, that there is no contradiction between the Qu'ran and Sunna, that the two sources complement each other hermeneutically, that legal rules derived from unambiguous and widely narrated texts are certain and subject to no disagreement, and finally that *ijtihād*, consensus, and *qiyās* are prescribed by revealed texts.[73]

We can further observe that Muslim scholars followed a methodology which was documented by Shāfiʿi but not created by him. Mālik, his master, used to follow some of these rules and even documented them, for example, the rule of public interest. A debate was recorded between Mālik and Layth b. Saʿd regarding the authenticity of the actions of the people of Medina.[74] This offers some evidence of the presence of principles of methodology of *uṣūl al-fiqh* that predate the influence of Shāfiʿi. In summary, we need to modify Schacht's claim that Shāfiʿi was a 'master architect' by stating that Shāfiʿi was in fact a classifier, documenter and master archivist. Shāfiʿi himself would never have claimed such a privilege; this represents a status which, according to Islamic theology, could only be held by the divine legislator.

It can be observed that the *Risāla* reveals Shāfiʿi's attempt to fill the systematic gap for Muslim scholars. This is confirmed by the lack of any other document which combines a basic guide for their legal disciplines. Perhaps this is why Shāfiʿi often analysed his own views in conjunction with those of other schools, such as Abu Ḥanīfa and Mālik. It is apparent that Shāfiʿi's *Risāla* aimed to provide a general scale for the various applications of Islamic legislation. This was the reason why Shāfi'i declined to touch on cases which indulged in deep debate or disagreement, focusing only on those that led to practical action. The structure of his book is often abridged and contains the formula 'he said and I replied', which reflects the style of his time yet achieves a flow that is often alien to contemporary Western scholars, who often assume that it is fictitious. But was it fabricated? We know that the entire *Risāla* was an answer to a series of written questions given to Shāfi'i, as previously stated. He would mention the legal rule, indicate its proof and then go on to cite a variety of examples. Years after its initial composition, two views were created from Shāfi'i's rewriting of his *Risāla*, the old and the new; and this produced a further source of Islamic legal deduction as perceived by Shāfi'i in both Baghdad and Egypt. Environmental jurisprudence was a fundamental factor leading to this rewriting of the *Risāla*, and it can be seen as an important guideline for contemporary Muslim scholars who attempt to blend Islam with the needs of a modern lifestyle.

Notes

1 Abu Zahra, *Uṣūl al-fiqh*, p. 8.
2 See Āmidi, p. 7. On defining the responsible individuals, see *maḥkūm 'alayh* later in this chapter.
3 Āmidi, 1, p. 84; Abu Zahra, *Uṣūl al-fiqh*, pp. 6–7.
4 *EI*[2], '*Uṣūl al-fiqh*', by N. Calder, x, p. 931.
5 Ghazāli maintains that, according to this definition, the title *faqīh* may not be assigned to a scholar of theology, philosophy, grammar, hadith and *tafsīr*; it is a title strictly reserved for the scholars of Islamic law. See *Mustaṣfā*, p. 5.
6 Qur'an: xcix: 6–7.
7 This is discussed later in the chapter (see *sabab*).
8 *EI*[2], '*Aḥkām*', by J. Schacht, i, p. 256.
9 Abu Zahra, *Uṣūl al-fiqh*, p. 26.
10 Qur'an: vi: 72.
11 Qur'an: xvi: 90.
12 Qur'an: ii: 183.
13 Narrated by Ṣahīh Muslim.
14 Qur'an: xxiv: 1.
15 For example, 'And pilgrimage to the House is a duty unto Allah for mankind', Qur'an: iii: 97.
16 For example, 'Such of you who die and leave behind them wives, they [the wives] shall wait without remarrying for four months and ten days', Qur'an: ii: 234.
17 For example, 'If ye do not, then be warned of war [against you] from Allah and his Messenger', Qur'an : ii: 279.
18 *EI*[2], '*farḍ*' by Th. W. Juynboll, ii, p. 790.
19 Abu Zahra, *Uṣūl al-fiqh*, p. 30; Āmidi, 1, p. 87.

20 Āmidi, 1, p. 103.
21 Qur'an: ii: 282.
22 Qur'an: ii: 283.
23 Ibn al-Jawzī, *Kitāb al-targhīb wa al-tarhīb*, Beirut, n.d.
24 Qur'an: ii: 275.
25 Qur'an: xvi: 90.
26 Qur'an: iv: 171.
27 Qur'an: ii: 222.
28 Qur'an: xxiv: 2.
29 Āmidi, 1, p. 98.
30 One of the traditions that Āmidi cites is when the Prophet suggested to a woman to continue her marriage with her husband after being freed and her husband remained a slave. She said: 'I will if you order me to do so'. He replied: 'no, I only recommend': Āmidi, 1, p. 105.
31 Āmidi, 1, p. 106.
32 An example of this is found in Qur'an: v: 5: 'this day are [all] good things made lawful for you. The food of those who have received the Scripture is lawful for you and your food is lawful for them.'
33 Āmidi, 1, p. 106. See also Ghazāli, *Mustaṣfā*, p. 60.
34 Qur'an: vii: 31.
35 Zuḥayli, *Uṣūl al-fiqh*, pp. 43–4; Zaydān, *Al-Wajīz*, p. 27–8.
36 Ghazāli, *Mustaṣfā*, pp. 52–3.
37 Shāṭibi, 1, p. 187.
38 Āmidi, 1, p. 85.
39 *EI*[2], '*Sabab*' by M. Y. Izzi Dien, viii, p. 666.
40 Ibid.
41 Zuḥayli, *Uṣūl al-fiqh*, 1, p. 93; Khallāf, p. 117.
42 Zuḥayli, 1, p. 98; Khallāf, p. 118; Āmidi, 1, p. 112.
43 Zuḥayli, 1, p. 109; Khallāf, p. 121
44 Zuḥayli, 1, pp. 108–10; Khallāf, p. 121.
45 Zuḥayli, 1, pp. 102–3; Khallāf, p. 120–1; Āmidi, 1, p. 67.
46 Zuḥayli, 1, p. 103; Khallāf, p. 125.
47 Al-Samarqandi, p. 35.
48 The founder of the Māturidi school is Abu Manṣūr al-Māturidi (d. AD 994). It stands halfway between the Mu'tazili and Ash'ari schools of theology and was generally accepted by the Ḥanafi school of law. Human actions, according to Māturidi's theology, occur by God's power; but those which are sinful do not occur with his pleasure or love. See Albert Hourani, A *History of the Arab People*, London, 1991, p. 167.
49 Ibid., p. 46.
50 Al-Samarqandi, pp. 156–60.
51 Khallāf, p. 134; Zuḥayli, 1, p. 133.
52 Khallāf, p. 135; Badrān, *Uṣūl al-fiqh al-islāmi*, Alexandria, 1992, p. 319; Zuḥayli, 1, p. 135.
53 Khallāf, p. 136.
54 Khallāf, p. 134–40.

55 Ghazāli, *Mustaṣfā*, p. 7.
56 M. Izzi Dien, in *Studies in Honour of Clifford Edmund Bosworth*, ed. R. I. Nutton, Leiden, 2000, pp. 354–5.
57 Hallaq, *History*, p. 36.
58 Ibid.
59 See Chapter 5, pp. 70–1.
60 Hallaq, *History*, p. 112.
61 Qur'an: xv: 79–82.
62 Shāshi, folio 5a.
63 Shāshi, folio 7b.
64 Shāshi, folio 6a.
65 Shāshi, folio 6b.
66 Shāshi, folio 8a.
67 Hallaq, *History*, p. 162.
68 Shāshi, folio 8b.
69 Abd al-Nasir al-Lughani, *A Critical Study and Edition of the first part of Kitāb Maḥāsin al-Sharī'a by Al-Qaffāl al-Shāshi*, Ph.D. thesis, Lampeter University, 2004, chapter 2.
70 Hallaq, *History*, p. 30.
71 Ibid., p. 22.
72 Nashmi, *Muqadimāt 'ilm uṣūl al-fiqh*, Kuwait, 1990, p. 174.
73 Hallaq, *History*, p. 30.
74 Yasin Dutton, *The Origins of Islamic Law*, p. 37.

8

Understanding the textual expressions

Scholars of *uṣūl al-fiqh* have detailed the means and methods for the deduction of legal injunctions from the possible meanings of the text. This work is very useful in assisting legal practitioners, for example *faqīhs* and *muftis*, to deduce a legal injunction. The main criticism that has been aimed at such classifications is that their inherent complexity could have the reverse effect on the deduction of a legal ruling. Furthermore, it has been pointed out that these classifications often reflect the view of only one particular school for their legal interpretation.[1] These linguistic rules are often studied from the perception of the expression, *lafẓ*, and its relationship to the definition that it provides. The specification for *lafẓ* is divided into specific, *khāṣ* (pertinent to one meaning); general, *'ām* (pertinent to all meanings); and collective, *mushtarak* (applicable to several meanings). Under the heading of the (figurative) usage of *lafẓ*, there is further division into actual use for the meaning stated, allegorical use and metonymy. The clarity of indication of the *lafẓ* is subdivided into the clear and the ambiguous. Most of the preceding classifications are further divided into categories, presumably with the aim of aiding in the ascertaining of the accurate detail of the meaning. Intricate discussion of these classifications is not our main concern here, as this would entail entanglement in the web of the linguistic rules of Arabic, a course which might well involve examination of the entire grammatical structure of the language.[2] Instead, I intend to focus on the linguistic methods that are concerned with the forms of textual indication for the meaning. These represent the heart of legal deduction and involve actual mechanisms that are employed frequently by scholars in the art of linguistic interpretation. These rules, in combination with the juristic ones, which will be addressed shortly, represent the entire interpretative operation used for legal deduction in Islamic law. The difference between the legal linguistic rules and the juristic maxims is that the former lead to the clarification of the meaning of the legal text, while the latter are ready-made legal maxims upon which new cases may be resolved. However, it is imperative to point out that the mechanism used by jurists to understand and classify legal knowledge requires the prudence of the jurist in order to avoid the mixing of sources or the utilisation of erroneous concepts. It can also be maintained that the legal rules are dependent upon linguistic ones, as the latter represent the first layer of knowledge required by the scholar to understand the text.

At the outset, it is important to point out the presence of two basic approaches to understanding the linguistic indication of text, *dalālat al-naṣṣ ʿala al-maʿna*: the approach of the methodical, *uṣuli*, as represented by the Ḥanafi scholars, and the approach of the debaters, *mutakallimūn*, as represented by the Shāfiʿi scholars.[3] These approaches delineate the foundation for interpretation when the text is not self-evident or in conflict with another text. The Ḥanafi scholars classified the forms of textual indications or expressions of the meaning into four categories:[4]

1. *ʿIbārat al-naṣṣ*, the explicit meaning of the words of the text.
2. *Ishārat al-naṣṣ*, the meaning of the text's words, as indicated by signs and allusions.
3. *Dalālat al-naṣṣ*, the meaning of the text's words inferred from the logical and judicial purport of the text.
4. *Iqtiḍā' al-naṣṣ*, the necessary meaning of the text's words, without which the text would remain incomplete.

Shāfiʿi scholars, on the other hand, approach textual understanding by using two modes of definitions: the pronounced meaning, *dalālat al-manṭūq*, and the understood meaning, *dalālat al-mafhūm*. The difference between the two is often seen to be more technical than actual.[5] However, a careful consideration can reveal that the difference is more than technical and can provide a completely different understanding of the meaning. The Ḥanafi are more concerned with the text itself and how it can be understood within the syntax of the language, while the Shāfiʿi target the meaning of the text that is derived from the words.

The most distinctive element of the first part of the Ḥanafi classification, *ʿibārat al-naṣṣ*, is the way in which meaning is expressed. The use of words and their formation articulates the meaning so that it is delivered in the immediate literal meaning of the text and what can be understood from it, thus leaving no room for further consideration of meaning. An example of *ʿibārat al-naṣṣ* may be found in the Qur'anic verse which states that God has permitted trading and forbidden usury.[6] This verse not only states that trading is allowed and usury is not, but also clearly highlights that the difference between them is that trading is permitted and usury is forbidden.[7] The value of *ʿibārat al-naṣṣ* comes from having the prime position of definite meaning, which implies the obligation of individuals to adhere to it.

Ishārat al-naṣṣ represents the manner in which wording indicates a meaning that is not intended from its sequence, either directly or indirectly. However, the indicated meaning, *lāzim*, is required in order to comprehend the meaning that is the subject matter of the statement, as illustrated by the following example. The Qur'an states: 'The poor people who have had to leave their homeland and their property for the sake of God would have a share of the booty'.[8] There is a non-deliberate meaning here that alludes to the fact that the poor people have already lost their property; but this is not the prime objective of the statement, which maintains that those people should have a share in the booty. A further example may be seen in the following Qur'anic verse: 'Consult them in your affairs'.[9] The original meaning here indicates that the governmental system should adopt the method of consultation, but the statement also alludes to the need for Muslim government to have available a group of people who can be consulted.[10] The value of *ishārat al-naṣṣ* is less than that of *'ibārat al-naṣṣ*, although Shukri maintains that they both indicate obligation.[11] This is confirmed by the fact that, when they are in conflict, priority is given to *'ibārat al-naṣṣ*.

Dalālat al-naṣṣ is employed when the indication of the wording of a statement is applicable by implication to another similar case, yet this is not stated directly. For example, the Qur'an instructs: 'do not say "fie" to your parents or raise your voice to them'.[12] The instruction here is clear, which is not to use expressions of displeasure, even ones as seemingly insignificant as 'fie'; but also it indicates that parents should not be treated in a worse way, such as with physical abuse. This is inferred, with no need for deep thinking or analysis.[13] As would be expected, the value of *dalālat al-naṣṣ* is less than that of *ibārat* and *ishārat al-naṣṣ*.

The fourth category, lower still in value, is *iqtiḍā' al-naṣṣ*, which represents an extra meaning for what has been stated in the words of the text. The intention is not literally stated, but is understood from the construction of the text. For example, 'prohibited to you (carrion, blood and flesh of pig)'.[14] Here 'to eat' is not actually stated, but is clearly intended, and the prohibition does not include other associations with pigs, such as keeping them to serve to others.[15]

A further concept in understanding the legal expressions is called the inverse meaning, *mafhūm al-mukhālafa*.[16] This is derived by analysis of the opposing meaning stated by the text. For example, the Qur'an states that the book is a guide for those who are aware of God.[17] The inverse interpretation is that those who are not aware of God will not be guided by the book. This category is surprisingly not accepted by the Ḥanafi scholars and treated as incorrect. This is strange, given their well-known academic analytical methodology.

The legal maxims

If the legal injunction cannot be deduced from the text and other forms of legal sources, the spirit of Islamic law will be resorted to with the aid of the legal maxims. The maxims are principles and concepts that could be applied to a wide variety of cases. They were not constructed at any one particular period in history, but evolved over time, most being established upon a recognised legal reference, such as Qur'an and hadith. It may be observed that these rules represent the basic legislative notions that express a general analogical trend in resolving legal cases and organising their injunctions.

These legal maxims are distinctive for their condensed nature and are often found to be coined in few well-structured words that provide a general definition of their principle. However, they do not represent basic theories (such as that of legal responsibility) which provide systematic topics relevant to one particular matter in Islamic law or legislation. Some Muslim lawyers, including Judge Ḥusayn,[18] claim that the entire Shāfiʿi school of thought is based on four maxims. These have been increased by other jurists to the following five:

1. Certainty cannot be removed by doubt.
2. Difficulty requires that matters should be simplified.
3. Harm is to be removed.
4. Custom should be respected.
5. All matters must be viewed according to their objectives.

It is not possible to ascribe these rules to one scholar, since they were not written at one time. The variation in style and language also indicates more than one compiler. It is more likely that they were edited several times by different hands to fit the changing needs of Islamic legal practice. The earliest name associated with these rules was Muhammad b. Muhammad b. Sufyān al-Dabbās.[19] His position was that of leader of the school of *ra'i*, individual opinion, in Iraq; and, according to Ibn Nujaym (d. AH 970), he compiled seventeen maxims reflecting the ideology of the Ḥanafi school.[20] Ibn Nujaym maintains that these rules represent the true essence of Islamic law and aid the scholar in attaining a stage whereby he can express a sound legal judgement.

These legal maxims are often cross-referenced and sectioned with those relating to *uṣūl al-fiqh*. They are also purely methodical rules functioning as deductive means for the legal injunction, and are not intended to provide practical principles for the use of lawyers. The two kinds of rules can often operate hand in hand to resolve complex legal situations, such as a clash of concepts. For example, there is a methodical maxim which states that when 'prohibition' and 'allowance' are in contradiction, then preference should be given to 'prohibition'; and, when two duties are in conflict, the more certain of the two should be observed. These two rules are often used when the injunctions based on legal rules could lead to positive as well as negative results. Accordingly, if a secondary public service, such as the building of a road or factory, could lead to adverse effects on public health or the environment, then such a road or factory should be sacrificed.

Various Muslim scholars, including Badar al-Dīn Muhammad al-Shāfiʿi (AH 745–94), appear to have combined both the jurisprudence legal principles.[21] These are useful in acting as conceptual loci for a variety of non-documented general injunctions and enable Islamic law to organise those issues that do not fit with any one general theory. According to Muṣṭafa al-Zarqa, the formation of these principles commenced towards the end of the third century AH.[22]

Ibn Nujaym says that the early twenty-five maxims that he collated were obtained from reliable Ḥanafi references. However, some of these maxims appear to be based on weak narrations, which Ibn Nujaym points out when the maxim is cited.[23] They can be subdivided into two categories: six maxims representing the basis on which the various schools of Islamic law are founded, and nineteen which are of a general nature. Ibn Nujaym's collection formed the basis for the legal maxims that were coined by the Ottoman Gazette of Legal Injunctions entitled *Majallat al-aḥkām al-ʿādliyya*.[24] Prior to Ibn Nujaym's work, there were earlier documents for these injunctions, such as the collection compiled by Abu al-Ḥasan al-Karkhi (AH 270–340).[25] Most references that have attempted to outline the principles, subsequent to the *Majalla* have deviated from the principles of legal maxims and provided general classifications and rules relevant to principal legal subjects. An example of this may be found in the book of ʿIzz al-Dīn b. Abd Salām (d. AH 660), which is an invaluable introductory work on law, yet which provides only main chapters of particular topics that are elaborated upon from the philosophical perspective of legislation. This is also applicable to the works of Shihāb al-Dīn Ahmad al-Qarāfi (d. AH 684) and Ibn Rajab, the Ḥanbali scholar. None of the previous books written after the *Majalla* provide legal rules that can be regarded as 'constitutional' general principles.[26] The *Majalla* is particularly valuable, as it has undoubtedly influenced the formation of later Islamic and Arabic law in the Muslim world. The *Majalla* sometimes contains maxims that are conceptually repetitious. These maxims, by and large, can be divided into primary and secondary, the latter being derived from the former. Despite certain principles bearing a relationship to one another, they can often be found scattered within the text of the *Majalla*. Zarqa, the latest editor of the *Majalla*'s rules, points out the weakness inherent in its disorganisation and lack of structure.[27] The following paragraphs will attempt to outline and translate selected maxims from the *Majalla*, as cited by Ibn Nujaym and commented upon by Zarqa and Zaydān.[28]

(1) All matters are by their intentions. This is based on a hadith which has a similar meaning. The legal application of such a maxim is very wide and could range from minor individual action to much more complicated notions relevant to economics or international matters. One classical application cites the case of a person who finds an object, *luqṭa*, in a public place; the law would consider him as the keeper, *multaqiṭ*, of that object, and he is thus not responsible for its

damage while it is in his possession, provided that he is not deliberately negligent. However, if his intention is to own the object, then he would be responsible for any damage, whether deliberately by negligence or not. It must be observed here that an abstract intention (not coupled with a responding action) does not lead to an injunction. Accordingly, a person who intends to donate or sell his house, even though no formal expression of this intention has been made, has no valid rights.[29] Intention and meaning are the prime aspects of a contract, not its wording or literary structure. Here the effect of intention is evident (as cited in the previous rules); however, the focus is on the contract and, if an individual states that he is giving an item on loan, then a contract of 'lease' has been entered into. This is applicable to all contracts.[30]

(2) Certainty cannot be annulled by doubt. This means that, once a particular matter is ascertained and doubt occurs about its continuity, then certainty would prevail. If an individual has died and is recorded as being in debt as a certainty, then he would be regarded as remaining in debt.[31] According to the *Majalla*, the definition of certainty, *yaqīn*, lies in the resolute acceptance of the mind for a fact, whereas doubt creates uncertainty in the human mind. Certainty suggests a definite mindset, whereas doubt creates an oscillation between the two, giving precedence to neither. Such a definition does not appear to stem from the concept of intention, and therefore the relationship between the preceding three rules seems to be somewhat inconsistent.

(3) Legal responsibility, *dhimma*, is not accountable until proved otherwise. This is based on the grounds that, when a human being is born, he is free of responsibility until legal actions are taken. Accordingly, if A accuses B of being in debt, this rule stipulates that B is not responsible until proven so. This application here is that 'doubt' is interpreted to the benefit of the accused.[32] Rules (2) and (3) are considered by Zarqa to be subdivisions of the first, yet he does not outline his reasons for this opinion. A relationship between (2) and (3) may be valid, but it seems less likely to incorporate the first rule.

(4) No statement can be ascribed to a person who is silent; and, when necessary, silence can be a statement. The reasoning here may be based on rule (3) and could be viewed as part of it. This is due to the fact that a statement made by a silent person cannot constitute a certainty, unlike a verbal response which indicates definite intention. An example for the first part of this rule can be as follows: A sees B selling A's property, but remains silent. In this case, silence is not an indication of approval, and A may reclaim his property from B. The classical evidence for the second part of this rule is cited by Zaydān. When a woman is asked if she will accept a particular man as her husband, a virgin girl indicates approval by her silence. If she does not consent to this, then she may say 'no'.[33]

(5) What counts in (legal) words is a reality.[34] This rule aims to differentiate between the metaphorical and literal usage of words. Accordingly, an individual

who refers to his grandchildren as 'my children' is using metaphor and, legally, the term may only be applied to his direct children. Also, if A informs B that he intends to 'donate' something and B takes it, but A then says to B that he meant 'selling' and requests payment, this is rejected as an invalid request because his initial words set the contract. However, if A had said he would donate it to B for a certain sum of money, then a contract of sale would have been entered into. This same rule applies to all contracts.[35] This rule is similar to the previous one and indicates that the meaning of words should be treated as effective and not ignored or avoided. Accordingly, if a person makes various statements on a similar matter, each should be taken on its own merits and treated as a different expression. For example, if an IOU is issued twice, the second should not be taken as representative of the first, even if the sum owed is identical. However, if someone makes a statement that is blatantly incredible, such as a man claiming to be the father of an older person, then his words should be ignored.[36]

(6) To offer proof is the responsibility of the claimant, and the giving of an oath lies with the person who denies such a claim. This rule is one of the fundamentals of Islamic legislative procedure in court or whenever a statement is required. The philosophy behind this is that if a person is making a claim that is not usual or that deviates from the norm, then the onus is on the claimant to prove his case. The accused remains innocent, and so he clears his responsibility with an oath. An example is cited in the *Majalla*: if the vendor requests payment from the person acting on behalf of the purchaser, holding the second party responsible as a representative, *wakīl*, then the vendor must prove the status of the second party if the purchaser denies him as *wakīl*.[37]

(7) Whatever is prohibited to take is also prohibited to give. This rule prevents the individual who acquires property in an illegitimate way from passing on his illegal booty.[38] It seems to be a limited rule which is applicable to transactions only, but it could have further applications relevant to rituals, particularly on zakah.

(8) Rulers oversee the public in order to fulfil public interest. This principle is more one of public administration, wherein governors are generally expected to act in the interests of the public. The *Majalla* cites that a ruler may not give any part of public property (e.g. public roads) for an individual to build on, unless there is no chance of such construction causing harm to others.[39]

(9) No harm should be inflicted on others, and no harm should be caused in retaliation. In this 'rule', the harm referred to should be severe and should never be initiated, even if it is inflicted by legitimate means; for example, the building of a septic tank close to the house of a neighbour, or the building of a wall that obliterates light from a neighbour's property and so on. However, if such an action affects someone adversely, the individual is not expected to retaliate and take the law into his own hands by knocking down the wall; such

cases are to be resolved in court.[40] This rule has many applications, and associated with it is a further maxim which states that 'harm should be removed'.[41] Also relevant to the concept of 'harm' is one that states: 'Public harm takes precedence over private harm'.[42] The application of this rule is cited in the example of an ignorant doctor who causes harm to patients. He may be prevented from future practice, despite the fact that this will cause him private difficulties. Individuals' property may be demolished in order to halt the spread of fire. The pricing of basic commodities is also subjected to this rule.

(10) Necessity justifies that which is prohibited.[43] This important rule indicates that there are times when it is allowed to pursue the prohibited under the principle of necessity. Although this is an elaboration of the previous rule, it offers procedure rather than the sole establishing of a concept; there, harm can be justified because further harm may be removed by doing what is normally forbidden. If an individual is starving, he may eat what is prohibited, such as carrion or pig meat, and a ship may offload its cargo into the sea to reduce the risk of sinking. This rule is, however, restricted by one which states that 'necessity should be judged according to its amplitude'. In this case, the sinking ship may only offload sufficient cargo to prevent disaster, since it is subject to this relation between necessity and appropriate amount.[44]A further related rule states that 'the removal of harm is preferred to the achieving of benefits'. This maxim indicates that the public interest of obtaining good is secondary to the avoidance of harm. For example, trading in drugs and alcohol is forbidden in order to avoid harmful and adverse outcomes, even though such transactions may well create commercial benefits. Here, Islamic law presents itself as a prevention against potential harm and, as Zarqa maintains, the immediate hedonistic joys of life are short-lived, while the pain of bereavement endures for ever. One stipulation is that the preference for the prevention of harm over any potential benefits should be weighed and balanced. This means that the prohibition will take effect if the harm outweighs the benefits, yet if the harm is minimal in comparison to the benefit, then the balance will be tipped.

(11) Customs, *'āda*, are to be referred to. The term 'custom' in this maxim equates with that which is repeatedly practised in any profession, culture or social group. For example, it is customary to pay one's bill after eating in a restaurant, and in contemporary societies this action is generally accepted. Customs can be either verbal or practical, and a few further similar rules have been derived from this notion. However, in principle, 'custom' has to have remained accepted and unchanged in order for it to warrant being referred to in law.[45] The *Majalla* added a stipulation that 'custom' is only referred to when there is no text to indicate otherwise. Also, 'customs' can vary within any one particular social group, which may result in the existence of both public and private customs.[46]

(12) Injunctions change over time. This rule accepts that injunctions may be affected by the passing of time, particularly those based on customs which are wont to change over the years. However, injunctions based on the text do not change.[47]

(13) What counts is that which is common rather than what is rare. The rule may be seen as a continuation of the previous one, but it is less specific in nature. It examines general acceptance of common practices, and an example of this is the variation in what is acknowledged as the age of puberty. This may be between fifteen and eighteen years old, depending on the culture.[48]

(14) The one who gains is the one who loses. This indicates that anyone involved in an action or contract that may result in profit must also be responsible for any losses connected with it. Partners in a company would all be liable for any loss incurred therein.[49] Zarqa cites another interesting example that is relevant to responsibility. In the case of a foundling child, the Muslim treasury is responsible for its upkeep, but if the parents are known, the treasury is then eventually entitled to that child's inheritance (were he/she to die childless).

(15) The individual is not responsible for damage incurred by his animal, unless he has not taken the required precautions to prevent such damage. According to this rule, if a man ties his horse in the correct allotted place and it kicks a neighbouring horse, then the owner is liable because he has been negligent.[50]

(16) No actions are allowed on any property without the consent of the owner. The *Majalla* specifies that the permission required is that of the owner; Zarqa states that the term 'permission' refers to legal permission, since 'permission' can suggest an unspecific notion that is more appropriate to general legislation. However, the *Majalla* states that it refers particularly to personal property.[51]

(17) He who hastens matters before their time will be deprived of them. This principle appears to be based on that of *sadd al-dharā'i'*, which means here that the person who utilises illegitimate means to achieve his objectives will be deprived of that objective once he is apprehended. For example, if a terminally ill man divorces his wife with a view to preventing her from inheriting his property, then she would nevertheless receive her share of inheritance if his intention was proven.[52]

In addition to the above selected legal maxims, there are other methodical maxims which are relevant to the principles of jurisprudence. Various scholars sometimes included them with the above maxims of law. An example is: 'No individual opinion can be exercised when a text is available'.[53] A practical example for this rule would be that no scholar can offer individual opinion on the prohibition of usury or fornication as to whether they are allowed or not. A further methodical maxim informs us that whatever is general in a private/personal injunction does not expire, although that part which is private can become invalid. The practical example of this maxim would be seen when an individual intends to fast on a Monday, but makes a mistake with the time and does so on Sunday; then his action would be invalid. However, in a general sense, his Sunday fast would retain its credit as a meritorious action. Also, when a representative is appointed conditionally yet he acts without respecting that condition, then his action as a representative would be invalid, although the general permission given to him would remain effective;[54] 'prohibition can be multiple, with multiple reasons'.[55]

Finally, it is observed that, despite the similarity in scholars' usages of the above methods to understand the text, there are often great variations in the final understanding of what the text means. The scholars themselves differed despite the similarity of their tools and principles, and this difference can be ascribed to many factors, such as the human difference in perceiving the facts of life, the obscurity of the topic itself, and the human instincts and wish for authority that can influence the legal conclusion. In this discussion, we have highlighted the practical legal methods and rules that Muslim scholars would use in understanding the text. These methods can be observed within the methodology of all the scholar whom we will discuss in the next chapter.

Notes

1 A very helpful summary of these classifications can be found in Zuḥayli's excellent textbook on *Uṣūl al-fiqh*, 2, pp. 195–415. For an English discussion and analysis, see Šukri Husayn Ramic, *Linguistic Principles in Uṣūl al-Fiqh and their Effect on Legal Reasoning in Islamic Law*, Ph.D. thesis, Lampeter University, 1996.

2 For a detailed listing of the grammatical rules relevant to jurisprudence, see Badr al-Dīn al-Zarkashi (d. AH 794), *Al-Manthūr fi al-Qawā'id*, ed. Taysīr Fā'iq Ahmad Maḥmūd, Qatar, 1985; Zaydān, *Al-Wajīz*, pp. 277–377; Zuḥayli, *Uṣūl al-fiqh*, 1, pp. 195–410.

3 Both titles reflect the nature of each group's approach towards the understanding of the text.

4 Ramic, p. 15.

5 Ibid., p. 66.

6 Qur'an: 11: 275.

7 Zaydān, *Al-Wajīz*, p. 355.

8 Qur'an: lix: 8.

9 Qur'an: iii: 159.

10 Zaydān, *Al-Wajīz*, p. 358; Āmidi, 3, pp. 61–2.

11 Ramic, p. 31.

12 Qur'an: xvii: 23.

13 Zaydān, *Al-Wajīz*, p. 362; Āmidi, 3, pp. 61–2.

14 Qur'an: v: 3.

15 Zaydān, *al-Wajīz*, p. 364.

16 Ibid., p. 366; Āmidi, 3, p. 63.

17 Qur'an: ii: 2.
18 Judge Ḥusayn is Abu Ali b. Muhammad Ahmad al-Marwazi (d. AH 462). See Badr al-Dīn al-Zarkashi, *Al-Manthūr fi al-qawā'id*.
19 Dabbās was a contemporary of Abu al-Ḥasan al-Karkhi (b. AH 260–340), who is reported to have practised *fatwa* at the year 214 while very young, Abd al-Qādir Mohammad b. Abi al-Wafā' al-Qurashi, *Ṭabaqāt al-Ḥanafiyya*, 1, pp. 116, 148.
20 Ibn Nujaym, *Al-Ashbāh wa al-naẓā'ir*, Damascus 1983, p. 10.
21 See Al-Zarkashi, *Al-Manthūr fi al-qawā'id*, p. 337.
22 Zarqa, pp. 955–6.
23 Ibn Nujaym, p. 10.
24 See Chapter 6, n. 4, p. 91.
25 Zarqa, pp. 955–6.
26 Ibid., p. 962.
27 Ibid.
28 Zaydān, *Al-Madkhal*, pp. 77–88.
29 *Majalla*, p. 17; Zarqa, p. 965; Zaydān, ibid., p. 77.
30 *Majalla*, p. 19; Zarqa, p. 966; Zaydān, ibid., p. 78.
31 *Majalla*, p. 20; Zarqa, p. 967; Zaydān, ibid., p. 80.
32 *Majalla*, p. 23, Zarqa, p. 970; Zaydān, ibid., p. 81.
33 *Majalla*, p. 47; Zarqa, p. 973, Zaydān, ibid., p. 79.
34 *Majalla*, p. 24; Zarqa, p. 1,003; Zaydān, ibid., p. 80.
35 *Majalla*, p. 24; Zarqa, p. 1,003; Zaydān, ibid., p. 79.
36 *Majalla*, p. 44; Zarqa, p. 1,001; Zaydān, ibid., p. 79.
37 *Majalla*, p. 51; Zarqa, p. 1,057; Zaydān, ibid., p. 81.
38 *Majalla*, p. 33; Zarqa, p. 1,013; Zaydān, ibid., p. 81.
39 *Majalla*, p. 34; Zarqa, p. 1,050; Zaydān, ibid., p. 82.
40 *Majalla*, p. 29; Zarqa, p. 977; Zaydān, ibid., p. 82.
41 *Majalla*, p. 29; Zarqa, p. 982; Zaydān, ibid., p. 83, see also p. 82 above.
42 *Majalla*, p. 31; Zarqa, p. 984; Zaydān, ibid., p. 83.
43 *Majalla*, p. 29; Zarqa, pp. 987, 995; Zaydān, ibid., p. 84.
44 *Majalla*, p. 30; Zarqa, p. 996; Zaydān, ibid., p. 84.
45 *Majalla*, p. 34; Zarqa, p. 999; Zaydān, ibid., p. 85.
46 *Majalla*, p. 35.
47 *Majalla*, p. 36; Zarqa, p. 1,001; Zaydān, ibid., p. 86.
48 *Majalla*, p. 37; Zarqa, p. 1,000; Zaydān, ibid., p. 86.
49 *Majalla*, p. 58; Zarqa, p. 1,035; Zaydān, ibid., p. 87.
50 *Majalla*, p. 60; Zarqa, p. 1,048; Zaydān, ibid., p. 87.
51 *Majalla*, p. 61; Zarqa, p. 1,038; Zaydān, ibid., p. 87.
52 *Majalla*, p. 62; Zarqa, p. 1,014; Zaydān, ibid., p. 88.
53 Zaydān, ibid., p. 80.
54 Ibid., pp. 111–12.
55 Ibid., p. 252.

PART FIVE

Legal authority and the future of Islamic law

9

Legal authority and the diverse faces of Islamic law

The 'establishment' face of Islamic law

To understand Islamic law, we need to look into the factors that contribute to its creation and continuity. Islamic law needs not only a state wherein it may be applied, but also the appropriate scholars to synthesise it. Without either of the two, the law could have no authority and would comprise only a set of instructions that the people could neither understand nor apply. At the present time, a few states claim to be Islamic, such as Pakistan, Sudan and Saudi Arabia. However, in this chapter, we will discuss some legal aspects of Saudi Arabia as an example of a state which claims to apply Islamic law. There is no doubt that many valid criticisms can be directed against such a claim. However, it must be emphasised that this choice of state was made because Islam started there, and the Saudi experience of an Islamic state can be seen as one of the earliest surviving states since the collapse of the Ottomans. Also, many Muslims still view its interpretation of the law as an important source for legal authority. In addition, this chapter will discuss some selected scholars who seem to hold some authority in interpreting contemporary Islamic law.

By the turn of the twentieth century, the Arab world was witnessing political attempts to present the 'Islamic solution' to various social and political problems. Such attempts would naturally have impinged heavily on Islamic law. One of the earliest attempts was that of the ancestors of the current Saudi ruling family. Muhammad b. Sa'ūd al-Kabīr joined forces with Wahabism[1] and later on was executed by the Ottomans. Years later, Abd al-Azīz b. Abd al-Rahman (b. c. 1880)[2] initiated his Saudi dynasty following in the footsteps of his grandfather. Despite all the controversy surrounding the Saudi dynasty and its method of interpretation of an Islamic state, this government has endured until the present day, proposing Islamic law as the main element for a contemporary state.

When the caliphate was officially abolished on 3 March 1924[3] Islamic law began operating within multiple political establishments. It became applicable by 'organic' states which were formed from the remaining fragments of the giant Ottoman 'Organisation'.[4] The non-conformation to one establishment and the support of the West could be the main reasons that have helped the survival of the Saudi dynasty until today. The young state was different from the devoutly religious state of Sudan[5] and the political Ottoman state; rather, the Saudis' interpretation of Islam was a combination of the two.

Abd al-Azīz bin Saud's first public speech offered insight into his perception of a future whereby legal scholars would be able to disagree with the rulers and could make an overt stance for what they believed to be right.[6] Ibn Saud shrewdly realised that his Islamic state could only exist with the support of the *'ulamā'*, which ultimately provided authority for both. Ibn Saud's 'Islamic totalitarianism' blended Islam with the Bedouin tribal principles of government; a major factor for the state was therefore held intact. His enemies often referred to him as the nomad, *badawi*, a term that reflected his nomadic tendency.[7] After so many years, the same term was used to criticise the religious politics of the Saudi state by a well-known contemporary scholar, Muhammad al-Ghazāli (AD 1917–2000), who maintains that Saudi Islamic law is based on a Bedouin jurisprudence and as such can only offer a puerile understanding of creed and law.[8] Was Ibn Saud thinking as a tyrannical Bedouin, or did he have an astute awareness of the relationship between a tribal culture and government politics? Whatever the answer, it has to be said that Ibn Saud's ruling paradigm provides us with an example of how Islamic law can be adopted as the main fabric of a state. The term *'aqīda*, creed, seems to have been pivotal to Ibn Saud's establishment of legal authority, and references to this are evident in most of his and his successors' speeches. However, Ibn Saud's secret of success lay not in what he proclaimed but in his wisdom and 'long sword'. He is reported to have once peered into the guest rooms, *majālis*, of his visitors, laughed and asserted: 'there is not one guest here with whom I have not previously fought'. A friend replied: 'Your sword is long, sire'.[9]

In addition to that, and perhaps more importantly, the authority of the Saudi state was established on the political understanding of its position as a small and weak state that could benefit from the support of the West on the grounds of the state *maṣlaḥa*. Despite this understanding, Ibn Saud was not prevented from making a stand for the Palestinians, because all Muslims regard the region of Palestine as central to Islam. In this case, political diplomacy had to take a back seat, and Ibn Saud wrote to President Roosevelt denying any support for the Zionists against the Muslim right to Palestine.[10] Ibn Saud had strong allies in the British government, who aided him in the fierce conflict between himself and his formidable enemy, the tribe of Al-Rashīd. There was intense rivalry between Al-Rashīd, supported by Turkey, and Ibn Saud, supported by Britain, and this eventually concluded with Ibn Saud as the victor. Although some authors portray Ibn Saūd as independent and balanced in his relations with Britain, the fact remains that his policy was not dissimilar to that of other rulers, such as the Kuwaitis and Persians in their acceptance of a British presence. Yet the opposite extreme of this policy was evident in Ibn Saud's ally, the Wahabi movement, who stood totally against the acceptance of any foreign influence, which evidently caused much embarrassment for the Saudis in front of their allies.

In modern Saudi Arabia, there has emerged a generation of Islamic activist youths who are in many ways similar to the Wahabis and can be seen as a continuation of the movement, in their turn causing embarrassment to the Saudis. Those youths are influenced by the radical waves that began in Egypt with Ḥasan Al-Banna (1906–49) and the Muslim brotherhood movement.[11] These youngsters grew up between the mid-1960s and the late 1980s, observing the writings and thoughts of scholars such as Al-Banna, who himself was influenced by the ideals of Muhammad b. Abd al-Wahāb. Saudi Arabia offered refuge to many Egyptian scholars who fled from Nāṣir, and later to the Syrian scholars who fled the pressure of Ḥāfiẓ al-Asad. These refugees enjoyed the homage of King Faiṣal and Khālid and exerted their efforts in the pursuit of academia, writing and the public teaching of Islamic law. The ultimate goal during this period was the divining of legislative solutions for major areas such as banking and insurance, as well as for penal law and a proper system of government.

The legal structure of the contemporary Saudi state based its foundation on the Sunni Islamic law, with special reference to the Ḥanbali school.[12] The same order of sources is employed as that of this school of thought. The codification of legal rules and principles is included in the system under the name of *niẓām* (plural *anẓima*), which designates acts, rules and regulations. *Niẓām* from a formal point of view is 'a document issued by the King and the Saudi council of ministers to regulate the behaviour of people and the interest of society'.[13] From a subject point of view, the document consists of articles that cover one particular subject. It has a number and date, and is signed by the king, these formalities being very similar to those of modern legal codes (particularly the Egyptian and French). The word *niẓām* is used to avoid the usage of the word 'law', the implication of this term being that it is made by humans and a non-divine source and authority. This echoes the influence of the Ottoman *tanẓimāt* issued during the time of Sultan Abd al-Majīd (r. 1839–61).[14] This was trying to justify the step of moving from the uncodified traditional methodology of Islamic law, which deals with cases on the basis of 'decision by cases as they occur', to the organisation of the Ottoman legal system by codification.

Perhaps this is why we find that in most Saudi legal literature the terms associated with legislation are converted to 'regulation'; thus the legislative authority is termed 'regulatory authority' and any new legislation is termed *niẓām* rather than legislation. However, it is observed that this is often done in an inconsistent manner that does not appear to maintain the actual difference between the meanings of the words 'regulation' and 'legislation'. The legislation that governs the relationship between a foreign contractor and his Saudi representative gives one example of such apparent inconsistency.[15] Various other 'regulations' are found in the Saudi legal system, governing various matters of trade industry or criminal law and proceedings. This separation between legislation and regulation is not only political; it could also stem from the difference in nature between Islamic law and human-made laws, particularly in the area of defining what the legal interpretation is. A human-made legal interpretation could accept the change of the legal philosophy of the law by or without following certain procedures such as referring it to the legislative authorities, in order to reinterpret the law. The interpreters of Islamic law could never change the philosophy of law. Even when resorting to means such as individual opinion, *ijtihād*, and the interpretations of the law on the ground of necessity, one cannot grant such a privilege to the legal interpreter of the law.

Saudi legal sources start with the sources of Islamic law, followed by the *anẓima*, which are also termed the ordinary rules. These include all the principal ordinances enacted by the state as represented by the king, in conjunction with the council of ministers. The lowest of the legal ordinances is termed 'tablet', *lā'iḥa*. This provides the details of the general principles that the *niẓām* has included. The *lā'iḥa* system follows an order of hierarchy whereby the lower cannot disagree with the higher *lā'iḥa* in either context or formality. These *lā'iḥa* rules are divided into three categories – *tanfīdhiyya*, implementation rules, *tanẓīmiyya*, regulation rules, and *al-ẓabṭ wa al-'amn*, security rules.[16]

The traffic implementation rules are an example of *tanfīdhiyya*. These deal with all aspects of traffic rules, such as driving licences and the rules that should be applied on the roads.[17] Normally these ordinances are published in the official gazette *Umm al-Qura*. The traffic law was first published on the 15th of the 8th of AH 1395; a few similar *lā'iḥas* are found, such as the hotels rules, which were enacted by the ministry of trade.[18] It is observed that these kinds of *lā'iḥas* are sometimes enacted directly by a royal decree without going through the ministerial hierarchy. This indicates a centralisation of power in certain aspects of state affairs, such as the civil service system.[19] While such a centralisation of power could be understood in conjunction with the appointment in the civil service of sensitive responsibilities, it is not clear why all appointments follow the same category of *lā'iḥas*. The only explanation is that there is no authority for appointment in the government service apart from that of the direct department, which operates within the umbrella of royal decrees, termed *dīwān al-khidma al-madaniyya*. Most other public services are ruled according to a ministerial level of rules, such as the *lā'iḥa* of customs.[20] The second category of *lawā'iḥ* is *al-tanẓīmiyya* or regulation rules, dealing with regulating public sectors, public services and administration of government. This kind of *lā'iḥa* differs from the implementation rules in the sense that it only specifies the responsibility and organisation of the public sector, without going into the implementation of the rules. An example is the *lā'iḥa* which organises private schools and defines the meaning of a school, its duties, conditions and objectives.[21] The third category of rules or *lawā'iḥ* are those relevant to public security and standards, which are termed *lawā'iḥ al-ẓabṭ wa al-'amn*. They include all the *tanẓīmi* rules for public security and health, such as the rules relevant to the supervising of food, wandering vendors and the controlling of businesses that can cause public disturbances.[22]

As regards the government administration system, the Saudis adopted three well-known Islamic systems: the judicial, the *ḥisba*[23] and the *maẓālim*.[24]

The judicial system in Saudi Arabia is independent, at least in theory, following a royal decree which granted the judges freedom of judgement and independence. This was established in 1935. The courts are divided into four: the council of supreme judgement, the court of appeal, public courts and small courts.[25]

From the above, it can be stated that the Saudi legal structure appears to be similar in many ways to contemporary legal structures. It is certainly similar to some other Arabic legal structures, such as the Egyptian and the old Iraqi ones, due to the fact that many legal advisors who built the Saudi system were employed from the rest of the Muslim world and brought with them their legal experience and knowledge, which was often influenced by the French and the British legal systems.

Authority and the law of resurgence

While Saudi Arabia provided a state form of Islamic law, in Egypt Islamic law was developing in the form of resistance and government opposition law. When Ḥasan al-Banna started his movement that called for an Islamic state,[26] King Fārūq (1920–65)[27] was the ruler of a state with a strong British presence. Fārūq's state acted in the capacity of defender of direct British interest in the area of the Suez Canal. An Islamic state would ultimately represent a threat to both the state and the British. After the death of Al-Banna, an event said to be linked to the king's secret police, the Muslim Brotherhood movement continued post-Fārūq and began a new phase of opposition under Nasir. Unlike the battle between rulers, as in the case of Ibn Saud and Al-Rashīd, a conflict arose between a popular religious movement, grounded on the claim of religious orthodoxy, and a military regime that was based on social reform and opposition to the dominating British presence. A clash was evident between the authority of the masses, as represented by the Muslim Brotherhood, and the authority of Nasir's government. Nasir's government was also a Muslim government which held the iron fist of the army but lacked the strength of religious authority.

The main strength of the Muslim Brotherhood lay in its academic writers,[28] like Sayyid Quṭb, who maintained the necessity for a new leadership based on original Islam. Quṭb's basic principle was that social reform could not be achieved without the removal of extraneous systems and their replacement with an Islamic government.[29] Quṭb was primarily calling for a revival movement that understood Islamic law on the premise of blending prophetic understanding with a contemporary attitude towards life. Nasir perceived the main threat posed by Quṭb and the Muslim Brotherhood as being their propounding of Islam as a total attitude towards life and not purely as a religion.[30] From Quṭb's perspective, a society of 'ignorance' was fast evolving which reflected the existing social structure before the time of the Prophet. By definition, this term describes a society that denies the absolute authority of God and thus submits itself to the power of other authorities, including communism and capitalism. Even societies which refer to themselves as 'a people's society', a nation state or a party state refute the ultimate authority of the Divine.[31]

An 'ignorant' society not only fulfils the aforementioned criteria but also extends to another one: that is, even though the society has an apparent belief in the worship of God, it does not apply Islamic law in its way of life.[32] A total Islamic system requires that God must be the ruling authority and that this principle should embrace all laws, customs and traditions. This concept of Ḥākimiyya[33] not only includes Islamic law but also extends to cover ethics, theology and all principles of government structure and rule.[34] Doubtless the views of Quṭb served to widen the existing chasm between the Muslim Brotherhood and the ruling political power, and a clash between the two was imminent. The suspicion of an attempt to assassinate the Egyptian President Nasir in Alexandria in October 1954 led to the Muslim Brotherhood's suppression, and six of its leaders were executed including Sayyid Quṭb. In the 1960s and 1970s, the movement was still active but was largely clandestine and spreading throughout the Muslim world.

The crushing of the Brotherhood by Nasir created a ripple effect of 'Islamic resurgence', 'government opposition' and 'Islamic hero movement' which was duplicated in most of the Muslim world that was formerly part of the Ottoman legacy, including Iraq, Saudi Arabia, Palestine, Jordan and Syria. The effect of the movement even went as far as the Malayan Archipelago and the Indian subcontinent. The influence of the writings of Quṭb may be discerned in the work of many contemporary scholars in the Islamic world. This is particularly evident in the terms and concepts that he inventively coined in his various writings, particularly his widely spread *tafsīr* of the Qur'an, *Fi ẓilāl al-Qur'ān*.

Authority and the liberal face of Islamic law

Muhammad al-Ghazāli (AD 1917–2000) may be seen as one of the recent post-Quṭb pioneers who have attempted to present an independent and more liberal

'Islamic solution' than that observed in the writings of the Muslim brothers. He was in clear disagreement with the radical traditionalist Saudi understanding of Islam. He may also be seen as a continuation of the earlier liberal scholars such as Jamāl al-Dīn al-Afghāni (1838–97) and Muḥammad Abdu (1849–1905).[35]

Muhammad al-Ghazāli wrote prolifically on a variety of aspects and related legislative issues. However, *Al-Sunna al-nabawiyya bayna ahl al-fiqh wa ahl al-ḥadīth* is a work that represents an enlightening summary of his independent and non-politically orientated thoughts and ideas. His main criticism of Islamic legal thought is that it has not given enough attention to the notion of rationalisation, particularly during the last few centuries. He maintains that the prevalence of weak hadith and problematic sects has resulted in stagnation and prejudice.[36] To him, sectarian fanaticism is an indication of ignorance that has led some short-sighted scholars to state that Mālik lacked full comprehension of many aspects of law, including the importance of *basmala*[37] and not perfecting the ending of prayer. Likewise, Ghazāli refutes the opinions of those who accuse Abu Ḥanīfa of failing to make ablution because he justified the action of prayer after touching a woman. Ghazāli reiterates that such claims are born out of ignorance and suggests that the only way to eradicate a one-tracked legal mentality is to implement a stringent educative policy that aims to generate a total understanding of Islamic law. It should refute the validity of merely resorting to nomadic law, and supersedes the simplistic and superficial comprehension of creed.[38]

Ghazāli states that Muslim jurists always remained close to the prophetic tradition, drawing attention to 'Ā'isha's attitude regarding the understanding of the Sunna's text through legal analogy and the circumstances of its occurrence. One of Ghazāli's main influences on modern Islamic law stems from his liberal criticism of the traditional scholars, who insisted on a literal interpretation of hadith. Such criticisms represent an important call to reform the legal methodology as well as the practical application of the texts on Muslim daily life. This was particularly important with regard to reforming the social position of women. Ghazāli rejects the claim that the blood money of a woman is worth only half that of a man. He maintains that such a claim displays ignorance and disrespect for the female sex; women should be held in esteem and treated with consideration by the Islamic faith. The covering of a woman's face was a further issue disputed by Ghazāli, who maintains that Islam does not require the face-veil, *niqāb*, as part of women's dress code. This can be found in the Qur'an, wherein believers were told to cast their eyes downward,[39] an action that could not be carried out at the time of the Prophet if the face was covered.

Ghazāli goes on to cite prophetic verses that indicate the non-requirement of face-covering in order to fulfil *ḥijāb*. He offers a new definition for female garb, which he terms the 'permitted exposure', *al-sufūr al-mubāḥ*, which grants women the right to uncover their faces and not to wear long gowns if they so choose. He also permits the making-up of a woman's face if she wishes to marry, referring to the Prophet's comments regarding a woman named Subay'a, who received criticism because she wore make-up while awaiting a further marriage proposal after the death of her first husband and the birth of her child. Some Muslims told her that she must not make herself up and that she should wait four months and ten days before remarriage. The Prophet disputed this reprimand and told her that, because she had already given birth, she was entitled to reveal her face. This hadith shows that, at the time of the Prophet, the revealing of woman to man, *sufūr*, was acceptable.[40]

Regarding the education of women, Ghazāli maintains that females have every right to study and further their education and also to be accepted to take employment and hold positions of public office. The Prophet held that women are equal to men, as the two sexes are the result of a division of the same essence. Ghazāli upholds the right of women to take up leadership and managerial posts, referring to 'Umar's practice of giving the higher post of *ḥisba*[41] to a woman named Shifā'.[42] In this capacity, she had absolute power over the market place, controlling and establishing justice for all concerned. Ghazāli further states that the legal testimony of a woman should not be worth only half that of a man, except in certain restricted areas wherein she does not possess the prerequisite skills that only men can possess. He also maintains that a woman can take public office as a governor.[43]

Ghazāli reveals yet another pioneering perception when he contests the prohibition of singing, maintaining that there are times when song has positive effects and can lead to higher goals, such as patriotic singing.[44] In general, Ghazāli recognises that there must be a careful balance between customs and the literal understanding of textually prescribed traditions. For example, the practice of sitting cross-legged on the floor to eat rather than reclining in a chair is not a requirement of Islam. Those who adhere to this as a set duty are mixing local custom with the textual tradition that it interprets, because such practices are not specified in the text. The Prophet has issued basic rules to propagate a correct Islam, but it is important to be able to distinguish between Arab tradition and custom, which may be accepted in different parts of the world as the interpretation of the same text.

Regarding clothing, Islam does not require a specific 'uniform', but garments are expected to be modest and respectable.[45] General housing and other buildings have to be constructed only to fulfil their purpose, and there are no legislative specifications for their design. On the same grounds of rejecting the literal interpretation of texts, Ghazāli highlights some common misunderstandings of the objectives of the legal text in Islamic society, such as the topic of personal hygiene. Some scholars maintain that it is not permitted for anyone to urinate standing up, nor is the use of toilet paper allowed. Ghazāli states that there is no proof of such prohibitions and that attention to cleanliness is the important issue, not the actual personal practices. He maintains that the usage of modern alternatives to the old means of hygiene, such as toilet paper instead of stones, is preferred since it provides more comfort and convenience for humans.[46] The toilets in modern mosques have upright urinating facilities, and these are acceptable so long as the Islamic cleansing and hygiene rules are adhered to.

According to Ghazāli, the actual objective of the law is of prime importance in an Islamic political system. He maintains that, to have a proper understanding of Islamic law, we must identify all objectives and means, whether rigid or flexible. A previous concept[47] of distributing spoils among warriors may be replaced by the modern notion of military conscription. Consultation, *shūra*, is an intrinsic element of the Islamic political system[48] whereby the definition of contemporary democracy may be seen as synonymous with the term 'consultation'. However, the practical implementation of a democracy may be fraught with problems if it does not agree with the Islamic ethos. Contradictions can only be eliminated through the stipulation and provision of set policies, such as the policy that grants people's freedom to choose whether or not to 'believe'.[49]

Many issues raised by Ghazāli have been the subject of discussion and often criticism among other contemporary Muslim academics. One example of this is a woman's right to give full legal testimony. Muhammad Ḥasan Abu Yaḥya[50] expressed his direct opposition to Ghazāli's stance, asserting that Islamic law perceives a woman's testimony to carry only half the weight of a man's. In response to Ghazāli's claim that such an attitude conveys and encourages disrespect for women, Abu Yaḥya maintains that such a legislation would not represent disrespect to women and that the status of the female has been endorsed in other areas of Islamic legislation.[51]

The 'middle way' face of Islamic law

Many of the issues raised by Ghazāli have been raised by another Egyptian scholar, Yūsuf Qaraḍāwi, who was closer to the school of the Muslim Brotherhood than Ghazāli. He seems to represent a new philosophy of the Muslim brotherhood that attempts to balance reason and moderation against the inherited legacy of the Brothers that was based on fanaticism, which they considered 'important' in the time of Fārūq and Nasir, but not suitable for the new millennium that witnessed the events of 11 September 2001 and the invasion of Iraq.

In understanding Islamic law, Qaraḍāwi's main thrust is placed on the principle of balancing the application of law and the understanding of Islam. According to him, the concept of the middle way, *wasaṭiyya*, is one of the main features of Islamic law.[52] Generally, he attempts to delineate the application of the legislative system in relation to its gradual process over time. He theorises that the application of Islamic law cannot be immediate and that legislation must reflect a step-by-step development that follows the initial establishment of the creed. The main duties of the Muslim have been prescribed and the prohibitions have been set gradually, as seen in the practices of prayer, fasting, the payment of zakah and the gradual prohibition of alcohol. The principle of gradual development became a major interest in the Muslim world, which was searching for a way to contain the growing Islamic fanaticism alongside a balanced contemporary approach towards life, coexisting with the rest of the world.

In Kuwait, a special committee was set up entitled The Supreme Consultative Committee for the Completion of the Application of Islamic law.[53] Such a move was in response to the repeated Kuwaiti public demands to apply Islamic law.[54] The title of the committee is an indication that Islamic law is not fully applied and that the aim is to achieve such an objective. The committee aimed to prepare the ground for the establishment of Islamic law and to search for alternatives to non-Islamic legislation.[55] A series of books that addressed this particular mode of thought appeared during the period 1996–2000. Al-Sharīf maintains[56] that the gradual application of Islamic law is a legal vision that stems from a variety of sources which represent the divine nature of Islamic law, based on public interest and ethics. Often, the gradual legislation of Islamic law is observed not only in its general principles but also within individual injunctions related to certain cases.[57] This new concept of partial application of the law is a new development in the understanding of Islamic law, contrary to that which has often been repeated by the writers of the Muslim brotherhood, echoing the instruction of 'Umar (the second caliph, d. AD 644) to take Islam as a whole or leave it. This is based on the assertion that Islam was finalised as a way of life and religion during the Prophet's life,[58] therefore it should be applied in full and not compromised on the grounds of necessity or non-availability of a suitable environment.

Abd al-Raḥmān Ḥabannaka al-Maydāni adds a further dimension to the concept. He maintains that rebuilding Islamic law is a process similar to building a skyscraper. It requires a gradual building of the foundation and application of contemporary systems. This can develop within an overall vision for the future, while the actual principles of Islamic law, whether ethical or theological, may be considered. Among cited examples of legal areas that warrant this gradual application are health, insurance, taxes, education, family law, banking and financial law.[59] According to Muhammad Bayanūni, the uncertainty of Muslims regarding the application of Islamic law may be ascribed to the psychological impact caused by Western civilisation. The division between religion and state also hinders the processes of Islamic law and increases objection to its developing application. Here, it seems that Islamic law needs to regain lost confidence by acting as a flexible system, implementing a practical element of law that can accommodate modern needs. This may be achieved through active recognition of the legal philosophy of *maṣlaḥa* and acceptance of the methodology of a gradual application of law.[60] On the latter point, Maydāni cites a statement made by the Prophet's wife 'Ā'isha which indicates the value of gradual application of the punishment for drinking alcohol. This was initiated during the early days, and Islam may never have been accepted by the majority of the converts had the total prohibition of alcohol been introduced immediately. Without such forethought, the public would have had great difficulty in abiding by the order. Bayanūni maintains that, despite the fact that Islamic law is not written in the form of legal articles, this does not detract from the validity of its injunctions, which are clear and easily accessed by legal experts. The task of writing the law in the form of clear articles could be achieved if undertaken by a specialised committee.[61] Bayanūni maintains that such a move is justified, since in the past there have been few attempts to set Islamic law in an articled format, such as *Majallat al-aḥkām al-'ādliyya* (1285/1869) and the Ottoman Law of Family Rights. The latter addressed all aspects of family law, including injunctions relating to Christians and Jews who were citizens of the Ottoman state.[62]

Islamic legal authority and Western methodology

Other groups of Muslim scholars aimed to re-establish the authority of Islamic law which they saw eroding under the attack of Western methods of criticism. Muslim scholars felt the need for a deductive methodology within modern Islamic law which self-examines the legal system of Islam and its sources. Akram al-'Umari,[63] questions whether a methodology of modern Islamic law should be based only on the four schools of law or should refer directly to the textual sources. He warns that a 'modern' deductive methodology has the potential for gross misunderstanding of legislation, particularly if the proper mechanisms devised by scholars are not utilised to access the Islamic sources.[64]

To discover the reasons for the weaknesses of Islamic law, a further group of scholars directed themselves towards examining Western Oriental Studies. Maḥmūd Ḥamdi Zaqzūq maintains that Western Oriental Studies have led to misunderstanding, and sometimes conclusions are reached that are deliberately misleading. This can be attributed simply to the fact that various orientalists have utilised methodologies that were devised for examining Christianity, an entirely different faith from that of Islam.[65] 'Umari moves the discussion onto a theological plane by arguing that the Christian perception of religion and creed is entirely different from the Islamic notion of faith, thus any error of methodology stems from a legacy that was generally formulated to interpret

Christian theological texts, these often being subject to problems associated with alteration during their translation. Islamic texts are different, particularly the Qur'an and a large amount of the correct Sunna, which have no such problems resulting from translation and narration. It is therefore inappropriate either to apply Christian methodology of interpretation to Islamic texts or vice versa, and any such attempts can have a devastating effect on the texts in question.[66]

'Umari also maintains that it is important to differentiate between epistemologies that exist in both Islamic and Western cultures. Islam cannot be understood within the secular epistemology devised by Western scientists, who stood against the Christian religion, but only by an impartial methodology that acknowledges objectivity yet also recognises that 'truth' may exist not only within the scientific approach but also within the spiritual one.

A further work by 'Umari addresses the non-compatibility of Islamic values *vis-à-vis* western ones. The title of the book can be translated as 'The values of Islamic society from a historical perspective'.[67] 'Umari maintains that the 'backwardness' in Muslim societies today is not restricted to one form of knowledge or methodology; rather, it is a comprehensive phenomenon that incorporates the entire intellectual and practical life of Muslims. This includes Muslim attempts to reread and evaluate the historical movement of Islamic society. These attempts have been largely affected by the borrowed Western methodology of knowledge, which is based on values that are totally different from Islamic values and culture. This has inevitably led to an evaluation of Islamic social history that has been considered within Western methodologies and moulds. Such an approach did not necessarily fit the understanding of Islamic intellect and history and often resulted in misreading the actual depth of Islamic values. 'Umari draws the conclusion that the main criticism of Islam made by Western-style studies was generally based on a methodology that measured Islamic principles against a totally alien set of values belonging to different a culture and civilisation.[68]

Western legal writers such as Schacht base their understanding on such a legal methodology. While a few such scholars have been successful with these methodological criticisms of Islamic law, difficulties seem to exist within other areas, particularly those relevant to understanding the essence of Islamic law and the position of the divine authority that makes the law functional and so different from other legal systems. To reproduce Schacht's words: 'However, the problem is by all means not only of external understanding of Islam, it is also of an internal nature'.

According to 'Umari, one of the main problems suffered by Islamic culture was the lack of careful scrutiny of social traditions, which control the historical movement in its general pattern. The observation of social trends in history has not been accorded enough value in social understanding of the law. Both the Qur'an and Sunna indicate clearly that their stories are examples for the people: for example, the story of Joseph.[69] This story indicates that history is not haphazard, but ruled by principles made by God, which are incomprehensible without an in-depth study of history.[70]

In 'Umari's view, the study of public opinion in early Islamic history continues to warrant further research, since the differing social classes have been only partially or superficially examined. He points out that this leads to a gap in the understanding of the transition of Islamic society from a tribal life-style to that of a complex community and the appearance of *khilāfā'* as a symbol of the unity of the Islamic nation.[71] However, it has to be clarified that such a social transition could not have been achieved without the presence of a reliable legal system, nor could the Muslim rulers have accomplished a balance between the various emerging social classes without the authority of the Muslim scholars, *fuqahā'*, who took the lead in influencing them.

Authority and the pious face of Islam: Singapore, Brunei and Malaysia

Among the writers who were indirectly influenced by Quṭb is Ahmad Muhammad Sonhadji (b. 1922),[72] one of the well-known scholars in Singapore, Brunei and Malaysia. From 1958–60, he was the official representative for the religious curriculum of the Association of Islamic Scholars and Teachers in Singapore (known as PERGAS), an organisation which represents the Muslim scholars, *'Ulamā'*, who were the backbone of Islamic *da'wa* and education in Singapore.[73] Sonhadji's main achievement was in the field of Qur'anic interpretation, *tafsīr*. His famous work, *'Abr al-Athīr*, began its days as a set of radio programmes that were broadcast with the aim of reaching the Malayan public, including the people of Malaysia, Singapore and Brunei.[74] Like Quṭb, Sonhadji deemed it important to simplify his *tafsīr* and avoid complexities of explanation that might alienate his audience. He kept to the 'basics' without venturing into the complex realms of obscure words and scholars' diverse views on what they mean, his objective being the addressing of an already 'believing' people. He intended 'to convey to them a full understanding and appreciation of the Qur'an. The contents of *tafsīr* should convey matters easily understood by the public. If this were not the case, the message of the Qur'an would fail to reach them.'[75] Also like Quṭb, Sonhadji employed the methodology of relating each verse to the other verses and pointing out the relationship between one chapter and another.[76] Furthermore, it is evident that Sonhadji was influenced by the Shaykh of Al-Azhar, Maraghi (d. 1952, Cairo) and indeed utilised the methodology from parts of *Tafsīr al-Marāghi*.[77]

Sonhadji's impact on Malayan society is evident, and he may be described as one of the contemporary scholars who has made a positive contribution in that part of the Muslim world, in a way similar to the modern Egyptian scholar, Muhammad al-Ghazāli, in the Arabic world. However, it is important to note that he, like most of the writers of that region, was influenced by his local environment, which treated the Arabic texts with respect and veneration. His deep humility and piety seems to have restricted Sonhadji from venturing into the pronouncement of *fatāwa* and the decision-making arena that was common in the rest of the Arabic world. When Sonhadji was asked the reason for his disinclination to reject the opinions of other scholars, he maintained that he lacked the expertise 'to decide, discuss and debate' with the supporters of other schools, all of whom had their solid arguments.[78] Despite that, Sonhadji made a challenging stand on one of the most controversial issues in contemporary Islamic *fatāwa*. The issue of music and singing has always been surrounded by controversy, particularly in the view of Saudi and some Egyptian scholars of *sharī'a*. Sonhadji appears to have mastered the art of music, and he was eventually able to form his own group, who sang religious Islamic songs, *nashīd*. However, the parents of the children began to complain, maintaining that the songs were reminiscent of a 'church' image. In Singapore at that time, no one else was teaching *nashīd* as Sonhadji was doing, yet among his students was a Mufti of Wilāya, Persekutuan Kuala Lumpur. Sonhadji's stance on this issue is deserving of respect; his justification was that it is preferable for youngsters to listen to Islamic *nashīd* than to the corrupting songs that are prevalent on the radio.[79] Such a statement reflects Sonhadji's awareness of the diversity of views of contemporary Muslim scholars of *sharī'a*, who appear to follow a variety of methodologies. Such methodologies range between the strict adherence to the text, the utilisation of rationale and the attempt to reconcile modern and classical understanding of Islamic law.

Conclusion

Islamic law, like other legal systems, requires a successful authority to justify its application. The success of the application of any legal system is dependent on the validity of its authority as well as on the commitment of the individual that the law rules. Muslim scholars argue that the authority of Islamic law in practice[80] is based on achieving the welfare of society. For this reason, it succeeds in winning the personal commitment of the subjects of the law and their reverence.[81] It may be observed that the legal authority in practice is also influenced by the application of the law, which follows two processes: the interpretation of the law and its application to daily life. It is during these two processes that the law can be misused or circumscribed, even with the availability of a state authority that supposedly takes care of both aspects. When there is no authority, as is the case in contemporary times, then every individual with some knowledge of Islam can claim the right to interpret the law and apply it. This statement may be less valid with regard to some sections of the law, such as ritual and set family practices; but with regard to most other areas, particularly those relevant to individual ethics, this statement is plausible. An individual is not able to perform a marriage contract without the minimum requirement of two witnesses and an imam, because this is the accepted and prevalent social practice. However, on an individual matter, such as the payment of zakah when no state exists, the individual may act as he wishes and pay as much as he wants to whom he sees fit.

The lack of central authority is probably one of the main reasons that has led to a weakness inherent in Sunni Islamic law, whereby many contrasting *fatāwa* are made by scholars who are said to be learned, *'ālim*. While diversity is important and represents a basic element of the spirit of Islamic law, this diversity seems to have backfired. There has been an emergence of many and often-conflicting views made by so-called Mufti and scholars, who pass easy judgement without careful consideration of the meaning of the text and, most importantly, the individual circumstances of cases. One often wonders, if there had been a central legal authority, would extremist ideas such as those that led to the events of 11 September 2001 exist? Perhaps the answer is in the affirmative, since the nature of any religious law expects the individual to partake in the decision-making of the law and the logistics of its application. However, a legal authority would reduce the incidence of chaotic legal decisions, which prevails in a Muslim society once there is a clear-cut division between the area of individual authority and what people can authorise for themselves. The principle of a central legal authority was practised and well documented in history during the time of 'Umar b. Abd al-Azīz,[82] when there were ten well-known scholars who represented the advisory *fatāwa* authority in Medina.[83] Those scholars were consulted on the major issues confronted by society.

At this juncture, we may pause to reflect upon the relationship between current public opinion and contemporary Muslim scholars and jurists. Juristic opinion can be profoundly influential upon public opinion. This legal influence in practical life is not engendered by the need of the community to decide on particular legal injunctions, but largely by the prevailing political leadership and also the ability of religious scholars to win a status of authority that can convince and compel a particular society to adhere to their opinion.

Notes

1 A puritan movement which adhered to the principles of Muhammad b. Abd al-Wahāb (1703–92). Wahābi doctrines do not allow for an intermediary between the

faithful and God, and condemn any such practice as polytheism. The decoration of mosques, the cult of saints, and even the smoking of tobacco were condemned. See *Encyclopaedia Britannica*, 1997.

2 In 1902, the young Abd al-'Azīz b. Abd al-Rahmān defeated the Rashidi governor and was hailed by the populace as their ruler. During the First World War he was aided by British subsidies to be relatively quiescent, though surrounded by enemies. In 1927, Ibn Sa'ūd was proclaimed king of the Hijaz and Najd and its dependencies. In the same year, the Treaty of Jiddah, negotiated by him with Sir Gilbert Clayton, placed his relations with Great Britain on a permanent footing as the British fully acknowledged Saudi independence. Ibn Sa'ūd found himself in difficulties with the more religious elements of Najd because of his association with Christian powers and his alleged complaisance in regard to the British-protected regimes in Iraq and Trans-Jordan. On several occasions, Ibn Sa'ūd violently suppressed political and military opposition by the Ikhwān. The civil war, however, dragged on into 1930, when the rebels were rounded up by the British in Kuwaiti territory and their leaders were handed over to the King. Ibid. (summary).

3 Mustafa Kemal initiated a policy of secularisation, marked by the suppression of the religious courts, Qurānic schools and sufi orders, the prohibition of the wearing of the traditional fez and the abolition of the article of the Constitution declaring Islam the state religion. See EI^2, '*Atatürk*', by R. Mantran, i, p. 734.

4 The Ottoman Empire entered the First World War holding all of western Arabia and supported in central northern Arabia by the Rashidis of Ha'il. Earlier Ottoman attempts to extend the empire to eastern Arabia, however, had been countered by the British, who were then paramount in the gulf and in treaty relations with the Arab sheikhdoms there. Sharīf Husayn b. 'Ali of Mecca, with assurance of British support, revolted against the Ottomans in June 1916, taking Mecca but failing to capture Medina. The British also supported the Idrīsi in Asir against the Ottomans. In Yemen, Ottoman forces entered the Aden Protectorate, but the war subsequently settled down to a stalemate. Two sons of Sharīf Husayn of Mecca, Faiṣal and Abdullah, stirred up the Hijazi tribes against the Ottomans and, assisted by British supplies and liaison officers, including the famous T. E. Lawrence (Lawrence of Arabia), moved northwards to Trans-Jordan along the right flank of the British armies and into Damascus (1918). Faiṣal set up an Arab government there, only to be dislodged by the French in 1920. In 1921 he was made King of Iraq, Abdullah emir of Trans-Jordan. *Encyclopaedia Britannica.*

5 Muhammad Ahmad b. al-Sayyid Abd Allah (1844–85) controlled a vast Islamic state extending from the Red Sea to Central Africa, and was founder of a ṣūfi movement that remained influential in the Sudan a century later.

6 Kishik, *Al-Sa'ūdiyyūn wa al-ḥall al-islāmi*, West Hanover, MA, 1982, p. 36.

7 Ibid., p. 39.

8 Al-Ghazāli, Muhammad, *Al-Sunna al-nabawiyya bayna ahl al-fiqh wa ahl al-ḥadīth*, Beirut, 1989, p. 11.

9 Kishik, p. 41.

10 Ibid., pp. 52–5.

11 *Al-Ikhwān al-Muslimūn*, a religio-political group founded in 1928 at Ismailiyya, Egypt, by Hasan al-Banna.

12 Al-Ḥafnāwi, *Uṣūl al-tashrī' fi al-mamlaka al-'arabiyya al-sa'ūdiyya*, Riyaḍ, 1977?, pp. 24, 36.
13 Ibid., p. 93.
14 Ibid., p. 91.
15 Published in the official gazette *Umm al-Qura*, no. 2,708.
16 Ḥafnāwi, p. 109.
17 This is a ministerial decision of internal affairs number 1, dated the 20th of the 7th of AH 1395.
18 Number 1,375, dated the 18th of the 4th of AH 1397.
19 This was enacted according to royal decree No. M/49 dated the 10th of the 7th of AH 1397.
20 Date 1391, amended 1395, by the minister, decision No. 1,703, dated the 13th of the 7th of AH 1395 and published in the official gazette, no. 2,587, dated the 22nd of the 7th of AH 1395.
21 This *lā'iḥa* was made by the council of ministers, decree No. 1,006 dated the 13th of the 8th of AH 1395 and published in the official gazette *Umm al-Qura*, Vol. 2,596, dated the 28th of the 9th of AH 1395.
22 Ḥafnāwi, p. 117.
23 A system which governs social-morality ethics and the market law.
24 A system which aims to control the injustice of governors and high officials of the state.
25 Ḥafnāwi, p. 151.
26 Al-Banna's vision for the Islamic state was repeatedly confirmed in his famous epistles that he wrote for his movement in the form of instruction. This was evident in the short treatises, *rasāil*, particularly *risālat al-ta'ālīm*, which called for *dīn wa dawala*, a religion and state, and *sayf wa miṣḥaf*, a sword and scripture.
27 Fārūq was the king of Egypt from 1936 to 1952.
28 Sayyid Quṭb and his brother Muhammad Quṭb were among a large number of writers on various Islamic legal literature. Also worth mentioning here among other works are Abd al-Qādir 'Awda, *Al-Tashrī' al-jinā'i fi al-Islam*, and Sayyid Sābiq, *Fiqh al-Sunna*.
29 Sayyid Quṭb, *Ma'ālim fi al-ṭarīq*, Stuttgart, 1978, p. 4.
30 Ibid., p. 83.
31 Ibid., p. 91.
32 Ibid., p. 90.
33 Qur'an: xliv: 60–5.
34 Quṭb, p. 124.
35 After an early infatuation with mysticism, in 1872 Muhammad 'Abdu fell under the influence of Jamāl al-Dīn al-Afghāni, the revolutionary pan-Islamic preacher of Persian origin who had settled in Cairo and who stimulated 'Abdu's interest in theology, philosophy, and politics. *Encyclopaedia Britannica*.
36 Ghazāli, *Al-Sunna*, p. 9.
37 See Glossary.
38 Ghazāli, *Al-Sunna*, pp. 7–11.
39 Qur'an: xxiv: 30.
40 Ghazāli, *Al-Sunna*, pp. 40–1.

41 See Glossary.
42 Ghazāli, *Al-Sunna*, pp. 47–8.
43 Ghazāli, ibid., p. 61.
44 Ghazāli, ibid., p. 70.
45 Ghazāli, ibid., p. 86.
46 Ghazāli, ibid., p. 89.
47 Ghazāli, ibid., p. 133.
48 Ghazāli, ibid., pp. 135–6.
49 Ghazāli, ibid., p. 137.
50 A professor of Islamic law at the University of Jordan-Amman.
51 *Journal of the Faculty of Arts*, Kuwait, 1990, 195–250.
52 Qaraḍāwi, *Al-ṣaḥwa al-islāmiyya bayna al-juḥūd wa al-taṭarruf*, Qatar, 1982 (AH 1402), p. 24.
53 The committee was formed according to royal decree No. 139/91.
54 Al-Bayanūni, *Mu'awiqāt taṭbīq al-sharī'a al-islāmiyya*, Kuwait, 1996, p. 72.
55 *Al-Lajna al-istishāriyya al-'ulya lil'amal 'ala istikmāl taūbīq al-sharī'a al-islamiyya*, published by the court of the Amīr of Kuwait, 1997, pp. 10–14.
56 Dr A. Al-Sharīf is one of the leading Kuwaiti scholars of Islamic law. He occupied the post of dean of the Faculty of *Sharī'a* at the University of Kuwait from 1998–2002.
57 Muhammad Abd al-Ghaffār al-Sharīf, *Al-Tadarruj fi taṭbīq al-sharī'a al-islāmiyya*, Kuwait, 1996, p. 37.
58 Qur'an: v: 3.
59 Al-Maydāni, *Al-Sharī'a al-islāmiyya bayna al-tadarruj fi al-tashrī' wa al-tadarruj fi al-taṭbīq*, Kuwait, 2000, pp. 20–1.
60 Ibid., p. 38.
61 Ibid., pp. 21–30.
62 Family law was the earliest section of Islamic law that began to take shape in the form of codified articles. This can be ascribed to the fact that concentration on this particular area of legislation was needed the most, since none of the colonising powers in the Muslim world was able to fully implement their own laws in such cases. All the Arabic countries codified their family law and became affected to some extent by the Ottoman Law of Family Rights. In Egypt, the law of Legal Statutes was enacted in 1929, i.e. *Qānūn al-aḥwāl al-shakhṣiyya*. In Lebanon, *Qānūn al 'Ā'ila* was established in 1933. The Syrian law was enacted in 1953 and went on to be amended in 1975. In Morocco, the *Mudawwana* of *al-aḥwāl al-shakhṣiyya* was enacted in 1957 and amended in 1993. In Iraq, *Qānūn al-aḥwāl shakhṣiyya* was published in 1959 and amended in 1980. In Tunisia, the *Majalla* of *al-aḥwāl al-shakhṣiyya* was published in 1967 and amended in 1988. In Jordan, *Qānūn al-aḥwāl al-shakhṣiyya* was also published in 1967 and then amended in 1981. In Algiers and Kuwait, *Qānūn al-aḥwāl al-shakhṣiyya* was published in 1984. In Libya, it was referred to as 'the law relating to marriage and divorce', published in 1984 and amended in 1991. *Qānūn al-aḥwāl al-shakhṣiyya* was published in Yemen in 1992 and in Oman in 1997. The Masqat document represents one of the well-developed, contemporary procedures that are based on Islamic law. It was prepared in 1996 by a group of legal experts on behalf of the General Council for the Arabic Gulf states. The Masqat

contains 282 articles regarding marriage, separation, custody of children, legacy and inheritance. As yet, it has not been implemented, and those states to which it is relevant continue to apply traditional legislative systems that depend primarily on the views of the judges. A.'Aṭāwi, *Codification of Islamic law in Bahrain*, Ph.D. thesis, Lampeter University, 2004.

63 Prof. 'Umari, born in Iraq in 1942, is considered to be among the pioneers of the idea of *mu'āṣara* or modernisation of Islamic thought without altering the roots. He worked for many years in Saudi Arabia, becoming King Faiṣal Laureate.

64 Al-'Umari, *Al-Turāth wa al-mu'āṣara*, Qatar, 1985, pp. 55–8.

65 Zaqzūq, *Al-Istishrāq wa al-khalfiyya al-Fikriyya li al ṣirā' al-ḥaḍāri*, Qatar, 1984, p. 119.

66 'Umari, *Al-Turāth*, 60.

67 Al-'Umari, *Qiyam al-mujtma' al-islāmi min manẓūr tārīkhi*, Qatar, 1994, p. 20.

68 'Umari, *Al-Turāth*, pp. 17–18.

69 Qur'an: 111.

70 'Umari, *Qiyam*, p. 25.

71 Ibid., pp. 73–4.

72 Born in Indonesia, he worked most of his life as a school *madrasa* teacher in Singapore and Brunei. He was appointed at Al-Junied School as Vice-principal and Principal, 1973–88. Most of his works seem to be educational, written for schools, such as *The Book of Fiqh and Tawiḥīd, Seeds of Religion, The Guiding to Understanding the Qur'an* (1 and 2), and other short popular works. See Zukifli M. Yūsuf, *A Study of Tafsīr 'Abr al-Athīr*, Singapore, 2002, pp. 26, 37, 40, 67–75.

73 Ibid., p. 30.

74 Ibid., p. 159.

75 Ibid., p. 17.

76 Ibid., p. 20.

77 Ibid., pp. 107–12.

78 Ibid., pp. 19–20

79 Ibid., p. 37.

80 The words 'in practice' are used to indicate that the discussion does not include the Divine authority.

81 Subḥi Al-Ṣāliḥ, *Ma'ālim al-sharī'a al-islāmiyya*, Beirut, 1982, p. 62.

82 'Umar b. Abd al-'Azīz (b. 682/683), a pious and reformist Caliph who attempted to save the *Umawi* caliphate by returning to the original prophetic principles.

83 Al-'Umari, *Qiyam*, 2, p. 61.

10

The *fatāwa* and legal authority

In this chapter, we will attempt to examine the Sunni religious authority as seen in the legal decisions, *fatāwa*, of various authorities. This examination focuses on samples of the Islamic legal authority and is not meant to be a full representation of it. The samples have been selected from what appears to be an 'acknowledged' authority in the Arabic world and Brunei as representative of the Malayan society.

In modern Islamic society, there are some forms of religious authority that influence the application of Islamic law, the official form being associated with political power and often derived from it, for example the Azhar in Egypt, the *Dār al-iftā'* of Saudi Arabia and the state Mufti of Brunei. The other form is the organisation's authority represented by public religious movements or groups that create authority and somehow elicit the adherence of the masses, such as the European Council for Research and *fatāwa*, which represents an offshoot of the Federation of Islamic Organisations in Europe and seems to be scholastically inspired by three main scholars. These are Yūsuf al-Qaraḍāwi, Abd Allah bin Bayya and Faiṣal Mawlawi.[1]

Although the second group appears to be independent and free from the political influence of a government, it does however remain influenced by the ideology of the political or social group of its founders. A third type of authority is that of single independent[2] scholars. This form focuses on one reputable scholar who is not associated with any particular government or group, who gives *fatāwa* individually, often following a public speech or within a compiled book.[3] These *fatāwa* provide a rich source of information for the understanding of various legal problems prevalent in Muslim society. In the following paragraphs, I will look at selected scholars, some of whom we have already discussed. The focus this time is not on their role as thinkers and writers but as legal decision-makers who obtained their authority from intellectual contributions, which qualified them in the eyes of the public to give *fatāwa*.

Muhammad al-Ghazāli[4] included 100 questions with their appropriate solutions in a book published many times since 1984. In most of his *fatāwa*,

Ghazāli seems to be employing *maṣlaḥa* as well as other inventive sources of Islamic law such as *qiyās* and *'urf*. He poses some challenging questions, such as one pertaining to the nature of government in Islam. According to Ghazāli, a government is neither about the supremacy of one race nor about the supremacy of a mundane philosophy, but rather about community authority. It is the authority that delegates power to a ruler who should act as a manager for the application of the divine order on earth.[5] The temporary election of a head of state, according to Ghazāli, represents a good modern basis on which to safeguard the rulers from tyranny if they are elected for an undefined period. Such a method does not violate Islamic law, since Ali was elected in such a way after 'Uthman, purely on the basis of public interest. There is no text or clear analogy, *qiyās jali*, which indicates that such a system is not acceptable.[6] The Islamic state, to Ghazāli, should unite all Muslims while providing authority and security for them.[7] His attitude to *fatāwa* reflects a flexible trend, allowing space for personal choice by not offering rigid decisions when no textual evidence is available; the converse of this attitude is often found in the legal decisions made by Saudi Muftis who insist on the strict textual interpretation of law. For example, one Saudi *fatāwa* prohibits smoking in any form because it can lead to serious illness.[8] On this issue, Ghazāli makes it clear that smoking is a dirty habit and can lead to health damage; however, he leaves the door open for individual choice by stating that he cannot make a judgement as to permission or prohibition. He maintains that smoking is *ḥarām* for some and abominable for others. Ghazāli's stance on legal decision-making may be classified as that of a realistic orthodox who recognises the needs of life within the boundaries of Islamic law without being influenced by position or political status.[9]

This realistic orthodoxy was evidently further developed into the concept of the *wasaṭiyya*, 'middle way', in Islamic law by Yūsuf al-Qaraḍāwi.[10] Although he is often seen as one of the figures of the Muslim brotherhood, he represents an independent scholar who created his own concept of Islamic law. His most famous book, 'the lawful and the unlawful in Islam', was written in 1960 and attempted to provide a response to a number of frequently asked questions in Muslim society without being strictly bound by one school.[11] The introduction refers to the principle of Islamic law that states: 'everything is permissible as a rule unless there is a text that indicates otherwise'.[12] His *fatāwa* have been published many times in the form of a book entitled *Contemporary fatāwa*[13] and can be found on the Internet. His views and activities have contributed to the formation of a new type of *fatāwa* group, mentioned earlier in this chapter, namely the European Council of *fiqh*.

This council works in coordination with the European Federation of Islamic Organisations, which is a non-governmental organisation with an Islamic popular nature inspired by the thinking of the early writers of Muslim brothers such as

Ḥasan al-Banna and Sayyid Quṭb. The council purports to hold a new modified Islamic philosophy which aims to understand and cooperate with the Western world rather than clash with it. The main objectives of this council, according to its constitution, are to bring together European scholars and to aim to unite legal injunctions on various issues, thus providing both legal injunctions suitable for Muslims in Europe and research for general, public *fatāwa*. The methodology of the *fatāwa* adopted by the council can be summarised (according to its publications) as the Qur'an, Sunna, consensus, analogy and other secondary resources such as *istiḥsān*, *maṣlaḥa*, *sadd al-dharā'i'*. The council does not clarify what the case would be if a clash occurred between public interest and any one of these sources, nor does it state to which area reference would be given. The schools of Islamic law that the council refers to in its legal decisions are the four Sunni schools of Islamic law. The council states that as a *fatwa* guideline it will include the awareness of what is unavoidable reality in order to reduce hardship to the public while targeting the objective of Islamic law.[14]

The cases discussed by the council provide us with an insight into the problems that face the Muslim community in Europe and into the form of authority that Muslims appear to accept in order to obtain solutions for their problems. By looking at the problems discussed, it is difficult to ascertain the social status and standard of living of the individuals targeted by these *fatāwa*. However, the European council *fatāwa* seem to provide some representation for cases pertinent to Europe, apart from some scattered examples found in the two collections of *fatāwa* which seem similar to cases found in a predominantly Muslim society. One of the main strengths of this council is the 'European' flavour of its *fatāwa* and having on its board scholars who belong to all the schools of Sunni Islamic law. It is observed that the authority of this council is restricted to Europe, although it seems to be growing with the use of modern media and Arabic channels that reach a worldwide audience. However, the influence of this council is far less than the influence of Muslim state Muftis who give judgement backed by governments that claim to apply *sharī'a* in one form or another. These include the Grand Shaykh of Al-Azhar, the *iftā'* authority in the ministry of *awqāf* in Saudi Arabia, the ministry of *awqāf* in Kuwait and the grand Mufti of Brunei. In the remaining part of this chapter, I will attempt to examine the subject matter discussed predominantly in these *fatāwa* and the legal structure and context utilised therein.

The Saudi and the Kuwaiti *fatāwa* target a similar society to that targeted by the state of Brunei. Both are oil-rich societies which are governed by a hereditary royal family. Despite the differences that one might expect between the Saudi and Kuwaiti Bedouin nomadic societies and the Malay society of Brunei, the *fatāwa* of all three are strikingly similar. All three present *fatāwa* which focus on personal issues such as handshaking between men and women,[15] the prohibition of picture-painting and figure-making, employment in banks, ornaments for women and the issue of music.[16] However, the attempt to present answers to questions posed by affluent Western culture can be observed more in the Brunei and Kuwaiti *fatāwa* than in the Saudi. This is reflected by the titles of *fatāwa* found in both Brunei and Kuwait, but not in those of Saudi Arabia, at least not within the collections consulted.

The Brunei collection includes the use of contact lenses during Ramadan,[17] paying zakah through a savings account,[18] sending a Christmas card to a non-Muslim,[19] trading in laser disc or video.[20] The Kuwaitis also tackle similar problems, for example the recording of Qur'anic verses onto children's toys, which is allowed according to them so long as such action is not disrespectful to the verses,[21] the prohibition of offering alcohol in an aeroplane, and allowing the consumption of chocolate even if it carries the brand name 'Rum' and a picture of a rum barrel so long as it does not actually contain alcohol. However, it is recommended to delete such terms and images from wrappers to avoid this indirect propagation of alcohol.[22]

Regarding methodology, the Saudi *fatāwa* appear to be based more on the *salafi*[23] and the strict Ḥanbali school. It is observed that, in general, only correct hadiths are used in their *fatāwa*. This observation is confirmed by the introductory remark made in the collections of the Saudi *fatāwa*.[24] The Brunei *fatāwa* adheres more to the Shāfiʿi school and employs free use of *qiyās*, analogy. One interesting example here is the case of *wilāya*, guardianship, of the father or a similar member of the family in a marriage, the presence of whom Shāfiʿi insists upon when a woman is to be married. The Brunei *fatāwa* appears to prefer the *wilāya* of the judge to that of a father, who refuses to act as a *wali*,[25] and regards the contract as valid without specifying why the father refused to act as a guardian and why the *wilāya* was not passed to other male relatives as the Shāfiʿi *madhhab* would expect. This in my opinion represents a preference for the government authority over that of the *fiqh* of the Shāfiʿi *madhhab*. It also represents a trend towards flexible *fatāwa*, evident not only in Brunei but also in *fatāwa* provided by the state of Kuwait, which also accepts the authority of the judge in performing marriage, despite the presence of a father who was not involved in the contract.[26] The philosophies of both the Brunei and Kuwaiti *fatāwa* seem to be more flexible than that of the Saudi, which insists on the literal meaning of the text and the traditional interpretation of the law. This echoes the methodology of the Ḥanbali school of law, which is seen as important in the preservation of the central core of the Islamic creed as based on the text and tradition of the Prophet. The Kuwaitis clearly indicate that their methodology of legal decisions is based on the concept of *tajdīd* or renewal of Islamic law, the general objectives and *maṣlaḥa*.[27] The main principles which seem to govern this group of *fatāwa* are:

1. Consideration of variation in customs, needs and public interest according to time and place.
2. Acceptance that the views of certain legal schools can be more appropriate in certain conditions and environments.
3. Cases are considered individually, and general principles and legal maxims might not necessarily provide an identical injunction for seemingly similar cases.
4. The political ruler of a country is better positioned to consider what represents public interest, and holds the authority to avoid chaotic legal disagreement.

These guidelines are extremely useful for the future application of Islamic law in a contemporary state. However, the last point needs to be modified in order to prevent the possible creation of Islamic legal dictatorship.

Finally, it is interesting to observe that this flexible trend is specifically mentioned by the writers of the Kuwaiti collection, who maintain that they are following the footsteps of scholars such as Yūsuf al-Qaraḍāwi, who asserts that Islamic legislation deliberately left some areas without legislation in order to accommodate individual opinion.[28] Qaraḍāwi's methodology was summarised in a book which was republished by the government of Kuwait in 1995. Qaraḍāwi maintains that in such areas, which he calls 'areas of *'afū*, permission', a scholar may refer to any alternative source such as *qiyās* or *istiḥsān*.[29] This interaction between an individual scholar and an official *fatāwa*-making authority offers insight into the process of a legal authority in an Islamic society where there is no religious authority at government level. Qaraḍāwi's views were initially individual; but, once identified as being suitable for a contemporary society such as that of Kuwait, his methods were utilised as a basis for legal decision. This highlights how an undeclared and informal Sunni authority can develop. An individual scholar can acquire undeclared authority once he obtains acceptance and popularity from the public. Qaraḍāwi has played a similar leading role in the non-governmental *fatāwa*-formation which was initiated by the European Council for *iftā'*. This further indicates the importance of individual scholars in influencing the Muslim public in the formation of legal authority. At this point, it is important to observe that this method of authority-creation could have the danger of single-mindedness of *fatāwa*, which was the very reason that caused Mālik to refuse enforcing his *Muwaṭṭa* in the Muslim state.[30] This undeclared publicly evolving authority seems different from the authority of Al-Azhar, which we will discuss next.

The authority of Al-Azhar is traditionally the oldest institutionalised authority in Sunni Islamic law.[31] It targets a larger audience than those previously mentioned, due to the fact that Al-Azhar represents an internationally acclaimed authority throughout the Muslim world. Al-Azhar *fatāwa* by and large are concerned with the 'lay' Muslim in both Egypt and the rest of the world. They do not target a particular class or society, and so one does not find many questions which deal with what we may term 'middle-class' *fiqh*. The main guidelines for these *fatāwa* provide evidence for the grounds upon which many contemporary scholars have based their methodology of *iftā'*, including Ghazāli and Qaraḍāwi.[32] The Grand Shaykh of Al-Azhar, Sheikh Jād al-Ḥaqq[33] maintains that a Mufti should deal with people's affairs in a middle way, neither with extremity nor with extreme leniency. When legal permission is to be weighed against the limitation of the strict jurisdiction, then the former should be followed. The Mufti should avoid passing any judgement which accommodates the desires and whims of the individuals.[34] The methodology that the Grand Shaykh suggests for legal decision is carefully stated to endorse all schools of Islamic law and incorporates *maṣlaḥa*. Thus he states:

> When a mufti is unable to find an answer to a question from within the available sources, then he may refer to any school to embark on a legal decision, provided that he does not select a view with a weak reference. To choose that which achieves people's interest, he should have good intention, bearing only God in his mind and not the ruler or the enquiring person. Finally, he should not give two optional views in one particular case, thus avoiding creating a third view. The *fatāwa* should not be made in accordance with the regional understanding of the scholar who is making the decision but according to the culture of the individual concerned.[35]

It can be observed here that the Shaykh of Al-Azhar does not focus only on the scholar who makes *fatāwa* and the cultural environment, but also pays attention to the person who enquires about the issue. This presents us with a useful insight into where the actual legal authority lies. He maintains that it is the individual himself who must make a commitment to obey the view given to him before he enquires about it and acts upon it.[36] In other words, it is up to the individual to decide when to enquire about the *fatāwa* according to his belief and personal conviction. If the enquirer is unable to find more than one scholar to answer his question, then he should adhere to the one *fatwa* that he has obtained. If another scholar gives him a similar *fatwa*, then there is no doubt that the enquirer should obey it. If there is some difference in the two *fatāwa*, then he may use his own sense and religious convictions. According to Shaykh Jād al-Ḥaqq, this is confirmed by the Prophet's hadith, which maintains: 'make judgment to your own soul, no matter what other people judge for you'.[37]

Upon reading the Egyptian *fatāwa*, it can be observed that they include general *fatāwa* as well as those relevant to individual cases. This is helpful in identifying the minute social problems and the legal methodology that was employed by Islamic law to deal with them, such as referring to custom in *fatāwa* number 446, which maintains that a man named Muhammad Abu Rās may not pay fees to his wife in return for her watering his date-palm trees. This is based on the prevalent custom that a wife does not normally charge fees for such an action unless those who are involved in similar actions would do so. And, since this is not the local custom, then her heirs may not claim payment after her death for such an action. However, if there is a contract between Abu Rās and his wife that he should pay her for such a service, then the case is different.[38] This tendency of giving the individual freedom of choice seems to be the source from which Ghazāli established his methodology of legal deduction.[39]

Another observation on the *fatāwa* of *Dār al-iftā' al-miṣriyya* is the presence of judgements which are relevant to Muslims and non-Muslims, in particular Christians. One example is the validity of a testimony of a non-Muslim that he is a Muslim before his marriage to a Muslim woman.[40] Such a testimony would normally require more evidence than the word of the individual, since it may be only a device to avoid the law which prevents the non-Muslim man from marrying a Muslim woman. Such a legal decision can be seen as a sign of evolution in the *fiqh* towards flexibility in accepting the individual's testimony on matters that can have affect on religious and public affairs. A similar flexibility is observed in some of the *fatāwa* given by the European Council of *fatāwa*, who accepted the testimony of a woman that sporting activity could have damaged her hymen, and therefore concluded that the tearing of her hymen is not enough evidence that she was not a virgin prior to her marriage and therefore this is not a ground for divorce.[41] The frequent occurrence of such an incident represents a major dilemma in a Muslim society, often leading to divorce on the wedding night. The main question to be asked is: what is the actual role of the Mufti here? Is he only rubber-stamping the wish of the individuals in order to make them happy? Or is he actually following the flexible spirit of Islamic law? If the answer is the first possibility, then that can be evidence that contemporary Islamic law is moving in an inverted direction by seeking its authority from the individuals themselves rather than deciding for them.

The frequent occurrence of similar cases can be ascribed to a combination of the lack of actual authority as well as the wish of Muslim scholars to accommodate the masses into Islam, which has no control over them except that which stems from their own faith and conviction. The Sunni schools of Islamic law continue to exist without an apparent unified authority, unlike the Shī'a school, which has a clear and defined form of clergy authority who take an active role in controlling and organising the society's life. This was clearly noticeable following Khomeini's revolution in Iran, and a similar influence may be observed in Iraq today. In Iraq, we are witnessing a rather interesting phenomenon which was previously unknown, that is, the public acclaim of religious authority, particularly among the Iraqi Shī'a. This could generate a powerful Shī'a Islam in Iraq, Iran and maybe Syria. This is no doubt due to the fossilised and clearly defined authority of Shī'a Islam, which poses the question of what the future of Sunni Islamic law is.

Notes

1 The European Council was initiated in March 1997. It includes a diversity of independent scholars of varying repute and backgrounds. Some are highly reputable and known in the Muslim world, such as the Egyptian Qaraḍāwi; Sheikh Abd Allah b. Bayya, a leading Māliki Mauritanian scholar and ex-first minister, and professor of Islamic law at King Abd Azīz University in Jeddah; and Faiṣal Mawlawi, who is the Mufti of the Lebanese capital Beirut. The council also includes Professor 'Ajīl Nashmi, professor of Islamic law at Kuwait University. Among the traditional and academic scholars are two further academics, Dr Majīd Najjār of the European Institute in Paris, and Dr Ṭaha Jābir al-'Alwāni, who is the director of the Institute of Islamic Thought in Virginia, USA. The council members also include religious practitioners such as Abd Allah Juday', a young traditional scholar and imam of a mosque in Leeds, and Mr Ahmad al-Rāwi, the current head of the Federation of Islamic Organisations in Europe. In 2002, the European Council was acclaimed when fasting in the month of Ramadan was made almost uniform in many Muslim countries. This was achieved by accepting that the beginning of the month can be ascertained by visual means or calculation at the observatory. This federation, with its many branches in Europe, regularly holds large meetings and seminars in various parts of Europe. On 19 April 2003, a meeting was held in Paris and was attended by approximately 100,000 European Muslims, who were addressed by Nicola Sarkosi, the French minister of internal affairs. This reflects a new trend of understanding between European Muslims and the West. The minister reiterated many of the French government's views on issues that concern Muslims in France, many of which met with conference approval. However, when he stated that the government could not accept the identification card of a woman wearing a headscarf, he was publicly jeered, despite the fact that he was pleased by the meeting (as the *Parisian* newspaper reported on 21 April 2003). Also see *Qarārāt wa fatāwa al-majlis al-awruppi li al-iftā' wa al-buḥūth*, Cairo, 2002, p. 11.

2 The use of the term 'independent' is only a working definition and naturally does not totally exclude those scholars from personal ties and influences caused by various factors.

3 Muhammad al-Ghazāli, *Mā'at su'āl 'an al-islām*, Cairo, 1989.

4 See above in this chapter.

5 Ghazāli, *Mā'at su'āl*, p. 266.

6 Ghazāli, ibid., p. 278.

7 Ghazāli, ibid., p. 283.

8 Ṣafwat al-Shādhili, *Fatāwā hay'āt kibār al-'ulamā' bi al-mamlaka al-'arabiyya al-sa'ūdiyya*, Riyaḍ, 1988, p. 136.

9 Ghazāli, *Mā'at su'āl*, p. 495.

10 See Chapter 9.

11 Qaraḍāwi, *The Lawful and the Prohibited in Islam*, English translation, Cairo, 1997.

12 Ibid., p. 15.

13 Qaraḍāwi, *Fatāwā mu'āṣira*, 2 vols, Cairo, 1993, p. 727.
14 *Qarārāt wa fatāwa al-majlis al-awruppi li al-iftā' wa al-buḥūth*, p. 11; see also *Al-Europiya*, vol. 30, 2002, 24–6.
15 Al-Shādhili, p. 73; Abd al-'Azīz Ibn Junayd, *Fatāwā mufti al-dawla*, Brunei, 1995, p. 73; *Majmū'at al-fatāwa al-shar'iyya al-ṣādira 'an qaṭṭā' al-iftā' wa al-buḥūth al-shar'iyya*, Ministry of *awqāf*, Kuwait, 1988, p. 353.
16 See Ibn Junayd; Al-Shādhili.
17 Ibn Junayd, ibid., p. 17.
18 Ibid., p. 21.
19 Ibid., p. 183.
20 Ibid., p. 188.
21 *Majmū'at al-fatāwa al-shar'iyya al-ṣādira 'an qaṭṭā' al-iftā' wa al-buḥūth al-shar'iyya*, p. 128.
22 Ibid., p. 363.
23 *Salafi* is derived from the word *salaf*, which designates the 'old' or the traditional methodology of deducing legal injunctions, such as the view of Ibn Taymiyya and that of his student Ibn Qayyim al-Jawziyya.
24 *Fātāwā al-lajna al-dā'ima lil buḥūth wa al-iftā'*, ed. Ahmad Abd al-Razzāq al-Ḍuwaysh, Riyaḍ, 1999, 1, p. 48.
25 Ibn Junayd, p. 970.
26 *Majmū'at al-fatāwa al-shar'iyya al-ṣādira 'an qaṭṭā' al-iftā' wa al-buḥūth al-shar'iyya*, p. 238.
27 Ibid., p. 6.
28 Ibid., p. 6.
29 Qaraḍāwi, *'Awāmil al-si'a wa al-murūna fi al-sharī'a al-islāmiyya*, Kuwait, n.d., p. 17.
30 See Chapter 2, p. 18.
31 Al-Azhar University is 'a chief centre of Islamic and Arabic learning in the world, centred on the mosque located in the medieval quarter of Cairo, Egypt. It is one of the world's oldest universities, probably older than Cambridge and Oxford. Situated in the heart of Cairo, Egypt's capital, Al-Azhar has been the greatest learning centre for Muslims since it was founded by the Fatimid dynasty in AD 970. The basic programme of studies was, and still is: Islamic law, theology, philosophy and the Arabic language. The Fatimids were of Shi'ah belief. They erected Al-Azhar as an institution to propagate the teachings of the *Isma'iliya* sect which could be a historical reason for the religious authority that it has gained. When the Ayyubids took over Egypt, they turned Al-Azhar into a school that taught the Sunni understanding of Islam. Rich in tradition and knowledge, Al-Azhar has produced brilliant *'ulamā'* such as Imam Suyūṭi, Imam Ibn Ḥajar 'Asqalani, Jamāl ad Dīn al-Afghani, Shaykh Muhammad Ghazāli and the modern Qur'an scholar Shaykh Mitwalli Sha'rāwi. Today, Al-Azhar is not just a university, but an institution that safeguards the teachings of Sunni Islam, and an umbrella body to which thousands of ulama affiliate themselves. The Head of Al-Azhar, called the Grand Imam (Al-Imām al-Akbar Shaykh al-Azhar), was previously appointed by a committee of Azhari top scholars. But now he is appointed by the Egyptian President according to the advice of the scholars committee. The current Shaykh of Azhar is Muhammad Ṭanṭāwi, born in Egypt in 1928, who learnt the Qur'an while still in elementary school. He studied in the Uṣūluddin Faculty of Al-Azhar University in Cairo in 1958. He

obtained his Masters in Education in 1959 and his Ph.D. in 1966. His doctoral thesis was on the Jews in the Qur'an and Sunna. On 28 October 1986, he was made the Mufti of the Government, and on 17 March 1996, he was appointed as the Grand Shaykh of Azhar. Shaykh Ṭanṭāwi has long been well-known for his frank views on various issues and problems confronting the Muslim world.' http://www.Sunnah.org/history/Scholars/maShaykh_azhar.htm

32 See Chapter 9.

33 'Shaykh Jad al-Haqq (1917–96) was born in the village of Batra (Daqahliyya Province) in 1917. He studied the Qur'an and memorised it at a young age, and had his early Azharite learning in the Ahmadi institute in Tanta. He worked as a judge in the *Sharī'a* courts and the Ministry of Justice, and was appointed as the Grand Mufti of Egypt in 1978. In 1982, he became the 42nd Grand Shaykh of al-Azhar.' http://www.Sunnah.org/history/Scholars/maShaykh_azhar.htm

34 *Al-Fatāwā al-islāmiyya min dār al-iftā' al-miṣryya*, 1981–93, vol. 1, pp. 15, 16.

35 Ibid.; see also Jād al-Ḥaqq 'Ali Jād al-Ḥaqq, *Buhūth wa fatāwa islamiyya fi qaḍāya mu'āṣira*, Cairo, 1994, introduction.

36 Ibid.

37 *Al-Fatāwā al-islāmiyya min dār al-iftā' al-miṣryya*, 1, pp. 21–2.

38 Ibid., 3, p. 910.

39 On Ghazāli and the realistic orthodox, see p. 145.

40 *Al-Fatāwā al-islāmiyya*, p. 623.

41 *Al-Majlis al-awruppi li al-iftā' wa al-buḥūth*, pp. 59–60.

11

The future of Islamic law

The removal of the Baath government in Iraq has led to many discussions between both Muslims and non-Muslims about the role that Islamic law can play in providing a stable Iraqi society which has been ruptured at all levels. Can Islamic law be valid in contemporary society, and if so what are the mechanisms and methodology that can be employed in such a process?

At the outbreak of the Second World War, the Arabic world witnessed a new era of change and challenges to its lands, culture and law. The American-led coalition invasion of Iraq was seen by many as a repetition of that action. The motto that was used at this time was the same used by General Maude when he entered Baghdad in March 1917[1] stating: 'we came here as liberators, not as conquerors'. However, the television footage representing an attack on the famous mosque of Abu Ḥanīfa and the consequent burning of the library of *awqāf* sent menacing messages to other states in the region which claim to be Sunni Muslim states, such as Saudi Arabia, Sudan and the Gulf states. Although no one can be certain as to the legal system Iraq is going to adopt, there is little doubt that the organic form of the law is going to be set in motion among the people and might well continue to coexist with any future law. The organic law is the mass law, which operates in a non-institutionalised form. It operates like a blade of grass which bends to the wind, but continues to survive either by itself or within clusters of its own kind. As has been seen in a previous chapter, the application of law primarily requires the understanding of the law through interpretation and then its application to various social and religious cases. Such interpretation and application does not cover all spheres of Islamic law, since individuals cannot control the applying of injunctions relevant to public issues such as the punishment of others for crimes such as *ḥudūd*. However, the idea of an organic law is valid for many injunctions, such as rituals, whereby a person can monitor him/herself to follow what he believes to be the law, thus fasting at the correct time and paying the right amount of zakah. This leads to a legal vacuum, whereby certain parts of the law are not applicable or are incorrectly interpreted by individuals to justify what they want to do. The thieves who were looting Baghdad after the war had neither a legal system to arrest them, nor individuals who were able to punish them, or indeed a conscience to stop them.

An interesting question here would be: what would be the response if the prevalent legal system maintains that the thief should be punished not according to Islamic law but by the principle of some other law? Can Islamic law accept such a ruling whereby authority does not lie with it? No doubt such a subservient legal position is not the ideal position under which Islamic law would like to operate. But it seems likely to occur as a *de facto* situation in which Islamic law coexists with another local law. Although Islamic law sometimes appears to be single-minded with regard to authority, it does accommodate itself to accept other legal systems, not only when it does not have an upper political hand, but also when it has full state control. The Turkish *Tanẓīmāt* reforms of the period 1839–76 are an example of this, whereby the commercial code promulgated in 1850 followed the French commercial code, which included provision of payment of interest. The same applied to the penal code of 1858 which abolished the punishment of *sharīʿa* law.[2] The result of the Ottomans' steps towards westernising the law forms a vital part of the legal system of most Middle Eastern countries. Therefore, the accommodation of Western principles of law does not mean the total abolition of Islamic law, despite the fact that secular laws were objected to by Muslim scholars when applied in their societies. But Muslim scholars felt that it was better to let *sharīʿa* pass peacefully away from the field of legal practice intact than to change its principles radically, as modern conditions required. At the same time, Islamic legal tradition has always recognised the right of the ruler through his *maẓālim* jurisdiction to supplement strict *sharīʿa* doctrine in the field of public and general civil law.[3] However, in practice this can be difficult since, as Coulson puts it, 'The adoption of Western codes in these spheres could appear as no more than a necessary extension of his admitted powers'.[4] The *Sharīʿa* law would then have to be fine-tuned to accommodate the power of the rulers, which could create a stalemate between themselves and the public.

The nature of Islamic law is such that it can operate as an organic law, even when the big tree of the organisation collapses and fails to function. History relates that this is what happened when the Mongols ravaged Baghdad and the Turkish defenders of the empire were not able to continue their role as the guardians and custodians of Islam. This is due to the nature of Islamic law, which is not a law in the Western sense of the word. *Fiqh*, as Laleh Bakhtiar maintains, is a 'praxic understanding', that provides an inside vision into how one is to act and live as a Muslim.[5] This probably explains Schacht's statement that we quoted earlier in this book, that Islamic law is a phenomenon so different from all other forms of law.[6] The phenomenal praxic understanding of Islamic law can be seen as the *raison d'être* behind the assimilation of Mongols, which turned them from being hostile invaders into believers who then participated in pushing forward the wheel of Islam.

The Western invaders from 1750–2004, as Karen Armstrong names them, had a different background from the Mongols. 'They came with the ideals of democracy, pluralism, tolerance, human rights and secularism, which were not simply beautiful but were dictated by the need of the modern state.'[7] However, these modern states required colonisation to expand, and that meant the colonisation of agrarian societies for raw materials and the exportation of their goods. The ideals of democracy, tolerance and human rights were valid within the state, but seemed to be totally void concepts when Western states had to subsume their colonised countries in order to survive. This whole process was experienced by the agrarian colonies as invasive, disturbing and alien. It was almost impossible to achieve modernisation, due to the rapidity with which it was being applied.[8] The problem was not only that, but also that the colonised had to adhere to someone else's programme of 'what is the meaning of modernisation'. Undoubtedly, this led to massive cultural problems in societies where industrialisation was being developed. A new culture was imposed with modern fast machines driven by the same individuals who had driven camels and donkeys only a few years before.[9] The result was a cultural 'rupture' that initially created a rejection of the traditional values; but ultimately there came the realisation that the only way forward was the rejection of the colonising alien culture. This rejection was translated by reverting to Islam, particularly to the rule of *sharī'a*; and, when the mass discovered that it was often not possible to apply the 'organisational' form of Islam, the alternative was the application of the 'organic' Islam.

The organic Islam is a form of Islam that is easy and convenient to apply, since all that it requires is an individual's or a small group's understanding of Islam. No doubt, Islamic extremism has found by this means a way to invade society, as Manson claims: 'Islamic fundamentalism is driven by an outrage at western culture and economic penetration perhaps more than political subjugation, since the former is pervasive and insidious'.[10] One cannot help but pose the question of the position that Islamic law will play in the future of the Islamic world and particularly the Arabic world which is largely Sunni, with new roadmap(s) being drawn up by 'the mother of all bombs', which led to the total disillusionment of Muslim believers in democracy, human rights and tolerance. One can sadly anticipate a mutant form of organic Islamic law which justifies all forms of illegitimate actions against democracy, human rights and tolerance. It is the mutant organic form of Islamic law that created radical and dangerous attitudes such as that of Usama Bin Laden; and one would not be too surprised to see the growth of similar forms of movement that have the potential to be even more violent and aggressive. Such movements, in my opinion, cannot be stopped by means of force; this appears to be exactly what their followers want.

Historically speaking, the principle of theological rebellion against the *umma* is not a new phenomenon. The *Khawārij* seceders rebelled against Ali because they interpreted Islamic law to justify their actions. They withdrew from the Muslim community, which they claimed had betrayed the spirit of Islam, and subsequently set up their own camp with an independent commander. The importance of the *Khawārij*, in a historical sense, comes from their having formed the first seed of a Muslim trend, whereby the politics that were affected led to a new theological argument.[11] The action of the *Khawārij* gives us an excellent historical example of how a cellular view can develop into a sectarian theological view with its followers and armies. The *Khawārij* disowned Ali and the entire Muslim community for the simple reason that Ali accepted the arbitration concerning the issue of who was entitled to be the leader of the community. In addition, the *Khawārij* perceived any person who had committed a mortal sin as an apostate.[12]

The danger of such a movement emerges not only from its temporary rise to power but also from its free interpretation of texts to validate a political stand, such as its interpretation of the Qur'anic verse 'Among the people is the one who sells himself desiring God's approval; these are those who have purchased error for the right guidance'. This interpretation led to the creation of another extremist splinter group which sprang out of the *Khawārij*. They called themselves 'purchasers', *shurāt*, because the members bought God's forgiveness in exchange for dedicating their souls to the elimination of the infidels, including any Muslims who disagreed with them.[13] More fanaticism was created by new splinter groups, which then interpreted theology with further extremism. The *Azāriqa*, who broke from the *Khawārij*, maintained that a person who becomes an infidel in this way (by committing a sin) cannot be readmitted to Islam.[14] Although Ali defeated the *Khawārij* at the battle of Al-Nahrawān, that battle later cost Ali his life at the dagger of a member of the *Khawārij* fanatic group named Abd al Raḥmān b. Muljim. Ibn Muljim's act was part of a conspiracy to expunge all the competing leaders including Ali, Mu'āwiya and the governor of Egypt, 'Amr Ibn al-'Āṣb. The extreme fanaticism of the *Khawārij* justified even the murder of women, because the movement did not have unity of military and political action.[15] Their views became more a collection of mutant organic theology that interpreted Islam according to their own opinions, despite the fact that, at that time, religious authority represented by Ali was available. Although he was a great scholar, the Prince of the Believers and the cousin of the Prophet, his authority was still questioned on the grounds of their fanaticism and blinkered perception, which could not see that the unity of the community was more important than the right of Ali to be the leader. One cannot help but perceive the *Khawārij* as historical forerunners to the Bin Laden movement, particularly with regard to how they saw themselves as being absolutely in the right and demonstrated their devotion to the cause by giving up all their property and belongings for its sake. The *Kharaji* movement was born after huge political upheaval, and it continued to snowball for a long time, attracting not only ordinary people but also intellectuals and many cultivated minds.[16] One might expect the same pattern to emerge from the movement of Bin Laden, which may well produce generations of fanatics and extremists, particularly as a consequence of the American invasion of the region and the errors committed therein. This will be inevitable unless Islamic law takes its proper position in the Muslim world, one which is stretching out its hand to the rest of the world in the hope of mutual understanding, cooperation and unity.

Notes

1 At the outbreak of the First World War, European political and economic penetration of Iraq was still very limited. In November 1914, an expeditionary force from India occupied the head of the Gulf and Basra. A first attempt to capture Basra ended with the surrender of the British at Kūt and 'Amāra, in April 1916, but a second advance succeeded in taking the city in March 1917. Mousil, however, held out until after end of the Ottoman Empire's participation in the First World War in 1918. Meanwhile an administration mainly composed of British and Indian officials had been established in the occupied Iraqi territory, and formed a transition to the formal assumption of British responsibility for the country under the Mandate of 1920. *EI*[2], 1, p. 250a.
2 Coulson, p. 151.
3 Ibid., p. 161.
4 Ibid.
5 Laleh Bakhtiar, *Encyclopedia of Islamic Law*, a compendium of the major schools, Chicago, 1996, p. xxxiii.
6 Schacht and Bosworth, p. 392.
7 Armstrong, *Islam: A Short History*, London, 2000, p. 123.
8 Ibid., pp. 123–4.
9 Izzi Dien, 'Islam and Environment, Theory and Practice', p. 51.
10 Henry Manson Jr, *The House of C. Abd Allah: The Oral History of a Moroccan Family*, New Haven, 1984, p. 19, quoted by Richard T. Antoun, *Muslim Preachers in the Modern World*, Princeton, 1981, p. 237.
11 Armstrong, p. 30.
12 *EI*[2], '*Khawārij* or Khārijite', by G. Levi Della Vida, lv, p. 174b.
13 *EI*[2], '*Shirā*', by M. Izzi Dien, lx, p. 470b.
14 *EI*[2], '*Khawārij* or Khārijite', by G. Levi Della Vida, lv, p. 174b.
15 *EI*[1], p. 907.
16 Ibid.

Glossary

Terms are in alphabetical order, ignoring the definite article *al-*.

aḥādīth. Plural of hadith (see hadith).
aḥkām. Plural of *ḥukm*.
ahliyya. The competence or capacity of an individual to fulfil a legal obligation. It is also termed *dhimma* by Muslim jurists and presents a 'legal persona' that is given for every individual, whether young, old, insane or ill.
'amal. An Arabic word referring to action.
'aqli (adjective). That which is relevant to deduction by human rationality.
aqwāl. Plural of *qawl*, which designates a word or statement.
asbāb al-nuzūl. The term comprises two words: *asbāb*, which is the plural form of the word *sabab* 'reason', and *nuzūl*, which designates the revelation of the Qur'an. The circumstances that accompanied the revelation of a certain verse were termed *asbāb al-nuzūl*, which literally designates the reasons for that revelation. This became a fundamental element in the Islamic exegesis of Qur'anic verses. However, there were a large number of verses unlinked to any historical context, these being revealed as general principles that were enacted without known or specified circumstances.

basmala (saying). *Bism Allah al-raḥmān al-raḥīm* means 'in the name of God the most merciful and most companionate'.
buṭlān. Incorrectness (see *ṣiḥḥa*, 'correctness').

dalīl (noun). From the root *dalla*, 'to show'. It designates an indicator, guide or evidence. Although the term is far from being unambiguous, it has a specific meaning in Islamic law, when it designates the sources of legislation. It is also used as the term designating the legally specified punishments for such offences as theft, drinking alcohol, fornication, highway robbery and slander.
ḍarar (see *ḍarūra*).
ḍarūra (noun). From the lexical root *ḍarar* that signifies 'harm' or 'damage'

Ḍarūra designates both the state of necessity and its cause, *sabab*, which justifies altering a legal injunction on the basis of avoiding imminent harm.

dhimma (see *ahliyya*).

farḍ (noun). A term which in general refers to the dutiful *wājib* action. However, the Ḥanafi school makes a distinction between *farḍ* and *wājib*, applying the first term to those religious duties which are explicitly mentioned in the Qur'an and the traditions of the Prophet.

fāsid (adjective). A technical term which refers to an object that is corrupt or false. When used in a legal contract, it designates a void contract.

fatwa. The term used for a legal decision made by a doctor of Islamic law, or *mufti*.

fiqh (noun). 'Understanding'. Originally, it included all forms of knowledge. However, the word became synonymous with religious and legal knowledge. It is briefly defined as the knowledge of legal injunctions that are applicable to the action of individuals.

furū' al-fiqh. The roots of the law, a term parallel to *uṣūl al-fiqh*, which designates the standards and norms of the *fiqh*. According to the EI^2, works on *furū'* set out the norms of the law, while works of *uṣūl* identify and classify the sources of the law, expound a methodology whereby these give rise to norms, and present a structure of authority which distinguishes the qualified jurist from the layman.

gharar. Refers to 'deception' which could occur due to the nature of the contract, the commodity or the contracting individual.

ḥadd. The boundary, limit or definition of objects and matters. Technically, this refers to legally specified punishments.

hadith. Lexically, meaning 'words or speech'. Initially in Islam, it referred solely to the words of the Prophet, but it developed to include all his words, actions and tacit approvals. This is very similar to the term *sunna*, which designates actions (*'amal*), words (*qawl*) and tacit approvals of the Prophet. The main remaining difference between the two lies in the fact that *sunna* is that which the Prophet has enacted for his people, while hadith comprises his legacy of words, actions and so on.

hajj. Arabic word designating pilgrimage to Mecca that should be undertaken by every Muslim at least once in a lifetime unless he is prevented by a compelling reason such as illness or poverty.

ḥaqīqa. The word for 'truth' in all its forms.

ḥaraj. A term literally meaning 'hardship', a condition or state that Islamic law aims to remove in human life. However, because the term is an abstract concept and as such varies in definition and severity from one individual to another, it cannot constitute a valid ground for analogy, *qiyās*, unless it constitutes serious necessity.

ḥarām. An action indicating that which has been prohibited by the legislator in a mandatory form.

ḥijāb. The dress code for Muslim women, which requires the covering of the body and hair.

ḥikma. Literally 'wisdom'; but it has complex Qur'anic connotations that carry a diversity of meanings, including wisdom, knowledge and acumen. Legally, it refers to the rational wisdom (*ḥikma*) of an injunction which is often mixed with *maṣlaḥa*, the main objective of Islamic law.

ḥisba. One of the complex administrative institutions developed in Islamic law. It supervises social morals and etiquette. It also censors the market adherence to weights, measures and ethics. The connotations of *ḥisba* have broadened rapidly through the ages to cover much more than it did originally. Sunāmi (thirteenth–fourteen century) defines it as every legal action practised in order to comply with God's commandments. See Izzi Dien (1997b: 25).

ḥiyal. Plural of *ḥīla*. It refers to legal manipulation.

ḥudūd. Plural of *ḥadd*.

ḥukm. The generic Arabic name for a legal injunction which is defined by Muslim scholars as the legislator's statement (relevant to the actions of individuals), which oscillates between allowing an action, banning it or leaving it optional.

al-ḥukm al-talkīfi. The dutiful injunction which focuses on the individual. It covers injunctions that are overtly proscribed by the texts, in the form of 'do' or 'don't do'.

al-ḥukm al-waḍ'i. The conditional injunctions which explain conditions and procedures required when certain actions are to be undertaken.

'ibāda (noun). 'Worship'. Normally in Islam, it designates the prescribed and voluntary rituals that a Muslim must perform. However, more specifically, it could include all human actions which are performed to fulfil God's order.

īḍāḥ. Clarification.

iḥtikār. Monopoly.

ijmā'. A consensus of academic opinion on any legal issue that arose subsequent to the death of Muhammad. However, usage of the term *ijmā'* was in evidence in pre-Islamic Arabic society.

ijtihād. Designates the utilisation of individual opinion to find legal solutions for a variety of cases. This methodology is a practical source based on the Qur'an, *sunna* and a general awareness of Islam.

ikmāl. Supplementation.

'illa. Effective cause, or *ratio legis*, of a certain injunction which can provide the ground that justifies the assimilation of a derived case with a basic one in the process of analogy, *qiyās*. A legal principle established by an original case is extended to cover new cases on the ground that they possess a common *'illa*.

'ilm. General reference to knowledge in Islamic law.

istiḥsān. An Arabic verbal noun derived from the term *ḥasan*, 'good', which designates the preference of one object or idea over another. Technically, it refers to juristic preference, which is associated with analogy, *qiyās*. In certain cases, it is found that it is preferable not to apply what seems to be the normal apparent analytical judgement, but to revert to a less apparent analogy due to the existence of stronger evidence.

istinbāṭ. The methodology of inducing a new piece of information from another.

istiqrā'. The methodology of deducing a new piece of information from more than one other source.

istiṣḥāb. An Arabic verbal noun derived from *ṣaḥab*, which means 'to accompany'. The word does not seem to be relevant to the concept of 'accompanying', except in that it represents the approval of an accompanying (i.e. existing) injunction until the presence of a viable alternative can be found.

istiṣlāḥ (noun). From the root *ṣ-l-ḥ*, which denotes improvement and reformation. *Istiṣlāḥ* is a concept that aims, on the ground of public interest, to provide a different and more appropriate answer for cases which are based on any source of legislation and not only on *qiyās*, as in the case of *istiḥsān*.

kalām. Dialectical theology.

khabar al-wāḥhid. The narration of hadith or legal view by one individual.

khabīth (adjective). From the root *kh-b-th*, denoting something wicked and soiled with sin.

khamr. The generic designation for the alcoholic beverage made exclusively from grapes. In this case, the text indicates that prohibition is related specifically to the drinking of grape wine. It is the Arabic word for 'intoxicant'.

Khawārij. Arabic for 'dissidents'. They were a group of Ali's followers who united when he was fighting Mu'āwiya. They rebelled against him for accepting the *taḥkīm* or arbitration in the dispute with Mu'āwiya, which concerned the issue of who was entitled to be the leader of the community. They became one of the most extremist sects in Islam, establishing a terrorist theology that justified killing others if they disagreed with them, even if they were Muslims. They withdrew from the Muslim community, which they claimed had betrayed the spirit of Islam, and subsequently set up their own camp with an independent commander. In addition, they perceived any person who had committed a mortal sin as an apostate. Muhammad Abu Zahra (1987: 60–7) observes that the reason for their rebellion could be ascribed to their naive sincerity, deprivation and nomadic background. Their understanding of Islam was derived from the text. Ali, in his argument with them, referred to the action of the Prophet, *'amal*, presumably to prevent them from interpreting the text as they wished. See also *EI*², '*Khawārij*', by G. Levi Della Vida, iv, 1133.

khilāf. 'Legal disagreement', a concept which was the result of the widening of opinion between various scholars, thus creating the opposite concept for 'consensus', *ijmā'*.

khilāfā'. Islamic rule of government which is based on the human vice-regency of the earth. The ruler of such a system is called *khalīfa*.

lā'iḥa. A minor legal regulation in some Arabic legal systems.

luqṭa. An object found that has no known owner.

madhab (noun). Referring to 'trend' or 'school of thought'.

maḥẓūr. Another name for *ḥarām* or that which is prohibited. Āmidi prefers to refer to the *ḥarām* as *maḥẓūr*. This concept is important in identifying the difference between an action or object which is intrinsically 'bad' and prohibited by the law, and one which is not intrinsically bad yet is prohibited by law.

makīl (adjective). From the verb *kāla*, which indicates measuring by the holding capacity of a measuring container such as the *ṣā'*.

makrūh (adjective). 'Abominable'; represents a minor form of the prohibited, similar in amplitude to the *mandūb*, which is a minor form of *wājib*.

mandūb (adjective). An action indicating that which has been requested by the legislator but does not carry compulsion.

māni'. The Arabic verbal noun which designates the reason for prevention. Legally, it is a concept or a status that nullifies an injunction, despite the availability of all validating causes and circumstances. In Islamic jurisprudence, it designates one of the reasons that formulates the *waḍ'i*, 'conditional injunction'. It represents factual evidence and circumstances that confer the non-validity of injunctions.

maqāṣid. Plural of *qaṣd* or *maqṣūd*, which designates the objective of an individual. The *maqāṣid* of *sharī'a* according to al-Imam Abu Isḥāq al-Shāṭibi (d. AH 790), represents the main foundation on which the understanding of legal texts can be achieved. His ideology was perceived by a few contemporary scholars as an alternative to the theory of Islamic jurisprudence in the understanding of Islamic legal texts.

maṣdar (adjective). A word which designates a source. The verb is *ṣadara*, 'to come up, move upward and outward, from the water hole' (opposite: *warada*). According to W. P. Heinrichs, it is not certain whether or not the word is associated with *ṣadr* meaning 'chest, breast or bosom'. See *EI*[2], '*ṣadr*', by W. P. Heinrichs, vii, 748b.

maṣlaḥa. Lexically, the word means 'public welfare or interest'. It is derived from the root *ṣ-l-ḥ* designating 'construction', 'restoration of good' and 'the removal of harm or corruption'. It is used by all sources of Islamic law as a guide and philosophy through which to deduce the legal injunction.

maṣlaḥa mu'tabara. A public interest which is acknowledged and recognised by Islamic law.

maṣlaḥa mulghāt. A public interest which is rejected by Islamic law.

maṣlaḥa mursala, A public interest which is neither acknowledged nor rejected by Islamic law.

mu'allaqāt. Plural of *mu'llaq*, which designates a suspended object. In Arabic literature, *mu'allaqāt* refers to the most celebrated pre-Islamic Arabic poems. They are generally numbered as seven and sometimes increased to ten. In recognition of their value, the Arabs used to write them in gold and suspend them on the walls of Ka'ba. The use of 'suspension' may also derive from the title of old anthologies which were admired as if they were suspended like a 'necklace or ornament'. See *EI*[2], '*mu'allaqāt*', by G. Lecomte, vii, 254a.

Mu'tazila. A group of Muslim theologians whose understanding of God and His relationship with humanity is defined through Hellenistic notions and a metaphorical interpretation of the anthropomorphic language that is used in connection with the Divine.

mubāḥ (also known as *ḥalāl*). Indicates an action which is allowed, whereby individuals have the option of 'doing' or 'not doing' such an action.

muḥarram. Passive voice of *ḥarām*.

mut'a (noun). Refers to indemnity payable to a divorced wife where no dowry has been stipulated. It is a quite different concept from 'temporary marriage', which shares the same name. See *EI*[2], '*mut'a*', by W. Heffening, vii: 75a.

mutawātir (adjective). Form of *tawātur*.

niqāb. Veil or the face-covering of a woman.

niyya. 'Intention'. It represents the central tenet for identifying belief in Islamic theology and 'responsibility' in Islamic law. Because intention is covert, no one can be absolutely certain of its existence except the individual involved. Islamic law uses similar evidence to that used by conventional law as a means of identifying intention.

niẓām (plural *anẓima* or *tanẓimāt*). All of these terms in Saudi legal terminology, denote the main legal regulation or articles of law.

qarḍ (noun). The Arabic word for 'loan'.

qaṣd al-ṣhāri' (see also *maqāsid*). The intention of the legislator, according to

Shāṭibi. This concept represents an important ground on which to resolve many unclear issues in Islamic law, such as the notion of *istiḥsān*. Although God's intention is not always clear, Shāshi (d. AH 365) maintains that 'the wise creator would only wish good for his creatures and He would run their lives according to the noble policy which was based on their mind and nature; welfare; mind and nature representing the attributes of God'.

qiyās. Literally 'measurement'. Technically, it designates legal analogy or syllogism, which assimilates the injunction of one case and applies it to a similar one that has no specified injunction.

ra'i. Individual opinion.

riba. Usury.

rukhṣah. In Islamic law, it designates permission to perform or not to perform an injunction. There is uncertainty as to whether *rukhṣa* is a part of dutiful injunction or conditional injunction.

ṣāʿ. A measuring instrument for grain or other amounts of objects. Its value was four *mudd* (*modius*) according to the custom of Medina. The value of the *ṣāʿ* was, from the canonical point of view, fixed in Islamic law by the Prophet in the year 2/623–4 when he laid down the ritual details of the orthodox feast of *īd al-fiṭr*. This carried with it the compulsory giving of alms called *zakāt al-fiṭr*, the value of which in grain represented one *ṣāʿ* for each member of a family. The *ṣāʿ* of Medina was subsequently chosen as the standard measure. See also *EI*[2], '*ṣāʿ*', by A. Bel, viii, 654b.

sabab (noun). Literally 'cause'. It designates a constant that leads to the injunction, normally accompanying it, but not necessarily creating it. It is often defined as the designation given by the lawmaker for an injunction.

sadd al-dharā'iʿ. The term comprises two words: *sadd*, a verbal noun meaning 'to close' and *dharā'iʿ*, which describes 'means' or 'causes'. The concept aims to predetermine any negative or evil future outcome of an injunction and aims to prevent such.

salah. Arabic for prayer, which follows a fixed series of words and movements, while facing in the direction of Mecca. Muslims are required to pray five times a day, the first prayer being before dawn and the last after dusk. Prayer must be preceded by ritual washing and may be said in any clean place.

sharʿi (adjective). That which is relevant to *sharīʿa* or law.

sharīʿa. The Islamic rules and regulations governing all aspects of human existence, including life after death. *Sharīʿa* also proffers a legal path that a lawyer may follow in order to extract the rules which correspond to Islamic beliefs and values.

sharika (noun). As a term of Islamic law, *sharika* or *shirka* takes different forms according to the contents and conditions. A partnership contract is controlled by the (central) principle of proposal and consent, *ījāb wa qabūl*. The classification of companies seems to be incompatible between the various schools of law, the incompatibility probably arising from the varying recognition of authentic sources, as well as from the question of what constitutes a valid partnership. See *EI*[2], '*sharika*', by M. Izzi Dien, lx, 348a.

sharṭ (noun). The Arabic word for 'condition'. In Islamic jurisprudence, it designates one of the reasons that formulates the *waḍ'i*, conditional injunction. It is an external matter that can occur without the presence of a legal action. However, without such an action, it is void. An example of *sharṭ* is found in the case of a divorce pronouncement, which would be void without the presence of marital status, although naturally marital status can exist without divorce.

shuf'a. Literally 'pre-emption', the right of the co-owner to buy out his partner's share which is for sale. Should the property be sold without his approval to a third party, the partner has the privilege to purchase the property, even against the will of the new owner, who should be reimbursed with the price paid. The Ḥanafi grant this privilege to the owners of adjacent properties and make it valid not only to non-fungible properties but also to appendages of the property, such as access and water rights.

ṣiḥḥa. 'Correctness' and its opposite *buṭlān*, 'incorrectness' or 'falsehood'. This influences the validity of the injunction and is part of the *waḍ'i* conditional injunctions. To validate or nullify an injunction, the legislator stipulates these circumstances or conditions.

Sunna. Traditions attributed to the Prophet, or the path which is directly relevant to his religious guidance.

Sunni (adjective). Referring to the individual adherent or the sect of Islamic law that bases itself on the tradition of the Prophet, in contrast to the *shī'a*, which also includes the notion of the leadership of the descendants of the Prophet or *imāma*.

sunnan al-'ādāt. The customary traditions, which would include Prophetic practices that formed part of his personal attributes, the following of which would constitute meritorious practice.

tabi'īn. The next generation to the Prophet's companions.

tafsīr. Interpretation. When used alone, the word normally refers to the discipline of Qur'anic interpretation.

tajdīd (adjective). In Islamic law, it refers to the renewal of Islamic law.

tawātur. 'Succession'. In Islamic law, the word is used to designate the narration of hadith or legal view by a large number of individuals who must have no predetermined intention to fabricate their statement.

ṭayyib (adjective). From the root *ṭ-y-b*, denoting something good and fresh.

'ulamā'. Plural of *'ālim*, which refers to a scholar of almost all disciplines. However, the term does refer more specifically to the scholars of Islamic law.

umma. The word is used in the Qur'an in the sense of religious 'community'. There are also instances where it means 'fixed term' (Qur'an: xi, 8; xii, 45) and communities of animals. In the ḥadith, it has a smaller range of meanings than that found in the Qur'an. However, the word occurs frequently there, most often with reference to the Muslim community. See *EI*[2], '*umma*', by F. M. Denny, x, 859b.

'urf (noun). Lexically, the term is derived from the root *'a-r-f*, which denotes knowledge. Legally, it refers to custom as a source of legislation. *'Urf* is often defined as the practice which has been incorporated into the social life of a community and known to be good and beneficial.

waḥi. The revelation of words, ideas or concepts. Normally, this term is used in Arabic to denote what God has revealed to His creatures. More specifically, it refers to God's revelation to His prophets and messengers, such as His instructions to Muhammad, either directly or through the verses of the Qur'an.

wājib (noun). An action that indicates an obligation/responsibility.

wakīl (adjective). Denotes the representative of a legal contract, such as marriage or sale.

waqf (noun). Derived from the verb *waqafa*, 'to stop'. The term designates the act of founding a charitable trust and hence the trust itself. A synonym, used mainly by Māliki jurists, is *ḥabs* (in French, often rendered *habus*). The essential elements are that a person, with the intention of committing a pious deed, declares part of his or her property to be henceforth inalienable and designates persons or public utilities as beneficiaries of its yields. See also *EI*[2], '*waqf*', by R. Peters et al., xi, 59a.

wasaṭiyya (adjective). From *wasaṭ*, 'middle'. A methodology for applying Islamic law. Accordingly, legislation must reflect a step-by-step development that follows the initial establishment of the creed.

wuḍu'. Ritual ablution expected before prayer. It includes the washing of hands, face, hair and feet.

zakah. Derived from the root *zakā*, to 'purify'. It refers to one of the main pillars and rituals of Islam which designates the contribution of one's appropriated wealth to the state or directly to the needy individual or organisation. Roughly, it is estimated to constitute about 2.5 per cent of the annually generated income of a Muslim.

Bibliography

Al'Ajami, Abu al-Yazīd, *Al-fuqahā' wa buḥūth al-'aqīda al-Islāmiyya*, Cairo, 1985.

'Ali Jād al-Ḥaqq, Jād al-Ḥaqq, *Buhūth wa fatāwa islamiyya fi Qaḍāya mu'āṣira*, Cairo, 1994.

Al-'Alih, Abd Allah Muhammad, *Marātib al-ijmā'*, *Al-dirāsāt al-islāmiyya, The Arabic Journal of the Islamic Research Institute*, Islamabad, 36: 3, July–September 2001.

Abd al-Raḥmān, Jalāl al-Dīn, *Al-Maṣlaḥa al-mursala wa makānatuhā fi al-tashrī'*, Cairo, 1983.

Abu Sulaymān, Abd-al Wahāb, *Tartīb al-Mawḍū'āt al-fiqhiyya*, Mecca, 1988.

Abu Yaḥya, Muhammad Hasan, 'Ḥukm shahādat al-nisā', fima siwa al-'uqūbāt mima yaṭali' 'alayhi al-rijāl ghāliban fi al-sharī'a al-islāmiyya', *Journal of the Faculty of Arts*, Kuwait, 1990, 195–250.

Abu Yūsuf, al-Qāḍi Ya'qūb b. Ibrāhīm, *Al-Kharāj*, ed. Muhammad Ibrāhīm al-Banna, Cairo, 1981.

Abu Yūsuf, al-Qāḍi Ya'qūb b. Ibrāhīm, *Al-Kharāj*, ed. Iḥsān 'Abbas, Beirut, 1985.

Abu Zahra, Mohammed, *Uṣūl al-fiqh*, Dār al-fikr al-'Arabi, no place of publication, 1958.

Abu Zahra, Mohammed, *Tārīkh al-madhāhib al-islāmiyya*, Cairo, 1987.

Āmidi, Sayf al-Dīn 'Ali b. Muhammad, *Al-Iḥkām fi uṣūl al-ahkām*, ed. Ibrāhīm Al-'Ajūz, Beirut, 1985.

Antoun, Richard T., *Muslim Preachers in the Modern World*, Princeton, 1981.

Armstrong, Karen, *Islam: A Short History*, London, 2000.

Al-Āsqalāni, Ahmad b. Ḥajar, *Fatḥ al-bāri fi sharḥ ṣaḥīḥ al-Bukhāri*, Cairo, no date.

'Aṭāwi, Ahmad, *Codification of Islamic Law in Bahrain*, Ph.D. thesis, Lampeter University, 2004.

Azmi, Mohammad Mustafa, *Studies in Early Hadith Literature*, Beirut, 1968.

Badrān, Badrān Abu al-'Aynayn, *Uṣūl al-fiqh al-islāmi*, Alexandria, 1992.

Bakhtiar, Laleh, *Encyclopedia of Islamic Law*, a compendium of the major schools, Chicago, 1996, p. xxxiii.

Al-Bayānūni, Muhammad Abu Al-Fatḥ, *Mu'awiqāt taṭbīq al-sharī'a al-islāmiyya*, Kuwait, 1996.

Al-Bilādi, 'Atīq b. Ghāyth, *Mu'jam al-m'ālim al-jughrāfiyya fi al-sīra*, Mecca, 1982.

Al-Bustāni, Salīm Rustum Bāz, *Majallat al-aḥkām al-'adliyya*, 3rd edn/reprint for the Istanbul original edition published AH 1304–5, Beirut, no date. (Quoted as *majalla*.)

Al-Būṭi, Muhammad Sa'īd Ramaḍān, *Ḍawābiṭ al-maṣlaḥa fi al-sharī'a al-islamiyya*, Beirut, 1982.

Calder, Norman, *Studies in Early Muslim Jurisprudence*, Oxford, 1993.

Calder, Norman, *Stvdia Islamica*, Paris, Ex fasciculo lviii.

Coulson, N. J., *History of Islamic Law*, Edinburgh, 1964.

Dutton, Yasin, *The Origins of Islamic Law*, London, 1999.

Al-Ḍuwaysh, Ahmad Abd al-Razzāq, *Fātāwā al-lajna al-dā'ima lil buḥūth wa al-iftā'*, Riyaḍ, 1999.

EI[1], *First Encyclopaedia of Islam*, 1st edn, 1913–36 (photomechanical reprint, Leiden, 1987).

EI[2], *The Encyclopaedia of Islam*, 2nd edn, Leiden, 1974– (in progress).

Encyclopaedia Britannica, 1997 (on compact disc).

Al-Europiya, vol. 30, 2002.

Fārūqi, Ismā'īl, *The Cultural Atlas of Islam*, London, 1986.

Fatāwā hay'āt kibār al-'ulamā' (see Al-Shādhili).

Al-Fatāwā al-islāmiyya min dār al-iftā' al-miṣriyya, 20 vols, Cairo, 1981–93.

Al-Ghazāli, Abu Ḥāmid Muhammad b. Muhammad, *Iḥyā' 'ulūm al-dīn*, 1st edn, Beirut, no date.

Al-Ghazāli, Abu Ḥāmid Muhammad b. Muhammad, *Al-Mustaṣfā fi 'ilm al-uṣūl*, ed. Muhammad Abd al-Salām al-Shāfi'i, Beirut, 1993.

Al-Ghazāli, Muhammad, *Mā'at su'āl 'an al-islām*, Cairo, 1989a.

Al-Ghazāli, Muhammad, *Al-Sunna al-nabawiyya bayna ahl al-fiqh wa ahl al-ḥadīth*, Beirut, 1989b.

Al-Ḥafnāwi, Abd al-Majīd Muhammad, *Uṣūl al-tashrī' fi al-mamlaka al-'arabiyya al-sa'udiyya*, Riyaḍ, 1977?

Hallaq, W. B., *A History of Islamic Legal Theories*, Cambridge, 1997.

Hallaq, W. B., *Law and Legal Theory in Classical and Medieval Islam*, Variorum Collected Studies Series, Ashgate, 1994.

Ḥassān, Ḥusain Ḥāmid, *Naẓariyyat al-maṣlaḥa fi al-fiqh al-Islāmi*, Cairo, 1981.

Hourani, A., *A History of the Arab People*, London, 1991.

Ibn Anas, Mālik, *Muwaṭṭa' al-imām Mālik, riwāyat Yaḥya b. Yaḥya al-Laythi*, ed. Ahmad Rātib 'Armūsh, Beirut, 1987.

Ibn 'Āshūr, Al-Ṭāhir, *Maqāṣid al-Sharī'a*, ed. Muhammad al-Ṭāhir al-Mīsāwi, Amman, 1999.

Ibn Ḥanbal, Ahmad b. Muhammad, *Al-Musnad*, ed. Ahmad Muhammad Shākir, 20 vols, Cairo, 1958–80.

Ibn Ḥazm, 'Ali b. Ahmad b. Sa'īd, *Marātib al-ijmā'*, Beirut, no date.

Ibn al-Jawzī, Isma'īl, *Kitāb al-targhīb wa al-tarhīb*, Beirut, no date.

Ibn Junayd, Abd al-'Azīz, *Fatāwā mufti al-dawla*, Brunei, 1995.

Ibn Māja, Abu Abd Allah Muhammad b. Yazīd al-Qazwīni, *Sunan Ibn Māja*, Istanbul, 1972.

Ibn Manẓūr, Muhammad b. Mukarram, *Lisān al-'Arab*, Beirut, no date.

Ibn Nujaym, Zayn al-'Ābidīn b. Ibrāhīm, *Al-Ashbāh wa al-naẓā'ir*, ed. Ibrāhīm al-Wakīl, Cairo, 1968.

Ibn Nujaym, Zayn al-'Ābidīn b. Ibrāhīm, *Al-Ashbāh wa al-naẓā'ir*, ed. Muhammad Muṭī' al-Ḥāfiẓ, Damascus, 1983.

Ibn Qayyim al-Jawziyya, Muhammed, *A'lām al-muwaqqi'īn*, Beirut, 1991.

Ibn Qayyim al-Jawziyya, Muhammed, *Miftāḥ dār al-sa'āda*, Riyāḍ, no date.

Ibn Qudāma, Muwafaq al-Dīn Abd Allah b. Ahmad, *Al-Mughni*, 14 vols, Beirut, 1984.

Ibn Qudāma, Muwafaq al-Dīn Abd Allah b. Ahmad, *Al-Mughni*, ed. Abd-Allah al-Turki and Abd al-Fattāḥ al-Ḥilu, 15 vols, Cairo, 1986.

Izzi Dien, M., 'Islam and Environment, theory and practice', *The Journal of Beliefs and Values*, 18: 1, 1997, 47–57.

Izzi Dien, M., *The Theory and Practice of Market Law in Medieval Islam*, E. J. W. Gibb Memorial Trust, UK, 1997.

Izzi Dien, M., *Maṣlaḥa*, in *Studies in Honour of Clifford Edmund Bosworth*, ed. R. I Nutton, Leiden, 2000a.

Izzi Dien, M., *The Environmental Dimensions of Islam*, Cambridge, 2000b.

Al-Juwayni, Imām Al-Ḥarmayn, *Ghiyāth al-umam fi iltyāth al-ẓulam*, ed. Abd al-Ḥamīd Al-Dāb, Qatar, AH 1401.

Khallāf, Abd al-Wahāb, *'Ilm Uṣūl al-fiqh al-islāmi*, Cairo, 1986.

Al-Khatīb, Muhammad Ajāj, *Uṣūl al-ḥadīth*, Beirut, 1989.

Kishik, Mohammad Jalāl, *Al-Sa'ūdiyyūn wa al-ḥall al-islāmi*, West Hanover, MA, 1982.

Al-Laythi, Yaḥya, *Muwaṭṭa Mālik*, Beirut, 1987.

Al-Lughani, Abd al-Nasir, *A Critical Study and Edition of the First Part of* Kitab Maḥāsin al-Sharī'a *by Al-Qaffāl al-Shāshi*, Ph.D. thesis, Lampeter University, 2004.

Al-Majlis al-awruppi li al-iftā' wa al-buḥūth, *Qarārāt wa fatāwa al-majlis al-awruppi*, Collection no. 1–2, Cairo, 2002.

Majmū'at al-fatāwa al-shar'iyya al-ṣādira 'an qaṭṭā' al-iftā' wa al-buḥūth al-shar'iyya, Ministary of *awqāf*, Kuwait, 1988.

Al-Maydāni, Abd al-Rahman Hasan Ḥabannaka, *Al-Sharī'a al-islāmiyya bayna al-tadarruj fi al-tashrī' wa al-tadarruj fi al-taṭbīq*, Kuwait, 2000.

Mubārak, Jamīl Muhammad, *Naẓariyyat al-ḍarūra al-shar'iyya*, Cairo, 1988.
Al-Nashmi, 'Ajīl Jāsim, *Muqadimāt 'ilm uṣūl al-fiqh*, typewritten notes, Faculty of Islamic Law, Kuwait, 1990.
Al-Qaraḍāwi, Yūsuf, *'Awamil al-si'a wa al-murūna fi al-sharī'a al-islāmiyya*, Kuwait, no date.
Al-Qaraḍāwi, Yūsuf, *Al-ṣaḥwa al-islāmiyya bayna al-juḥūd wa al-taṭarruf*, Qatar, 1982 (AH 1402).
Al-Qaraḍāwi, Yūsuf, *Fatāwā mu'āṣira*, 2 vols, Cairo, 1993.
Al-Qaraḍāwi, Yūsuf, *The lawful and the prohibited in Islam*, English translation, Cairo, 1997.
Al-Qarāfi, Shihāb al-Dīn Ahmad b. Idrīs, *Anwār al-burūq fi aḥkām al-furūq* 'Ālam al-kutub, no date.
Qarārāt wa fatāwa al-majlis al-awruppi (see Al-Majlis al-awruppi).
Al-Qaṭṭān, Mannā', *Mabāḥith fi 'ulm ūm al-Qur'an*, 3rd edn, Beirut, no date.
Quṭb, Sayyid, *Ma'ālim fi al-ṭarīq*, Stuttgart, 1978.
Quṭb, Sayyid, *Fi ẓilāl al-Qur'an*, 9th edn, vol. 2, Cairo, 1980.
Ramic, Šukri Husayn, *Linguistic Principles in* Uṣūl al-fiqh *and their Effect on Legal Reasoning in Islamic Law*, Ph.D. thesis, Lampeter University, 1996.
Raysūni, Ahmad, *Naẓariyyāt al-maqāṣid 'inda al-imām al-Shāṭibi*, Herndon, VA, 1995.
Al-Ṣābūni, Muhammed Ali, *Ma'āni al-Qur'an al-karīm*, 2nd edn, Mecca, 1988.
Al-Ṣāliḥ, Subḥi, *Ma'ālim al-sharī'a al-islāmiyya*, Beirut, 1982.
Al-Ṣāliḥ, Subḥi, *'Ulum al-ḥadīth wa muṣṭalaḥuhu*, Beirut, 1995.
Al-Samarqandi, 'Alā' al-Dīn Abu Bakr Muhammad b. Ahmad, *Mīzān al'-uṣūl fi natā'ij al-'uqūl*, ed. Zaki Muhammad Abd al-Barr, Qatar, 1994.
Schacht, Joseph, *The Origins of Mohammadan Jurisprudence*, Oxford, 1950.
Schacht, Joseph and C. E. Bosworth, *The Legacy of Islam*, Oxford, 1974.
Al-Shādhili, Ṣafwat, *Fatāwā hay'āt kibār al-'ulamā' bi al-mamlaka al-'arabiyya al-sa'udiyya*, Riyaḍ, 1988.
Al-Shāfi'i, *Al-Umm*, vol. 7, Beirut, 1983.
Al-Shāfi'i, *Al-Risāla*, ed. Ahmad Muhammad Shākir, Cairo, 1993.
Al-Shanqīṭi, Ahmad b. Amīn, *Al-Mu'allaqāt al-'ashra*, Cairo, 1993.
Al-Sharīf, Muhammad Abd al-Ghaffār, *Al-tadarruj fi taṭbīq al-sharī'a al-islāmiyya*, Kuwait, 1996.
Al-Shāshi, al-Qaffāl, *Maḥāsin al-sharī'a al-islāmiyya* (see Al-Lughani).
Al-Shāṭibi, Abu Isḥāq Musa, *Al-Muwafaqāt fi uṣūl al-Sharī'a*, 4 vols, ed. A. Drāz, Cairo/Beirut, 1975.
Al-Sibā'i, Yūsuf, *Al-Sunna wa makanatuha fi al-tashrī' al-islāmi*, Beirut, 1998.
Al-Suyūṭi, 'Ābd al-Raḥmān, *Tanwīr al-ḥawālik sharḥ 'alā muwaṭṭa' Mālik*, 3 vols, Beirut, no date.
Al-'Umari, Akram Ḍiyā', *Al-Turāth wa al-mu'āṣara*, Qatar, 1985.

Al-'Umari, Akram Ḍiyā', *Qiyam al-mujtma' al-islāmi min manẓūr tārīkhi*, Qatar, 1994.

Where, Hans, *The Hans Where Dictionary of Modern Written Arabic*, ed. J. M Cowan, London/New York, 1960; new edn 1974.

Yūsuf, Zukifli Muhammad, A *Study of Tafsīr 'Abr al-Athīr*, Singapore, 2002.

Zaqzūq, Maḥmūd Ḥamdi, *Al-Istishrāq wa al-khalfiyya al-fikriyya li al-ṣirā' al-ḥaḍāri*, Qatar, 1984.

Al-Zarkashi, Badr al-Dīn Muhammad b. Bahādir, *Al-Ijābah li īrād ma istadrakathu 'Āisha 'ala al-ṣaḥāba*, Beirut, 1970.

Al-Zarkashi, Badr al-Dīn Muhammad b. Bahādir, *Al-Manthūr fi al-qawā'id*, ed. Taysīr Fā'iq Ahmad Maḥmūd, Qatar, 1985.

Al-Zarqa, Muṣūafa Ahmad, *Al-Madkhal-al-fiqhi al-'ām*, Damascus, 1968.

Zarqāni, Muhammad, *Manāhil al-'Irfān fi 'ulūm al-Qurān*, no date, Cairo.

Zayd, Muṣṭafa, *Al-Maṣlaḥa fi al-tashrī' al-islāmi*, 2nd edn, Cairo, 1964.

Zaydān, Abd al-Karīm, *Al-Madkhal li dirāsāt al-sharī'a al-islāmiyya*, Baghdad, 1966 and Beirut, 1990.

Zaydān, Abd al-Karīm, *Al-Wajīz fi uṣūl al-fiqh*, Baghdad, 1987.

Al-Zirikli, Khayr al-Dīn, *Al-A'lām: qāmūs tarājim li ashar al-rijāl*, 10 vols, Beirut, 1954–9.

Al-Zuḥayli, Wahba, *Naẓariyat al-ḍarūra al-Shar'iyya*, Beirut, 1995.

Al-Zuḥayli, Wahba, *Uṣūl al-fiqh al-islāmi*, Damascus, 1998.

Al-Zuḥayli, Wahba, *Al-Tadarruj fi al-tashrī' wa al-taṭbīq fi al-sharī'a al-Islamiyya*, Kuwait, 2000.

Index